What, Why, How

WHAT, WHY, HOW

Answers to Your Questions about
Buddhism, Meditation, and
Living Mindfully

BHANTE GUNARATANA

Wisdom Publications
199 Elm Street
Somerville, MA 02144 USA
wisdomexperience.org

Library of Congress Cataloging-in-Publication Data
Names: Gunaratana, Henepola, 1927– author.
Title: What, why, how: answers to your questions about Buddhism, meditation,
and living mindfully / Bhante Gunaratana.
Description: Somerville, MA: Wisdom Publications, 2020. | Includes index.
Identifiers: LCCN 2019030067 (print) | LCCN 2019030068 (ebook) |
ISBN 9781614296164 (paperback) | ISBN 9781614296171 (ebook)
Subjects: LCSH: Buddhism—Miscellanea. |
Meditation—Buddhism—Miscellanea.
Classification: LCC BQ135 .G85 2020 (print) | LCC BQ135 (ebook) |
DDC 294.3/4435—dc23
LC record available at https://lccn.loc.gov/2019030067
LC ebook record available at https://lccn.loc.gov/2019030068

ISBN 978-1-61429-616-4   ebook ISBN 978-1-61429-617-1

23 22 21 20 19   5 4 3 2 1

Cover design by Phil Pascuzzo. Interior design by James D. Skatges.
Set in Fairfield LH and DGP.

Printed on acid-free paper that meets the guidelines for permanence and
durability of the Production Guidelines for Book Longevity of the Council on
Library Resources.

Printed in Canada.

Contents

Editor's Preface

Bhante Henepola Gunaratana, Mahathera, has spent his life spreading the Buddha's teachings. Known and beloved worldwide by the affectionate nickname "Bhante G.," he was born in Sri Lanka in 1927 in the village of Henepola, was ordained as a novice monk at the age of twelve, and received full ordination at twenty.

He was invited to America in 1968 and served as the general secretary of the Buddhist Vihara Society in Washington, DC—a group he would later come to lead. He went on to earn a doctorate in philosophy from the American University. In 1985, he founded the Bhavana Society in the hills of West Virginia, a Theravada Buddhist monastery and retreat center that continues to attract retreatants from around the world.

Bhante G. is a noted Buddhist scholar and author of numerous books on Buddhist meditation practice and the Buddha's teachings. These include his classic introductory guide to meditation, *Mindfulness in Plain English*, as well as *Eight Mindful Steps to Happiness*, *The Four Foundations of Mindfulness in Plain English*, *Loving-Kindness in Plain English*, and many more. His life story is told in *Journey to Mindfulness: The Autobiography of Bhante G.*

When I think of Bhante G., I invariably envision him sitting on a maroon meditation cushion. He is seated in front of the big golden Buddha in the meditation hall at the Bhavana Society in the back hills of West Virginia. In my mind's eye, he seems larger than life, just like that oversized Buddha in the monastery and retreat center the Sri Lankan native founded in the early 1980s.

I am always surprised when we meet him in the sangha hall or monastery library at how slight his physical frame is. It is a measure of the authority, breadth, and bigheartedness of his teaching of the Dhamma that when he is in the meditation hall, the largeness of his spirit and erudition makes his physical presence seem larger, too.

Of all his books, he is perhaps best known for his remarkable primer on establishing a meditation practice, *Mindfulness in Plain English*, a book that Jon Kabat-Zinn dubbed "a masterpiece." More than two decades after its debut, it has been translated into nearly thirty languages. (On a recent visit to the Bhavana Society, Bhante G. was pleased to show me a copy of the book recently translated into Russian.)

I don't think it would be an exaggeration to suggest that that single book has perhaps guided more people to explore meditation in depth than any single Buddhist book of the last few decades.

This book is a bit different. It is an attempt to capture some of Bhante G.'s off-the-cuff style when asked questions at retreats, public events, live interviews, and questions e-mailed to him. Our hope is that this book, with its themed chapters, will be an accessible guide both for beginners coming to insight meditation and the Buddha's teachings for the first time and for experienced meditators wishing to learn deeper aspects of those teachings.

This book condenses into one volume a half-century of Bhante G.'s answers to common questions, both introductory and advanced. How do you deal with pain while meditating? How long and how often should I meditate? What is spiritual friendship and why is it important? How does one uproot the hindrances? What are the stages of jhana and how do we know we have achieved them?

Bhante G.'s wit, honesty, and learning are a delight to experience live. He is known for his plainspoken instruction and guidance on meditation and Buddhist teachings as well as a deep command of passages from the Pali canon of Buddhist scripture, which he can pull up from memory in their original Pali.

He is also known for his wit, erudition, and good humor in answering questions about Buddhism and meditation and incorporating the practice of mindfulness and meditation into busy, modern lives.

This book is an attempt to capture a portrait of him thinking and responding on his feet (and on his cushion), as he parses and presents the Buddha's teachings to an audience of dozens or an audience of one.

Throughout, he offers insights into his own personal experiences and challenges. These include his arrival in America, the attempt to ordain Buddhist nuns at the Bhavana Society, challenges faced in establishing a traditional forest monastery in the West Virginia hills, and even how he got the nickname "Bhante G." He talks about the Buddha's core teachings on meditation and spiritual practice, and responds at length to a host of questions posed to him through the years by lay followers and retreatants. Bhante G. also offers up some candid thoughts on the state of Buddhism today in the West and offers insights into how his understanding of the Buddha's teachings and his own practice have developed.

Our hope in creating this book is to offer deep yet practical insights into Buddhist practice and the spiritual life from a Buddhist monk who has lived that life both on and off the cushion for nine decades.

May all beings attain Nibbana.

EDITOR'S ACKNOWLEDGMENTS

Thanks for additional editing help from Judy Larson and Patrick Hamilton. And to Bhante G., for checking the manuscript and ensuring we got his responses and Pali words and phrases right.

—Douglas John Imbrogno

1

On Meditation

How Much Effort?

How much effort should we bring to our meditation practice? We hear the phrases "just sit" or "effortless effort" when it comes to meditating. How hard should we be trying when meditating?

When it comes to meditation, your effort should not be haphazard or blind. It's a committed effort. Before you even start, you should consider, "Is this the right moment for me to practice?"

Suppose it's a busy time, the TV is blaring somewhere, people are running around. No matter how hard you try, you can't seem to do the practice. You have to understand the situation, you have to be mindful of when to sit.

But once you've chosen the place and time to practice, by all means, apply every ounce of effort to overcome laziness, drowsiness, restlessness, worry, and so on. These are very common, ordinary obstacles. In Buddhism, we call them hindrances because they hinder our progress. When hindrances arise, we shouldn't be lazy. We shouldn't think, "Well, this is just way too hard. I'm wasting my time. This stuff always comes up and blocks me when I try to meditate. I give up."

You must encourage yourself and always renew your effort at sitting. You might tell yourself, "I can do this. This is possible. I can overcome my sleepiness, I can work with this restless mind. I see other people who have learned how to do this. I can do this myself!"

So, you must exert yourself. You must try to shake yourself awake and tell yourself, "Hey, you! Don't chicken out of this!"

As for "effortless effort," well, that's a lazy man's advice. There is no such thing as effortless effort. Things don't come to us just like air. However, laziness, drowsiness, lust, greed—they come to us very naturally! Good things often don't come to us naturally. We have them in us by our nature, but we must work hard to arouse them.

The trouble is that our mind is like water. Water always finds its way to the lowest place. In a similar way our mind tends to drag us down into the lower state of things—to base ideas, lazy practices, the easy way out.

Yet if we head that way, we'll end up going down the drain with all the rubbish in the mind! So, we must turn up the volume on our effort. We repeat the same thing, again and again and again, until we achieve it. We bring commitment to our meditation practice, in spite of whatever happens in any one sitting.

There are actually three stages of effort. In Pali the first stage is called *arambhadhatu*, which means the element of beginning. When you read an inspiring book about meditation or have an enlightening discussion with a friend or teacher on Buddhist practice, you may become enthusiastic and start meditating right away. Yet a few weeks or months later, your effort may wane. You slide right back into the same old same old. How do you avoid that?

That's where the second stage of effort comes in— *nikkamadhatu*, which essentially means proceeding with your effort. You stick to it, you work at your meditation practice with dedication and regularity. Even then, you can become lazy or may waiver in your resolve.

Then you have to play your last card. You have to give yourself a pep talk, but also be firm with yourself: "This is it! I won't budge from this cushion even if my back is killing me! OK, so I'm restless—I've seen that before. All right, now my knees hurt—I've experienced that too. I can sit through this. I can work with this. Reduce me to a skeleton and still I won't budge!"

That is the third kind of effort called *parakkama*, or valor. In the armed forces, you are encouraged to bring valor and bravery to your work. Meditators also need that kind of effort.

Sometimes people come here to the Bhavana Society with all good intentions to meditate. They book a place to stay months in advance and come for a week, or two weeks, or a month. Then a few days later they tell me, "Um, Bhante, I have to go. I forgot I had to get back because I have this job to do and . . ."

Or you may experience an inspiring meditation retreat, return home, and start practicing. Weeks or months later your resolve may waiver in establishing a daily practice. Remind yourself: You can do this. See the example of your teachers and fellow meditators. Seek out the support of sitting groups. Attend retreats regularly.

Really, it comes down to this: when you take the time to practice, when you make that commitment, stick to it with all the energy you can muster.

METTA AND MEDITATION

Some teachers recommend generating a feeling of metta, or loving-friendliness, in advance of meditation, bringing to mind a time you were very happy or acted with compassion and then beginning with a wish for yourself, "May I be happy." Do you think this is a good practice?

I think this is a benevolent thought—that you have done something very meaningful to help people, you practice metta, and by doing so you make others happy. When you think of your actions that made others happy, you are happy. With this happy feeling you can practice meditation. I think that's a good thing and there's nothing wrong with that.

Best Meditation Object

What is the best meditation topic or object?

There are many meditation topics. But I think if you have a teacher, they would recommend you start your practice with focusing your mind on the breath. Most meditators find the breath easy to focus the mind upon for many reasons. It is readily available. It goes wherever you go. You don't have to pack it in a bag. It is right there with you. You breathe all the time, and it will be present anytime you want it. That is the subject of meditation I recommend for everybody to start with in their practice.

Then you can see feelings—the feeling of the breath, the feeling of your body, the feeling of your cushion, the feeling of the temperature in the room. "Feeling" means some sensation you experience—another very good subject of meditation.

You may then become aware of passing thoughts. Don't let your thoughts proliferate by adding more thoughts. Just become aware of any particular thought arising, for instance, a thought of anger. You feel it. It arises in your mind. You remember a certain person, certain situations in which you had an encounter, some kind of exchange of words that triggered your resentment, your anger, which is one of the three unwholesome roots.

You try to pay total attention to how you feel when anger arises in your mind. You see it is not a very pleasant feeling and then tell yourself, "Why should I allow my mind to experience this unpleasant thought, which is harmful to my peace and my health and that hurts me in many ways? It eats me up inside, it disturbs my peace, it increases my blood pressure and disturbs my sleep. I lose friends when I experience this anger all the time. I might even lose my job." You can see the many disadvantages to anger. And so you let it go. You come back to your breath and meditate upon it.

LAYPERSON'S DAILY MEDITATION

In daily life how often should we meditate and for how long? If I am serious about committing to a meditation practice, what do you see as a minimum amount of meditation for a layperson?

I think every day—at least thirty minutes in the morning, thirty minutes in the evening—you must meditate. That is not a fixed or mandatory limit, of course. But given people's active and busy lives, that is the minimum for someone who is serious about meditation practice. I encourage meditators to try to maintain that schedule every single day without fail.

I also encourage everyone to add the one-minute hourly meditation during their daily lives. Set aside one minute of every hour to stop and take about fifteen breaths—that's about one minute. This will add a short but regular mindfulness reminder throughout your day.

And when you have the time, you should make the effort to go on meditation retreats at a meditation center. In all these ways you will always be in touch with a regular meditation practice. The commitment to practice is important. And the opportunities for mindfulness are there every moment of the day. Even as you lie in bed at night, go to sleep keeping the mind on the breath.

As for regular sitting, it's good to get into the habit of sitting in the morning and also in the evening. In the morning it may be easier to meditate, as your senses are not yet bombarded by the day's sense stimuli. It can be quite enjoyable to get up before anyone else, to have this time for yourself. In the evening it can seem a little more difficult to meditate, especially for laypeople. The TV and computer may be blaring, your children may be fighting, and your cellphone is right there, offering endless distractions.

But after things have quieted down or if you're able to go off by yourself to a quieter place, meditating in the evening can be wonderful. After all, dealing with all the nitty-gritty problems of fast-paced contemporary life can be nerve-wracking! Yet all that stress and overstimulation can be handled more easily, more calmly, more wisely if you commit to a regular daily period in the evening when you allow the agitation from the day to settle. This will give your mind and spirit time to rest.

People often collapse when they get home and think that a good night's sleep is all they need. But while a good sleep is revitalizing to the body and mind, a good evening meditation can be far more powerful in clearing the mind of the distractions and agitations of the day.

It is also important to grow used to sitting regularly for longer lengths of time. That's because when you try to meditate, even if you're able to sit for one hour, your real, true meditation may be no more than fifteen minutes. So, as you work with your practice, work on sitting a little bit longer each time. This is another reason why it is important to go to retreats regularly and also to find a supportive sitting group in your area, where possible. These will all help you in deepening your practice.

Many people come here to the Bhavana Society and hope to maintain a regular link to the center and to the monks here. We ask them, "How much time do you spend on meditation? How frequently?" These are essential matters. The answers help us to help them.

But what if that person doesn't keep up their regular meditation practice? All of a sudden problems arise and they consult us for help. It will be hard for us to give them the necessary help— because they haven't been doing their homework!

MEDITATION AND RELAXATION

What is the goal and purpose of meditation? Is feeling relaxed and peaceful a good goal?

The purpose is to reach the highest goal of Nibbana, or enlightenment. Along the way there are various other fringe benefits. Feeling peaceful certainly will occur. Becoming relaxed will be a result along the way. These experiences should not be overlooked. But they also should not be taken as the final attainment.

We have to look for the red herrings in meditation. You know about red herrings? Originally they were used to deceive hunting dogs because their smell is so strong the dogs would be thrown off track. Similarly, in meditation we have to look for deceptive moments and experiences.

Don't worry about miraculous attainments and powers, such as being able to read another's thoughts or astral traveling. Don't look for them. These can be red herrings. They can deceive meditators.

What you have to look for is how you get rid of certain psychic irritants in order to cleanse the mind. When the mind is clean and clear, some of these supernatural things may be possible. But they are not the goal of practice.

So, when we understand the truth—especially the Four Noble Truths—we begin to see the real path developing in our mind. When we meditate we always remember to pay attention, that we must develop our mindfulness, concentration, and equanimity.

These factors have to be developed in tranquility meditation as well as insight meditation. Cultivate your attention, sharpen your attention. Pay attention always to your experience. Develop your mindfulness and use concentration to deepen your mindfulness. And try to have equanimity, an unbiased state of mind, so you can look at your experience clearly.

Just try to stay in a balanced state of mind. Then cleansing the mind becomes easier. Buddha said cultivating the mind is possible. Otherwise, we will get lost in the jungle inside our minds.

PAIN AND DISCOMFORT

While sitting in meditation, I try to keep at it when pain and discomfort arise. But after a while I feel I just have to change my position. How do you handle pain and discomfort while trying to sit for longer periods of meditation?

Normally the first and immediate reaction to pain and discomfort is to want to change position. That can be conquered if you have a little patience and if you stay with the pain. Pain that arises in meditation is not going to kill you. But if it does kill you, well, that is the best way to die—while meditating! After all, there are a whole lot more miserable ways to go.

But you won't die. You just need to work with the pain or discomfort. When you have a pain in your back, your knee, or somewhere else while meditating, just watch it at first. Pay mindful attention to it. If you think you will lose your leg or something like that, watch even that reaction—since the way you react can intensify your perception of the pain.

As the Buddha taught, the first "dart" that you experience is the physical sensation of the pain. But the second dart is your attitude toward the pain. That second dart is optional! So, try to have a positive attitude by looking at the pain and seeing it exactly for what it is. Try just sitting with the pain without immediately shifting your position. Say to yourself, "Let me sit with this pain and see how it increases and what happens after that."

You will be surprised as you pay careful attention to the pain. It seems to increase in volume and intensity. It increases until it reaches its painful climax—then it breaks down and even disappears. It becomes a neutral sensation. It becomes weak and blurred. Then your mind is able to return its focus to the breath.

If you stay with that neutral feeling, it turns into a pleasant feeling. As you watch that pleasant feeling, it turns into a neutral feeling again. That neutral feeling may again turn into the unpleasant feeling of discomfort. So it goes, in a cycle like that. Try to see this whole cycle of pain and your reaction to it ebbing and flowing throughout your meditation.

Suppose you are sitting and after thirty minutes you start to experience a lot of pain. If you tolerate the pain for five or ten minutes with this wholesome, positive attitude, you will see the pain or discomfort change into neutral and then pleasant feelings. Then it may become unpleasant for a while. Then it's neutral again. When you come to that neutral feeling a second time, you have spent perhaps forty-five minutes meditating.

Through such effort, you can overcome the immediate desire when encountering discomfort to shift away from it. Sitting through these cycles of pain and discomfort, seeing how the mind reacts, can be a very powerful experience. In this way, you can really get to deeper levels of meditation.

The trouble is that many people don't have a lot of patience, or they have not developed it enough. This difficulty is always coming up in meditation practice for them. I just advise them to stay with the pain and see the whole cycle.

Certainly, if you feel you really need to, you can mindfully shift your position. Or get up quietly and do standing meditation for a while, and then return to sitting. Working with pain and discomfort in meditation can offer deep insights into how our minds work.

Plus, as you learn to sit longer, your body will grow used to the posture, and discomfort will not be such a big issue. Please don't get discouraged when you have discomfort as you sit. That is a part of the deal. Accept it and work with it.

Beginning Buddhism

You've been teaching beginning students a long time. What advice might you have for a person newly interested in Buddhism?

People who are interested in Buddhism must first pick up the right books, especially Theravada books. As I am a Theravada monk, somebody might think I am prejudiced. Surely, I am prejudiced. But I don't condemn other sects and say other sects don't have many wonderful things to teach.

But Theravada Buddhism is the oldest branch of Buddhism; therefore, if somebody wants to learn about Buddhism, first they must learn Theravada Buddhism.

I must tell you a little story I heard about a famous Tibetan teacher. One very cold winter night he called his students together, maybe sixty or seventy of them, from the grounds of the center they were all at. According to the story, in the middle of the night he woke up his bodyguard and asked him to gather the students. They all came to the big meditation hall and were sitting there, trembling from the cold.

This teacher came about a half-hour later and sat down. Everybody was silent. They all were waiting. They thought he was going to make a very serious announcement. Very serious! He sat down and waited for another fifteen minutes. Finally he lifted one finger and said, "Don't forget Theravada Buddhism! Now, go and sleep."

To make this one statement, he created this scene! That means even a Mahayana Buddhist sees the significance of Theravada Buddhism. So, I would say if somebody wants to learn Buddhism, first they must pick up good Theravada books and good translations of the Buddha's teachings.

There are many beautiful translations, especially Bhikkhu Bodhi's translation of the Majjhima Nikaya, Samyutta Nikaya, Anguttara Nikaya, and Sutta Nipata. He also has written some very good books on the Digha Nikaya and separately published one book titled *The Buddha's Teaching in His Own Words*. People should read first at least one of these books to gain the background and grounding for the practice.

And when it comes to meditation, they must also pick up meditation books that give clear instructions on meditation. I don't want to pinpoint any particular books, but the instructions must be easy to follow.

Second, they must choose a teacher who teaches in a clear, comprehensive language. By associating with that person, they will learn very sincerely. While learning, they must practice. Practice, practice, and practice! Then they will see how these meditation instructions work very well. The person will come to have a good knowledge of meditation through experience.

Ultimate Aim of Meditation

Are we trying to empty the mind when meditating? What is the ultimate aim of meditating?

Sometimes people think insight meditation is just sitting on a cushion doing nothing. This is *not* mind-emptying meditation! This is *mindfulness* meditation. There is more to it than just sitting there. After all, you can devote 100 percent of your attention to what you are doing and still not gain any insight. A cat or a tiger pays total attention to its prey but doesn't gain an iota of insight about anything. Why? All they have is simple concentration as they focus intently on their prey in their minds.

But in insight meditation we pay total attention with mindfulness. We work on gaining the ability to look at everything that arises with the clearest state of mind—without greed, hatred, or delusion.

That is not how we normally pay attention to things. Usually our minds are obsessed or distracted by some variation of greed or desire for things or a rejection of things. We feel annoyance, dislike, or dissatisfaction with our current state. We want to be someplace else, anyplace other than where we are. Or there is ignorance about what is really going on around us and inside us.

But when we start to pay mindful attention to our moment-to-moment experience, we learn to see the mind's restlessness and distraction, its illusions and desires, more keenly. That is where letting go comes in.

Very often you hear about "letting go of things." Sometimes meditators become confused by this phrase. We must remember what is meant. We learn to let go of those things that are harmful to our practice, but we keep those things that are beneficial.

What is harmful to us? Greedy thoughts are harmful. Hateful thoughts. Jealousy, fear, worry, confusion—we must train ourselves to abandon these states by cultivating their opposites. When we have mindful reflection, what do we see? What do we gain? We gain clear comprehension.

Clear comprehension or clear understanding of the purpose, according to the Buddha, means we understand our aim. It means that we meditate not just to gain a little relaxation or to temporarily feel good. Those are certainly nice byproducts of meditation practice. But the ultimate aim of practicing meditation is the purification of our being. We aim at no less than overcoming suffering, treading the path that leads to liberation, and finally attaining that liberation. Our mind and body are our laboratory for this effort.

In the Four Foundations of Mindfulness the Buddha repeated something so many times that it is like a chorus: "This body is not something to cling to. This body exists for me to gain knowledge and insight." That is really what we are doing in meditation practice—not just blanking out.

SAMATHA AND VIPASSANA

I am interested in your thoughts about a certain way of viewing meditation: that samatha meditation with a primary object of the breath is preparation for vipassana, a type of meditation that technically has no primary object and in which everything is the object. I wonder if you think there's a place in the meditative journey where a meditation that focuses on a primary object becomes something to put aside in favor of seeing the three characteristics in everything that arises?

There seems to be some confusion in the question itself. We must understand the difference between samatha and vipassana meditation. Samatha meditation—*samatha* is the Pali word, in Sanskrit it is *shamatha*—means calming and making the mind peaceful to gain concentration. That is the meditation system we use to gain deep concentration, culminating in attainment of what is called *jhanas*.

To gain that state of concentration, we need one single object to focus the mind. So selecting one single object to focus the mind to gain concentration is samatha meditation.

For vipassana meditation any subject is acceptable. Anything—your body, feelings, perceptions, sounds, sights, tastes, whatever. We can use anything to gain insight. That is called mindfulness practice. Anything we focus our mind on is clearly marked with the three characteristics of impermanence, unsatisfactoriness, and selflessness. Therefore, vipassana meditation can use any subject, while samatha meditation uses only one subject at a time.

Having said this, which of these two do we practice first? In your question you say samatha meditation is to be practiced to prepare for vipassana. To some extent that is true, because some people are very good at gaining concentration. It is easy for them. At other times, or for a different person, they cannot gain concentration that easily or quickly. For that time, for that person, practice vipassana first.

There are four ways actually. You can practice samatha first and then vipassana. The other method is to practice vipassana first, then samatha. The third method is practicing the two parallel to each other. The fourth method is to just inwardly settle your mind. That is neither samatha or vipassana but a combination of both.

Practicing concentration meditation, the mind becomes calm, peaceful, and relaxed. Once you gain concentration, you don't stop there. You use vipassana to deepen your understanding. When these combine together you can see things more clearly. As the Buddha said, the concentrated mind can see things exactly as they are.

So, if somebody likes to practice tranquility or concentration meditation because they have good powers of concentration, then that is fine for them. But he or she should not stop there. The person must then go to vipassana meditation.

GOOD AND BAD MEDITATION

Do you have good and bad meditation sessions? If so, what is the difference?

Actually, when you practice mindfulness there is no difference. There is no "good" meditation or "bad" meditation. Why? No matter how "bad" we think our meditation is going, we can use those so-called bad experiences as the object of our mindfulness, right then and there.

Why do we think a meditation session is a bad one? Maybe it's because the mind is wandering. Or it's full of worries and fear, distracted and agitated by anger, tension, lust, or restlessness. But in fact, these are the actual materials we have to use in meditation. These are called mental objects.

During a bad meditation session, if some really unpleasant feelings or distracted states arise, then use them, then and there, as the object of your meditation. If anger at your spouse or your boss arises, examine it. Don't do anything. Learn to watch the anger without getting carried away by it. Don't let it obsess you. Try to be aloof around it. Be mindful of the focus of your mind at that second, noting, "This is anger. This is how anger is! This is what it does. It disturbs my peacefulness. I can feel my heart beat faster."

As soon as anger arises in the mind, marching orders go out to the heart: "Get that heartbeat racing! Elevate that blood pressure!" We can see this connection, we can see this happening. So, we just keep watching, watching. As the seconds and minutes pass, the anger, the fear, the anxiety, the lustful thoughts that have come to dominate our attention slowly subside. Perhaps not very quickly. It may take a while. But they will if we watch it from start to finish. This process of mindful observation of mental objects is part and parcel of what we do during meditation. So how can it be "bad"?

And when you say "good meditation," what do you mean by "good"? Perhaps your mind is not so busy. Yet maybe a good meditation lulls you to sleep. Someone might say, "Ah, now *that's* a good meditation." That is not good meditation! That is bad meditation.

If you do feel sleepy, by the way, just watch that sleepiness, too. And do something to rouse your energy, to wake you up and get rid of your drowsiness. Take three deep breaths and hold them to oxygenate the blood. Do standing meditation to wake your body up from its drowsiness. Even that situation, if we handle it mindfully, is not bad meditation.

So, I would not say there is good meditation and bad meditation. It all depends on how we handle each moment. If we handle a moment mindfully, any situation is a good meditation.

THE LOTUS POSTURE

Should I try to meditate in the lotus posture? Is it important?

When it comes to posture, if I say one thing is important or better, other people who cannot do that position may feel bad about their own posture. Since you asked the question, I must say, yes, the lotus position is the *best* posture. Once you sit in lotus posture, you see how steady your body is, how easy it is for you to breathe, how easily you gain concentration.

The lotus posture is not something impossible. Once you sit in that posture, you feel how comfortable it is—that is why it is called the yogic posture, the diamond posture. The lotus is considered to be the best flower among flowers. Yogis use this posture to sit for hours—no other posture can keep you steady and enable you to sit that long without moving. For these reasons, this is the best posture.

If you cannot go for the best, go for the second best: half-lotus. And so forth, scale it down to the easiest posture, so that you will not be deprived of the practice of meditation. Sitting in a chair is fine too, if that is all you feel your body can manage at the moment. The important thing is just to start a regular meditation practice.

As for the challenge of attaining the lotus posture, I can talk about that. When I was sixty-five I decided to sit in full lotus. Before that I had never sat in full lotus. I sat only half-lotus. One day I thought, "Gee, I've been sitting and meditating for so many years, let me try it—full lotus." That day I sat only five minutes. Boy, I thought I was going to die! It was *so* painful.

But my determination was stronger. I said, "No, I must try this!" The next day I sat in lotus posture. And the next day. And the next day. Each time I increased my length of sitting. Finally I could sit in full lotus for more than an hour without any trouble.

So, from my experience I can tell you this is not something impossible. Anybody can do it if I could start doing it at age sixty-five! Ever since then I have been sitting in that posture.

REACTION TO PAIN

I deal with chronic lower back pain. How do we work with such pain in meditation so it is not worsened through mental suffering and our reaction to it?

If you have chronic pain, try relaxing your back muscles and then put your entire attention on the breath. During the time that your mind is focused on the breath, you may not experience acute pain. As soon as your attention shifts from the breath, you may feel the pain again.

Also, try alternating between sitting and walking meditation. It would be better if your sitting was limited to a half-hour or less and that you do more walking meditation. You can also try changing your sitting posture to an easier posture or try sitting on a chair.

I have back pain when I sleep on a very soft mattress. Sleeping on a hard mattress might also help. If none of these suggestions works for you, then see your doctor again and he or she might make a better recommendation.

OTHER MEDITATION POSTURES

Many in the West, when they think about Buddhism, think about sitting meditation. But what about walking meditation, especially given the fact that the Buddha and his monks walked everywhere?

The Buddha used all four postures in meditation practice: sitting, walking, standing, and lying down. The easiest and most familiar is sitting, because most of the time people sit in the office, they sit at home. Therefore, they use that as an easy posture, especially to gain concentration. But for vipassana meditation all the four postures can be used.

In walking meditation some of us emphasize the movement of our feet and coordinating with the breath, noticing the movement and the feeling we have when we walk slowly. That part is emphasized.

But there is another part of walking meditation—that is the mental state. While walking we must understand every part of our body is moving. Every part! In walking meditation all the aggregates—our bodies, our feelings, our perception, our volitional formations, our thinking and consciousness—all these five aggregates are involved. Every aggregate is changing at every fraction of a second when we walk.

It is a more dynamic meditation than sitting meditation. In sitting meditation the body is relatively still, but the mind is working very hard. In walking meditation the mind and body both are working in cooperation with each other. They have to cooperate.

So, when we walk in silence we focus our mind not on just one aggregate. Instead, we focus on all of them working together simultaneously. Awareness of that simultaneous movement of every aggregate, the changing nature of every aggregate, is a very good meditation.

That is why the Buddha used these four postures. They are akin to the four wheels of a vehicle. When you balance your vehicle, you have to balance all four wheels. So, sitting, standing, walking, and lying down, all these four postures can be used equally for vipassana meditation because in all these postures the same thing is happening.

MEDITATING OUTDOORS

I have been meditating outside. It occurred to me that when meditating outside things in nature—animals, insects—they often come to you. What are your thoughts about the benefits of meditating in nature?

Well, at the very least you get a lot of oxygen from the trees! You merge with nature when you meditate outside. You know, in the Buddha's life, he was born under a tree and he attained enlightenment under a tree and passed away under trees. And whenever he gave his followers instruction on meditation, his bhikkhus and bhikkhunis, or monks and nuns, he would say, "Bhikkhus! There are trees. Sit under them and meditate!"

When we are very peaceful, the trees that surround us—

although they don't have feelings like ours—somehow receive the peaceful vibrations from us, and we feel the peaceful vibrations out in nature. So, practicing outside is a very compassionate and meaningful way to practice.

MISUNDERSTANDING MEDITATION

Meditation is taught in different ways by different Buddhist schools. Then there is the lay mindfulness movement in the West. Can you talk about the differences among these ways of teaching meditation?

Meditation is the heart of Buddhist teachings in all of the sects. Whether it is Mahayana, Theravada, Vajrayana—in all sects the practice of meditation is emphasized.

Though it has become a very popular subject, there also is a great deal of misunderstanding about meditation. Either it is overly simplified or it is made very difficult to practice.

When it is simplified, people become so complacent and don't take it seriously. Some people think they just need to be aware of what is happening around them. So you don't have to do anything, just be as you are. Go with the flow. Take it easy. Don't worry, don't make effort! It's your nature. You don't have to worry. You are enlightened, but you just don't know. That is one way of looking at meditation.

However, that is not actually what we learn in the Buddha's teachings from the scriptures. Maybe some individuals come up with various ideas just to throw around very catchy phrases. I think that is too simple.

There is another way of looking at meditation that can become almost impossible to follow. That is, an analytical system. You keep analyzing, analyzing, analyzing. This approach breaks it down to very nitty-gritty details that go on and on as if meditation is something like microbiology.

When we look at the Buddha's suttas, we don't see that kind of a detailed system. We have to look at the Buddha's suttas for guidance.

Unfortunately, that is the very thing that people don't want to look at! They don't want to study; they simply want to meditate without knowing the Buddha's guidelines. If we try to meditate, we will get bewildered and confused and we won't know what we are doing. And that is what has happened to so many people. This is why I always quote the Buddha's suttas on meditation and always refer people to them.

MEDITATION PROGRESS

How do we know we are making progress in meditation?

This is a very common question because people don't know what they are doing. They follow this system, then that system, this teacher's instruction, then that teacher's method.

They spend many hours sitting on cushions and counting their cushion hours. How many hours, how many days? How many retreats have I gone to? They go from retreat to retreat. If they hear that in such and such a place there's a good meditation teacher, they say, "Let's go there!" And then they hear there's another teacher—"Let's go there!"

They keep window-shopping. You might call it meditation window-shopping. Yet when they look at themselves, they find themselves at the same place. They have gained nothing. They never look where they are supposed to look. They never do what they're supposed to do. One doesn't have to go that far to practice meditation. Buddha has laid down the plan. And they just ignore that.

When we try to explain meditation from the Buddha's own words, they say, "Who cares about that! Tell me what you know, what you have experienced!" But we only know what we experience by following the system. If we don't follow a method, we cannot tell what we've experienced.

Buddha asked us to look at our own mind. That is exactly what we are *not* doing. In order to see how far we have developed in our meditation, we must look at our mind.

Hearing the Heart

During meditation I can hear my heartbeat, and it competes with my breath during meditation. What should I do to overcome this?

If you hear or feel your heartbeat while breathing, you just pay attention. You don't have to divide your attention between the breath and the heartbeat. You let your breath be almost automatic. You just let it go—in and out—because it is happening anyway. Then, when you feel the heartbeat, it is something you don't normally experience all the time. But the breath is going on all the time. So let that breath continue in its natural rhythm. And when the heartbeat arises, you pay attention to the heartbeat—don't try to divide your attention.

When you do not feel the heartbeat, then the breath becomes prominent. In anapanasati meditation, you become aware of any sensation that arises as it arises. For instance, joy. Feeling joy, you breathe in, and feeling joy, you breathe out. So you feel the joy while you are breathing in, you feel the joy while you are breathing out. The attention is on the joy, and the breath is moving in and out, because it's a constant object. Since it is repeating itself, it doesn't need any attention—it goes on and on. But joy is not going on all the time. It is something you have not noticed before. And suddenly you experience joy.

Pay attention to the things you experience anew. That is not a hindrance, don't try to overcome it.

PAIN WHILE MEDITATING

Can the pain we experience in our legs and backs while sitting help us to understand the noble truth of dukkha?

Just feeling physical aches and pains itself does not explain dukkha or unsatisfactoriness. We experience dukkha in our own minds. Physical sensations will not go away even if you attain enlightenment. Even arahants have pain, even the Buddha experienced pain. But they do not suffer from their pain. Suffering is a psychological mental state, and that is what we want to get rid of—and it can be gotten rid of!

MEDITATION FOCUS

What should I focus on when I do vipassana meditation?

If you do vipassana meditation correctly, you should be able to see very clearly impermanence, anicca; suffering, dukkha; and nonself, anatta. Everything else should be ignored. Stay with your awareness of anicca, dukkha, and anatta.

You experience the changes in your breath, the feeling of inhaling and exhaling, the perception of inhaling and exhaling. There is our intentional attention to the breath and the feeling and consciousness associated with the whole process of breathing. You may experience the hardness and softness of your breath. You can feel the moisture and dryness of the breath. You can feel the heat and coolness of the breath.

In so doing you experience the characteristics of the four elements—earth, water, heat, and air. You notice them changing every fraction of a second. This is impermanence you are experiencing. You can notice also that any thought arising in your mind is changing. This is impermanence, too.

Some of our experience is pleasant. Then the mind attempts to grasp on to it. Some of our experience is unpleasant. Then your mind attempts to reject it. Some of our experience is neither pleasant nor unpleasant.

Notice how greed, hatred, and delusion arise in your mind. Any attempt your mind makes to grasp anything ends up in frustration or disappointment. Not being able to grasp any impermanent thing—whether it is form, feeling, perception, thoughts, and consciousness—brings about suffering.

This is why all impermanent aggregates are called aggregates of suffering—*dukkhakhandha*. Seeing this truth is called "knowledge and vision of everything as they are"—*yathbhutananadassana*.

If you are meditating correctly you should be able to focus your mind on impermanence, unsatisfactoriness, and nonself. When you see the truth of impermanence, unsatisfactoriness, and nonself, you are able to let go of greed, hatred, and delusion.

TRAINING THE MIND

During meditation my mind sometimes becomes very active, thinking of the past or future or planning things I need to do. I attempt to overcome this by concentrating on the breath, but lately this has been causing headaches when trying to counteract an overly active mind. Do you have any suggestions?

When the mind is wandering you have to train it to stay in one place. I suggest counting—you count from one to ten. Breathing in and breathing out, count one. Breathe in and breathe out, count two. Breathe in and out, count three. In such a fashion go to ten and stop there. Then, do the same in reverse and come down from ten to one. Breathe in and breathe out—ten. Breathe in and breathe out—nine. And so on.

In the second round you go from one to nine and come down to one. In the third round you go from one to eight, then back to one and so forth, until you come to one and stop. Then you repeat it again. You go to ten and count down to one.

When you do it several times, your mind gets so tired of counting—it is so boring! You lose your count, and then you think, "I was counting and what happened? Where was I when my mind started wandering?" Then you remember it started wandering when you were at six and you wonder whether you should go from six to seven or six to five. You get confused! Then you start all over again.

In this way you make your mind very tired. When the mind is tired, it cannot wander anymore. Then, start focusing the mind on the breath. This seems to work for some people—it may not for everybody. But try it and see if it works for you.

Another way to deal with the wandering mind is to say, "If you want to wander, I will provide an object to focus on." Then you focus your attention on the thirty-two parts of the body. Memorize them and go from the crown of the head to toes, focusing the mind on each part. Say, "Head hair is impermanent, unsatisfactory, and selfless. Body hair is impermanent, unsatisfactory, and selfless. The nails are impermanent, unsatisfactory, and selfless," and so forth.

Say also, "This is not mine, this is not I, this is not myself." You focus your mind on each of the thirty-two body parts using these six sentences. See what will happen.

The mind is so agitated and excited that it wanders. So give it a subject! And at the same time you learn something meaningful. You gain insight into your own body. All the notions about the body will slowly fade away. This is really a mindfulness practice. There are six sentences for each body part. Head hair, for instance, is impermanent, unsatisfactory, and selfless. Plus, head hair "is not mine, it is not I, this is not myself."

You may say your hair is yours. But if it is yours, you should be able to do anything you want with your hair aside from cutting, washing, and shampooing it. But as you age, can you stop your hair from turning gray and falling out? Can you control that? No.

Therefore, head hair is not yours, along with body hair, teeth, nails, and the other parts of the body. For every part of the body we focus our mind on we can use these six sentences as a way of analyzing the thirty-two body parts as described by the Buddha. And the wandering mind will learn something. That's a good meditation.

BREATH AS AN AGENT

Insight meditation instructions recommend letting distracting mental formations arise and fall away, and to simply return one's awareness to the breath. How does a meditator gain insight regarding aggregates and mental formations if anything other than the breath is to be seen as a distraction and allowed to fall away?

Actually a meditator gains insight and wisdom not just by focusing the mind on the breath. The breath is used at the beginning, and through the breath we can notice various types of things in our mind and body. This is a very big subject, and sometimes I hesitate to start talking about it, as I can go overboard since the subject is very deep and profound. Talking about it is difficult.

But we start with the breath and through the breath we can see impermanence, unsatisfactoriness, and selflessness, of our body, feelings, perceptions, thoughts, and consciousness. These are what we call the Five Aggregates. These are all we have.

The breath is called a body conditioner. When we breathe in and out, oxygen is distributed through our blood circulation to keep our cells alive and to keep the body functioning. Unlike all the kinds of conditioners you might buy at the store, the Buddha talked about the real conditioner that conditions our living. This is the breath.

And then we have thoughts, feeling, perceptions, and consciousness, and all these are constantly and consistently changing. When we start with the breath, the breath shows this sign of change because the breath is constantly changing, bringing in new oxygen to replace the old air in the body.

It is changing all the time. Therefore, everything else is impermanence. Everything in the universe is impermanent, and because of impermanence, things can exist. Nothing can exist if things are not impermanent.

Friends, impermanence is the only thing that keeps us alive. If we understand impermanence exactly as it is, then we reach a permanent state. We can see this through the breath.

Therefore, we use the breath as an agent, and through that our mind opens to see impermanence and to free ourselves from attachment. To gain insight we use the breath, the body, feelings, perceptions, and so forth.

Light Show

During today's talk you mentioned that seeing a light or brightness that comes by itself is dangerous. Why is that?

Because it confuses the meditator. The meditator thinks, "Oh! I am going to attain jhanas!" As soon as you sit for ten minutes, a bright light appears. "Oh, I am done! I have attained jhanas!" That very light can confuse you.

But if the light arises through the development of mind, and through overcoming hindrances just before gaining concentration, that is not dangerous, because you have prepared your mind to accept it.

As for the light that appears all of a sudden for no reason, you don't know how you got it and so you get confused. That is the danger.

Sensations during Meditation

During most meditation sessions, I feel a throbbing between my eyebrows. It is not painful, although it makes it harder to

be aware of my breath at my nostrils. Should I pay any special attention to this throbbing?

If you feel throbbing between your eyebrows, if it is very strong and significant, pay attention but relax. Don't get upset. This can be interpreted as a headache or something else. Don't do anything else, just keep paying attention to it and relax your mind. Don't be afraid of the sensation. It will disappear.

HANDLING JOY AND BLISS

How should we deal with joy and bliss when they arise during meditation?

When you have feelings of joy and bliss, watch them mindfully and see how they rise, peak, and pass away just like any other feelings or emotions. No feelings stay still. Feeling arises when there is contact. When the senses and sensory objects come together, then feeling arises. Feeling cannot arise on its own without any contact. So, don't get attached to any feeling. Let them come and let them go.

Attachment, after all, is a mental state. It, too, comes and goes. Feeling comes and goes as fast as can be. If you try to grab a feeling, it slips away. It is already past. If pleasant feelings and states such as joy or bliss arise, just note them. When you try to cling to them, they will slip from your grasp. This unending attempt to grab and hold on to feelings we like leads to endless frustration. This is the essence of suffering.

To put it another way, stress results from when we feel unable to cling to desirable feelings. I would also put it this way: the insatiability of desire is suffering.

Stay unattached to any feelings that arise—even delightful ones such as joy and bliss. That way, you will not end up in frustration. They are all impermanent. They are unreliable. Just stay mindful and watch them come and go.

STRIVING TOO HARD

Why does the body heat up in deep meditation?

You may be doing something not recommended to have this experience. Normally, in deep meditation, you feel calm, relaxing, peaceful mental states rather than heat. You may be striving very hard with unnecessary pressure. Next time when you meditate, if you have that sensation, just relax and see how much unnecessary exertion you may be applying. Then relax and reduce it.

COUNTING BREATHS

How do we deal with restlessness during meditation? Is it OK to count the breaths?

You have to pay total mindful attention to the breath and breathe very mindfully to calm your mind. Restlessness and worry come as a pair because when you are restless, you worry. Or when you worry, you become restless.

Restlessness and worry result in what we call monkey mind. We are born with monkey mind because we evolved from monkeys. And that process is still going on in our mind! We still have that tendency. The first thing you have to do is think of the noble qualities of the Buddha to calm yourself and make your mind very peaceful.

As for counting, there is a very beautiful and mindful way of counting to deal with restlessness. Breathe in and breathe out and count one. Again, breathe in and breathe out, count two. Again, breathe in and breathe out, count three. You count up to ten in this fashion. And then come down from ten to one.

The second time go from one to nine. Then nine to one. Then one to eight, eight to one; one to seven, seven to one; one to six, six to one; one to five, five to one; one to four, four to one; one to three, three to one; one to two, two to one and stop.

When you do this kind of counting, your mind stays on the breath. But because of the habitual nature of our mind, our attention still drifts away and goes somewhere. All of a sudden, your mind is on the moon or in South America.

Suddenly, you remember, "Ah! I was counting, what happened to my counting?" Then you can't recall at which point your mind wandered away. Was it six or seven? Or maybe eight? Then you remember you were at six. When you come back to six, then you don't remember whether to go from one to six or six to one! Right?

Just start all over again from the beginning. And then go to ten again. When you come down, the mind wanders again. The mind does not stay on the counting. Then you realize, "Ah! I lost the counting again!" So you start all over again.

When you do this exercise many, many times, then your wandering mind will stay on the breath. And that will help you overcome your restless, monkey mind.

THE DOUBTING MEDITATOR

How do we deal with doubt arising in meditation?

The Pali word for doubt is *vicikiccha*. The cure for the hindrance of doubt is trust. You've got to trust your own practice, number one. Look at yourself. You have overcome other hindrances like restlessness and worry. That gives you confidence that you can do it.

You are not hopeless, you are not helpless. You are a person who can do something. The very fact that you came to practice indicates that you have a wonderful intention. That gives you strength that you have achieved something from meditation. Your own personal experience gives you confidence.

Then you begin to trust the Dhamma because it is this Dhamma that brought you to this practice. It gives you this self-confidence. And then you have a deeper confidence in the Buddha who introduced the Dhamma. Your doubt gradually dies away and disappears.

MEDITATION AND MANTRAS

You have said that one should not use a mantra. Some Theravada Buddhist teachers recommend using the word "Buddho" with the in- and out-breath. What do you think about this?

To be honest, using the word "Buddho" itself is not enough. We have to deepen our understanding. Repeating the word "Buddho, Buddho, Buddho" does not deepen your understanding. That also would be stimulating your mind as you verbalize in your head. When you verbalize and stimulate the mind, gaining concentration can be difficult.

The Buddha never recommended anywhere to repeat his name to attain any jhana. The word "Buddho" itself does not open our mind to understanding. Perhaps this practice helps you to attain some control of your mind at the beginning, to reduce distraction and focus the mind. But then later on you've got to get involved in the real serious practice. I have never come across anywhere in the Buddhist suttas where somebody recounted the word "Buddho" to attain any stage of enlightenment.

PEACE IN SOLITUDE

Should I be concerned that my practice of meditation is causing me to spend more time in solitude?

Any serious meditator likes solitude. A deep understanding of Dhamma comes to us when we are in solitude. Solitude offers plenty of time for us to have a good hard look at ourselves. When we are in the company of others our attention is drawn to countless distractions. We can more easily experience peace in solitude. For this reason the Buddha always praised solitude.

"Solo" Practice

With no access to a nearby practicing sangha group or a meditation teacher, and little opportunity for meditation retreats, I have an isolated "solo" meditation practice. Given those circumstances, if I were to simulate an occasional private intensive meditation retreat at home, how important or valuable might restricting eating solid food to just the morning be?

If you are a solo meditator and train yourself to be disciplined and decide not to have solid food in the evening, I think you will benefit just as well as somebody who is in a community of meditators.

Actually, if you can do it as a solo meditation practitioner, your training of not taking solid food in the evening would be even more effective because you have achieved this without any guidance or encouragement. You have made the commitment on your own. Therefore, your practice would be even better. I would recommend that you go ahead and do this practice.

2

Morality and Discipline

SIGNIFICANCE OF SILA

Buddhism teaches that three things, *sila*, *samadhis*, and *panna*—or morality, concentration, and wisdom—are key to a successful meditation practice. And we must have good sila or morality as a first step toward a successful meditation practice. Could you elaborate?

In addition to using the word "morality" for *sila*, I would also suggest the words "discipline" and "restraint," perhaps even in place of the word "morality," which has a philosophical connotation. And, yes, it is correct to say that practicing sila—acting with discipline and restraint in daily life—lays an essential foundation for a good meditation practice.

Depending on how disciplined we are, our practice becomes successful. When we don't have sufficient discipline, our practice will be difficult. Mindfulness may then be hard to attain or sustain.

We must have good discipline to be mindful. Most of the time we don't remember to be mindful—we are not mindful of mindfulness! It's harder yet when our minds are distracted or bothered by unwholesome actions we may have undertaken or become involved in.

33

The Pali word *sila* recalls the word "sealant" in English. When you want to fill a crack, you use a sealant and seal it off. You lay the foundation for a house and cover all the cracks, so no water will seep in, no insects will enter, and the foundation won't collapse. As a result, the foundation for your house remains firm and sturdy enough to build upon. Sila is like that when it comes to meditation. It's the foundation. Through restraint, through wholesome actions and decisions made in our daily lives, we lay this foundation.

If we don't lay a good foundation for meditation, we can directly see the results in our practice. You may be meditating regularly, sitting a half-hour or hour. All of a sudden, one day you can't sit for even ten minutes. Your mind is agitated, you're constantly distracted, you simply can't focus. Something you have done in your life—becoming enraged with someone, sexual misconduct, addictive behavior of all sorts, or some unwholesome action of body, speech, or mind—has deeply registered in your subconscious mind. It keeps coming back up, making you feel remorseful, guilty, restless, full of worries. You just can't sit!

However, it's unrealistic to expect people to become paragons of virtue before they ever begin to meditate. If we wait until we are saints, if we put off meditation until our sila is perfect, then we will never meditate! Whatever our moral situation, we must begin.

We make the commitment to root out unwholesome behavior and to encourage wholesome habits in our lives. It helps to make the commitment and to come back to it time and time again: "OK, from now on I'm going to undertake this meditation practice and I'm going to try not to break my principles." If you do, then learn from those consequences. Feel the heaviness in your mind and in your life. Our goal is to make the mind light, to make our life light. After all, we are seeking to attain en-*light*-enment, aren't we?

Sila, though, should not be confused with a set of commandments. It is something you undertake by yourself, of your own accord. If you don't make the effort, if you commit some unwholesome behavior, you reap the consequences and it affects your meditation practice. If you do make the effort, you'll also see the positive consequences. It's very cause and effect.

We practice sila for our own self-confidence and to overcome our weaknesses. Sila is a way of behaving that we ourselves choose. We undertake it by ourselves for the sake of a steady state of mind, for the sake of progress in our practice. Good sila strengthens our courage and ability. It gives support to our meditation practice and provides psychological strength. It is this foundation that is absolutely necessary to gain concentration.

No Regret, No Remorse

How do skillful actions affect our concentration?

Think of a large tree. When you look at a tree, you can see the leaves, the canopy, the branches, the bark. Yet the whole tree stands on its roots buried in the ground. If the roots are very strong, deep, and powerful, you can depend on a tree's steady growth.

Deep roots are similar to ethical, moral principles or wholesome spiritual habits. Some habits are called *akusala sila*, or unskillful. Wholesome habits are called *kusala sila*. Everything depends on our moral principles, just like the roots of that large tree.

When you observe the precepts, the mind will not be shaken or full of regret and remorse. When you go to sleep you can sleep well and you get up well. At night you will not have nightmares because your moral habits are good ones.

When you reflect on how you spent your day you have no regret. As a result the next day you are full of joy. With joy you live your daily life, observing the same moral, ethical principles. Then you will be very calm, relaxed, and peaceful. Tranquility will easily arise. It happens naturally. You don't have to wish to be calm and relaxed.

That is the nature of Dhamma. When you have this calm, relaxed, peaceful, joyful state, then you become happy. Happiness arises naturally in a mind free from remorse.

We also should remember the difference between happiness and excitement. Some people equate the two. When excitement arises, you will laugh and jump up and down. You win the lottery and get a lot of money and get excited. And you say, "I'm happy!" But that is not happiness; that is excitement.

But when you experience happiness based on moral, ethical, wholesome habits, then your mind is very calm, relaxed, and peaceful. There is nothing to agitate and excite you. When you are happy, you don't have to strain to gain concentration. Buddha said the happy mind naturally gains concentration.

This all happens very naturally, and you don't have to wish for it to happen. You just have to take that first step—that is, undertaking moral, ethical, wholesome, skillful habits.

MEDITATION GROUNDWORK

How exactly does wholesome sila affect our ability to meditate?

It's important to understand that restraint and discipline are just one side of the coin. Observance—which means undertaking wholesome actions and encouraging positive states of mind—is the other side of that coin.

Restraint is called *samvara*; observance is called *rakkhana*. For instance, we give up killing and harming other beings. That's a wonderful thing. But we also practice loving-friendliness. We give up stealing. That's a wonderful thing. But at the same time we cultivate generosity. We abstain from telling lies. But we also strive to tell the truth. We choose to abstain from abusing alcohol and other drugs. Then, we do all we can in our daily lives to maintain a steady, peaceful state of mind.

So, while sila means abstaining from unwholesome actions or

habits of mind, it also means observing other wholesome practices and habits of mind. As we restrain our senses, on the one hand, we cultivate positive, opposite tendencies in working with the senses, on the other.

Having gained some confidence in how you live your daily life, as soon as you sit to meditate, you are better able to gain concentration since your mind is clear, clean, and steady. There's no remorse, no regret, no guilty feelings, no shame.

So, you shouldn't consider sila as some kind of burden imposed upon you. Sila lays the groundwork in meditation and is a springboard to concentration. And concentration is then a springboard to wisdom. Each links with the other.

The Buddha repeatedly mentioned it: "The concentrated mind knows things as they are." Concentration is like training a spotlight on something. Wisdom or insight is like eyesight—which then sees and understands what has been caught in the glare of that spotlight of concentration.

These two—concentration and wisdom—become strong when we have a strong moral foundation or good sila. And these three elements are the three main pillars of Buddhism. Actually, the entire teachings of the Buddha can be contained in these three categories: sila, samadhi, panna. They are like a tripod—one leg cannot stand without the other two.

That is why we emphasize these things in meditation practice, especially at an advanced level. If people really want to stick to meditation practice, they must—they must!—undertake this kind of commitment. They must begin to take total responsibility for how they live their lives.

RIGHT LIVELIHOOD AND RESPONSIBILITY

When it comes to Right Livelihood, most of us probably don't work at slaughterhouses or weapons manufacturers. However, many of us find ourselves working, for example, for companies that make most of its revenue from sugary drinks. Or a company that fires someone who just had a child. Or as a janitor at an advertising firm whose job is to create desire for products. Are we complicit in such work?

The way people use revenue from your work is not your responsibility. You have no intention to do something to hurt somebody. And your intention is to do your job. While doing your job you can have thoughts of metta in your mind: "Let my work be beneficial to all people."

THE SIGNIFICANCE OF PRECEPTS

What is the significance of the precepts in Buddhist practice?

In order to remind ourselves of our ethical principles, we repeat these precepts—the Five Precepts for laypeople or the Eight Lifetime Precepts, or the monastic precepts, that we offer at the Bhavana Society.

We repeat them very often, sometimes daily, in order for people not to forget. When we repeat something again and again, it stays in the mind and automatically comes into play. The person will remember them when a situation arises. If it is unethical behavior, the person will not become involved in it, recalling the precepts they have taken.

For this reason, the precepts are repeated again and again.

With the Five Precepts, a layperson undertakes the training rule to abstain from taking life; to abstain from taking what is not given; to abstain from sensual misconduct; to abstain from false speech; and to abstain from intoxicating drinks and drugs causing heedlessness.

The precepts also provide the basis for concentration in our meditation practice. When we maintain ethical principles the mind is calm, and when we sit to meditate we gain concentration quickly. When we break the precepts a person feels remorse and regret and the mind grows unsettled and restless and cannot gain concentration.

Therefore, to encourage self-confidence and concentration, these precepts are important.

THE EIGHT LIFETIME PRECEPTS

At Bhavana you offer the Eight Lifetime Precepts, with an additional focus on false speech, harsh speech, malicious speech, and gossip or useless speech. Why do you offer this expanded list of precepts?

These are all elements of the Noble Eightfold Path, and the Eight Lifetime Precepts bring a greater attention to them.

In Right Speech, we have the four aspects of speech. That means abstaining from telling lies, divisive talk, harsh speak, and gossip or useless speech.

Right Action involves abstaining from killing, stealing, and sensual misconduct. I use "sensual misconduct" instead of "sexual misconduct" because the original phrase is given in the plural and so includes the eyes, ears, nose, tongue, body, and mind.

People habitually abuse their senses by seeing so many unnecessary things: videos and TV shows, movies, and such. And then they abuse their ears by listening to all kinds of unnecessary things. And the tongue is one of the most abused organs by all the things we consume, eating all kinds of junk food and the like.

And by speaking, a person can also abuse their tongue, saying wrong, hurtful, insulting things. The last of the Eight Lifetime Precepts includes abstaining from drinks and drugs that cause heedlessness, and abstaining from wrong livelihood, which means not dealing with livestock for meat, selling and buying weapons, selling and buying poisons, and cheating in measurements. These are some of the examples of how people do not know how to choose a Right Livelihood.

These are precepts anybody can observe provided the person has the will. By following these precepts, the person is following three steps of the Noble Eightfold Path. Therefore, we use the Eight Lifetime Precepts, and lay followers recite them as part of the daily morning puja.

3

Buddhist Principles and Practices

The Buddha's Teachings

Why should we work on mindfulness and study the Buddha's teachings? How is it any different from other philosophical systems that talk about the nature of reality and the problems of existence?

Well, there is a big difference between the Buddha's teaching and mere philosophical speculation about the nature of reality. The Buddha's teachings are not a philosophy to study just for the sake of knowledge and intellectual curiosity. The Buddha taught a way out of samsara, meaning the repeated round of birth and death. He found a solution to the recurrence of suffering in life after life after life.

It's not a speculative method at all but a practical and realistic one. His teaching of morality is a systematic training to discipline the mind, to simplify life, and to clear the way to enlightenment. His teachings on ethics offer definite guidelines for dealing with the rest of the world. And his psychological teachings help us to see how the mind actually works.

That's not just interesting and stimulating stuff to know. Instead, these teachings offer a means of ending those habits of mind and behavior that cause us so much grief and pain. In short, it's a complete system for liberation and enlightenment, not just a system of ideas or interesting insights into reality.

Of course it's possible for individuals to gain some wisdom from their own life experiences without knowing the Buddha's teachings about insight meditation. Obviously, this happens all the time. If they're lucky or wise, people do learn from their mistakes! Anyone with some common sense can learn to stop stubbing their toes on the same table leg or to stop making the same ill-advised comments that lead to conflict with a parent or sibling.

Unfortunately, the world is also full of confused teachings, confused people, and confused influences. People are made dizzy by all these confused ideas and teachings. They may have a hard time sorting out what to accept and what to reject in this world.

So the Buddha points out a path, a very definite direction, through all this confusion. It's a path with morality as its foundation. It has concentration as its strength to keep us focused on that path. And wisdom is the guiding light we follow while walking that path. At the end of that path lies nothing less than enlightenment, liberation, and a final end to suffering.

Not a bad deal!

THE TRIPLE GEM

Please explain the Triple Gem.

The Triple Gem means the Buddha, Dhamma, and Sangha. The Buddha is an embodiment of wisdom and compassion and a fully enlightened individual. Dhamma is the truth that Buddha realized through his own practice. He practiced Dhamma to realize Dhamma. Dhamma is also the Buddha's teaching, and the Buddha's teaching is the truth. The Sangha signifies the eight noble individuals. These are those who have attained stream entry—on the path, and at its fruition. Then there is the once-returner—on the path, and at its fruition; the never-returner—on the path, and at its fruition; and arahants—on the path, and at its fruition.

These eight individuals don't necessarily have to wear robes like I do or have shaved heads and live in monasteries observing celibacy. They can be men, women, monks, and nuns in any society, anywhere in the world, if they have attained these eight stages.

They are called the Sangha. And anybody can gain membership in the Sangha club by qualifying themselves. The qualification is attaining the stream-entry path, the first stage of enlightenment. Then you get the key and go on to the once-returner path and fruition, and so forth.

THE ILLUSION OF "SELF"

How does the mind create the illusion of a permanent self?

That's just a built-in system. We cling to something, thinking it is permanent. That is an illusion—that it is something lasting.

I would recommend that everybody look at one's own mind to see how true this established illusion of "self" is. We don't really need to ask anybody this question. Just honestly, sincerely, impartially look at yourself, pay attention to your experience, and see how true this sense of a self is.

THE IMPORTANCE OF VOLITION

Can you explain the significance of the Fourth Aggregate of mental volition?

Volition—in some places it is called *kamma*, in other places it is called *sankhara*—changes our life. It makes us happy or unhappy. It can make us healthy or ill. Volitional formations are the thoughts we generate in our minds that drive our actions. If our intentional thoughts are motivated by greed, hatred, and delusion, the volition is unwholesome. If our thoughts are motivated by nongreed, nonhatred, and nondelusion, it is wholesome volition.

According to these intentional thoughts, we speak, we act. If our volitional formations happen to be motivated by greed, hatred, and delusion, then the results will be very painful and unpleasant.

But if our volitional formations are motivated, supported, or backed by nongreed and nonhatred such as metta or nondelusion, then the results will be very pleasant and pleasing and they will make us happy. So, volitional formations are very important.

A CREATOR GOD

One thing about Buddhism that confounds many people of traditional religious backgrounds is that there is no main creator god. Buddhist cosmology does speak of gods and higher realms, but even these gods are subject to impermanence.

If there is a creator god, how did he come to exist? Who were his parents? If he had no parents, did he come into existence by himself? People normally describe God as a male—they rarely talk about a she. He should be genderless. This genderless being must have come from something. In order for that so-called God to come about as an individual, he has to change places to be here—and he has to go through a process that was changing to allow him to be here. Therefore, even that individual does not have autonomous power to control everything.

So many things are happening in the world that not everyone likes. A few days ago there was a shooting in a high school. Every week brings news of tsunamis, earthquakes, typhoons, epidemics. We have science and the marvels of technology that seemingly perform miracles. But can they perform any miracles to stop all these disastrous things from happening?

Since there is not one being to control everything, so many undesirable things are happening. But in the United States it is often very difficult for people to say, "I do not believe in God!" Even the dollar bill says "In God We Trust."

If something is there that can control everything, then it is very sensible to trust it. But there doesn't seem to be such a force. In Buddhism there is a belief in causes and conditions. Due to certain causes and conditions, certain things happen. When this exists, that occurs. When this does not occur, that does not exist. For example, when two things touch each other, feeling arises. If these two things do not touch, no feeling arises.

You ask, is it going to rain? It depends. It depends on what? Clouds, moisture, wind, the barometric pressure—so many factors are required. So you wonder if is it going to rain today. Well, it depends.

Nothing exists by itself. Everything depends on something else. This whole universe is in motion. This earth revolves around the sun depending on gravity. The moon goes around the earth because of the earth's gravity.

Everything from the tiniest subatomic force to the largest object in the whole universe is always depending on something else. We Buddhists believe in that law—this is called the law of dependent coarising.

Now, a perfect understanding of dependent coarising is almost impossible for an ordinary person. The Buddha said it is deep, it appears to be deep, and it *is* deep—it is the law of the universe. And if somebody without any bias investigates the way the world operates, they will come to see this principle in action.

Many scientists are impartial—they just want to know what is there. With such an attitude, if somebody looks at Buddhism exactly like a true scientist, that person will find what the Buddha said is 100 percent true.

But the person has to be impartial, unbiased, and unprejudiced, without greed, hatred, fear, and delusion. With a clear, impartial state of mind, that person can look at what the Buddha really taught and see this teaching of no god, no creator, is true.

BUDDHA NATURE

In popular Buddhism and Mahayana Buddhism there is much mention of buddha nature. That is not a part of Theravada Buddhism, is that correct? And is the focus more on each human's potential for obtaining buddhahood?

I don't quarrel with the term "buddha nature." We must understand what is meant by this term.

We say we have the potential of attaining liberation because everybody wants to be free—free from all suffering and sickness and hunger and so forth. That is universally true. So, buddha nature is the nature of wisdom. The root of the word *Buddha* in Sanskrit and Pali means wisdom. One who attains the highest level of that wisdom is called Buddha.

We all have that nature. Even non-Buddhists have it—Muslims, Christians, Jews, and even somebody who doesn't espouse any religion at all. It means we all have the potential of liberation from suffering. Therefore, I don't quarrel with the term. But I try to interpret the phrase in a Theravadan way of understanding.

LUMINOUS MIND

What is meant by "luminosity of mind"?

Luminosity doesn't mean 100 percent pure, but you can see the potential of purity in the luminosity of the mind. The mind can be purified. That potential is within us, and that is a luminous state, meaning a shining state.

Whenever the external defilements invade the mind, that luminosity will be polluted. Luminosity here means a mind without excessive greed, hatred, and delusion. Once the mind is perfectly clean, that is the state of arahanthood, and after that you will not be reborn. If it is perfectly clean and clear, nothing can defile it.

But for the rest of us, the potential of cleansing and purification is there.

TRICKY BUSINESS

Could you please give more detail about how consciousness tricks us into believing that there is a permanent self?

The speed of change in our consciousness is so rapid that we think it is not changing at all. One day, the Buddha said that consciousness changes very quickly, all the time. Somebody asked, "How quickly? Can you describe the speed?"

Buddha said that there is no way to measure the changing speed of consciousness. The monks asked if he could give an example. Buddha said, suppose you take a spider's web and bring it close to a candle to burn that web. How long does it take to burn one single thread of a spider's web? Even before you bring the candle close to it, the strand disappears. Buddha said that during even that briefest time the mind will change a hundred thousand times. Millions of thought moments arise and pass away! That is how speedy consciousness is.

Yet since consciousness is changing so quickly, you cannot see its speed. It is like when water is pouring from a pipe—is it the same water that pours from the beginning to the end? No. The water is composed of so many tiny little drops connected so closely that we cannot see the drops. Yet they look like one cylindrical object coming from that pipe. A river is another example.

Our consciousness changes so quickly; therefore, it is not easy for anyone to distinguish one moment of consciousness from another.

And this is why consciousness tricks us into believing it is permanent, because of its speed.

DOMINANT THOUGHTS

In the Conch Blower, or Sankha Sutta, the Buddha talks about a person who has engaged in unwholesome behaviors coming to the realization that they can stop these behaviors and beam metta in all directions. Can you talk a little more about that?

The Buddha gave a very beautiful simile in that sutta. Suppose somebody has done something they regret, say, killing an animal. Then the person recognizes and remembers that action. And after remembering, the person thinks, "This is a thing I should have not done. Now it is done. I must now practice more metta." So the person keeps practicing metta again and again and again and has compassion for all living things. And then that would be his dominant thought in the mind, not that killing.

But if somebody were to kill an animal and think about it again and again and again in spite of all the other wholesome things they have done, then that thought of killing would become the dominant thought in the mind. One can deliberately set aside that thought: "I was unmindful because of certain circumstances and so this happened. Now I am more sensible, more reasonable, wiser. Now I will not commit this act again. From now on I keep practicing more mindfully, I share more metta, more compassion."

And so this person keeps honestly practicing, undertaking more wholesome behavior. Then the mind will become charged with these wholesome thoughts—and the unwholesome things will be forgotten.

That is what one should do.

If somebody has done something only once in their entire life, something bad, if that person were to think of it again and again all of their life, that would become their dominant thought, even at the moment of death. That would be their last thought.

However, if they keep thinking of wholesome things, if they keep returning the mind to skillful actions, then that is the thought that will come to the forefront of the mind.

LIFE'S PURPOSE

What is the purpose of our life?

Some people might say "We are a cosmic accident." Others would say "We don't have any purpose. We were thrust into this world through our parents' decision."

I would say that there is a very definite purpose to our life. We all know it. We all are striving to achieve it. But we don't know how to put our finger on it and say "This is the purpose of life." In fact, we all have one purpose in life. I have asked many people, what do you want in your life? Money? Wealth? Status? Education? Sex? Recognition? What?

None of them is the answer.

All of us, all living beings, want to live in peace and happiness. How do we accomplish that? Everybody loves being happy. If you are peaceful and happy, would you hate yourself? Definitely not. When you hate yourself, are you happy? Not at all. Then why do you hate yourself? The very moment you hate yourself, you suffer.

Don't use anger as a defense mechanism. It makes you more miserable. When you use it to defend yourself, your happiness runs a million miles away from you. When you hate yourself, not only do you suffer, you inflict suffering on others as well. By the same token, if you love yourself, you wish to bring happiness to others.

Read Dhamma books with skillful intention. Read with the intention of helping yourself. Then think of others whom you can help with your Dhamma knowledge. That is how you read Dhamma teachings, with loving-friendliness. With loving-friendliness in mind, learn a skill to help yourself and help others. It is always best to not think of money when you learn or do a job. Think of loving-friendly ways of helping yourself and others when you do any kind of job.

Speak with the intention of filling your mind with loving-friendliness and sharing that feeling with other people. Let go of lustful thoughts because these inevitably end up in suffering.

Remember that lust or greed is a primary cause of suffering. Because of lust, you will blind yourself to your actions and not notice you are sowing the seeds of suffering in your mind and in the minds of other people.

When you talk with loving-friendliness, you sow the seeds of happiness in your mind and in the minds of other persons. If you need a purpose in life, practice loving-friendliness. Live in a way that brings peace and happiness to yourself and others.

DISPASSION EXPLAINED

Please explain "dispassion" versus "compassion."

Dispassion comes from understanding and it leads to disenchantment. Nibbida means you become dispassionate. *Nibbida* is a Pali word that means you see reality exactly as it is. When you have a deep understanding of the impermanent nature of all things, then you will no longer be attached to anything. Nonattachment is not anything negative; it is becoming fully aware of what is happening.

It is just like when you were a child you were attached to various kinds of toys. When you grow up you are not attached to them anymore. You let your children play with toys because that is what they like. You see them playing with toys and you understand their mentality. And you stay aloof without becoming attached to toys. When you understand things, you are not attached to anything—that is called dispassion.

Compassion arises when you see suffering beings. That is a very wholesome emotion that arises in the mind. Your heart melts. Indifference is negative—you just don't care. That is a negative emotion.

AN INTELLECTUAL UNDERSTANDING

How important is in-depth study of Buddhist teachings in my spiritual practice? The teachings seem so voluminous and complex. Is a deep intellectual understanding of the teachings necessary?

It is possible to attain even enlightenment without too much learning. All one has to do is study oneself and practice mindfulness and concentration. Without having any academic knowledge, one can certainly attain a high spiritual level. After all, everyone who attained enlightenment in the past didn't have a PhD in "Enlightenment Studies"! They just studied the Dhamma. Where did they learn Dhamma? They learned Dhamma from within themselves.

The mind and body are like a huge encyclopedia. If one wants to study things very carefully, the mind and body provide ample source material. But there has to be some guidance, somebody to offer guidelines. There has to be some instruction in how to undertake that study of oneself. That is where teachers and spiritual friends come in.

SPIRITUAL FRIENDS

What do you mean when you use the phrase "spiritual friend"?

A spiritual friend—a *kalyana mitta* in Pali—is someone who is full of loving-friendliness and compassion and is willing to help you in your spiritual growth. Spiritual growth means to grow in peace and harmony. Such a person helps you develop your mind and body in a harmonious way.

A spiritual friend can be a teacher, relative, or friend who is willing to help you without expecting anything from you. They understand your need and willingness to grow. This friend would sacrifice their own comfort to make you peaceful and happy.

A spiritual friend demonstrates an enormous amount of patience and dedication toward you. They are available to give you advice and listen to you. They would not turn you away until you are satisfied with their help. This person is a good listener and good communicator. They would not encourage you to do anything detrimental to your peace and happiness. They would never encourage you to do anything unwholesome that might bring you pain and suffering, now or in the future.

There is no big difference between a spiritual friend and a teacher because one plays both roles in spiritual matters. Someone who strives for liberation from suffering needs a spiritual friend until they attain liberation.

A spiritual friend would not say, "I have played my role. Now you are on your own." Rather, this friend would say to you, "Come anytime you need help. Don't forget to ask me any question. I am available to you any time. Whenever you have any difficulty, remember, I am here waiting to help you. Don't think you are alone. I am here."

Spiritual friends give you a sense of security. You always feel someone is paying attention to your spiritual needs. You feel there is somebody to help you. You don't feel as if they will ignore you. A spiritual friend is there to guide you in the right direction.

HINDRANCES AND FETTERS

Buddhist teachings speak of "hindrances" and "fetters," those things that keep us from mindfulness. What do these terms mean and what is their significance to our practice?

Hindrances are mental obstacles that block your way forward. It's like you are driving down a road and suddenly there's a roadblock.

You can't go on. The roadblock is lifted, you drive on awhile—and then there's another roadblock! And another after that one. You're trying to go somewhere, but you're having a difficult time getting anywhere. Hindrances are like that.

The Buddha spoke of five specific hindrances that keep blocking our way, which constantly prevent us from achieving a concentrated mental state and from seeing things clearly. They are ill will, sensual desire, a slothful or lazy mental state, restlessness, and doubt.

Fetters are the deep, established roots from which these hindrances grow. Hindrances come and go in the mind repeatedly. We may think we have dealt with them, but then they rise up again and again. That's because we haven't dealt with the roots from which they spring.

For instance, say that you get really angry with a colleague at work or with a friend or spouse. You want to wring their neck! You try to calm yourself down. You take a couple of breaths, you go do something else. You think you have dealt with your anger. The next day comes and you have another encounter with that person. Something is said and your anger flares up hotter than ever. You hate them! Your face turns red. Your blood pressure goes through the roof. "What happened?" you wonder later. You thought you had dealt with your anger.

Well, superficially, you had. But you haven't gotten to the root source of your feelings of dislike or hatred. You haven't dug up and destroyed those roots. And these are some tough roots! They grow deep. Until you do that, those roots will keep throwing off new shoots.

The Buddha identified ten fetters, ten sets of deep roots that keep causing us grief. We won't get into the meaning of all these fetters in detail because that would take awhile. But these fetters are what tie us to samsara and the wheel of repeated existence. They are a belief in an enduring self, skeptical doubt, clinging to rules and rituals, sensual desire, ill will, craving for fine-material existence, craving for immaterial existence, conceit, restlessness, and ignorance.

So, the difference between hindrances and fetters is that fetters are firmly rooted, they're very strong. Hindrances are temporary things that return, arising from these deep roots. When we ultimately eliminate these fetters, then new shoots can no longer grow from them. We've eliminated the roots once and for all by attaining liberation and enlightenment.

The Buddha spoke about two kinds of reflection: mindful reflection and unmindful reflection. Wholesome or mindful reflection is a great fertilizer if you want to grow strong, healthy roots. If we want to stunt the roots of our unwholesome states of mind, then cultivate mindfulness.

Unmindful reflection, however, nourishes some pretty unwholesome roots. It's why ignorance, hatred, and greed keep shooting up again and again.

Uprooting Hindrances

Can you talk in more depth about the nature of the hindrances?

You uproot hindrances when you have uprooted fetters. Fetters are underlying our hindrances. The fetters are the deep roots from which the hindrances arise. How deep are those roots? I will give you an example.

Somebody once planted bamboo at the Bhavana Society outside my window. I said, "Don't do that because it will grow very fast and it will block my view." And he did not listen. He said, "This is not Sri Lanka, this is America—bamboo will not grow like that."

And so he planted it.

Believe me, after about a year—as I predicted—my window was completely blocked! So I said to him, "I told you. Now we have to remove it." He started digging and digging and removing the bamboo. After about six months the bamboo grew back again. He got a bulldozer and removed the bamboo. After another six or seven months, it grew again!

Then a woman came to the monastery, a very strong woman. One morning after breakfast, she started digging. She dug into every inch of that bamboo plot and found this long root. And she removed it. After that the bamboo did not grow anymore.

Now, hindrances are like those bamboo plants. Fetters are like that bamboo root in the soil. Underground there is a network of deep roots. From this network of roots, shoots come up. These shoots coming up are like the hindrances.

There are ten fetters. They are belief in a permanent self, doubt, believing liberation can be obtained by following rules and rituals, greed, hatred, desire for existing in fine-material form, desire for existing in immaterial form, restlessness, conceit, and ignorance.

As long as these ten fetters exist, hindrances grow out of them. The hindrances are sensory desire, *kamacchanda*; ill will, *vyapada*; sloth and torpor, *thina-middha*; restlessness and worry, *uddhacca-kukkuca*; and doubt, *vicikiccha*.

So you cut down the hindrances by attaining jhana, or deep states of absorption. And they grow again. You attain jhana and then they later grow again. You attain mundane jhanas to remove the five hindrances temporarily. It is just a Band-Aid.

You've got to do the real surgery to remove the roots. That's what you do when you attain supramundane jhanas. When you attain supramundane jhanas, you eliminate the roots. Otherwise, you cannot remove these hindrances completely.

APPRECIATIVE JOY

Can you explain appreciative joy, or mudita?

When you appreciate somebody's success, you show how great your heart is. Similarly, in this life you will be appreciated by others, who will come to see you are generous in your thought and have a great heart. This is called appreciative joy.

When somebody is successful, you must have a good heart,

thinking he or she deserves it. Not only in this life will you be popular among people, but in the next life, too. You will become very popular for your good deeds. The Buddha said jealousy can make you unpopular in this life and the next life.

Therefore, cultivate appreciative joy—to appreciate others' success, no matter how big it is. We cultivate this wonderful, wholesome mental state. Just out of our own clean, pure heart we appreciate what other people have accomplished.

The Meaning of Mara

What does the figure of Mara represent in Buddhism, because he follows and taunts the Buddha even after enlightenment?

Mara means several things. The number-one thing is "that which kills wholesomeness." Mara means death. Anything that kills wholesomeness is called Mara.

Second, Mara means all the defilements. In the Sutta Nipata, Buddha listed the ten armies of Mara. The first is desire, the second is dislike, the third is thirst and hunger, the fourth is greed, the fifth is sleepiness and drowsiness, the sixth is restlessness, the seventh is conceit, the eighth is jealousy, the ninth is false reputation (a reputation you gain by wrong means), and the tenth is praising oneself and disparaging others.

And the one that followed the Buddha until he passed away? Death followed him. There is no question about it—one day he would die.

There is also the belief in Mara as a sort of mythological divine being, as the deity of death who dominates others. These other aspects of Mara I mention, anyone can experience.

Which Suttas?

I am going on a three-week retreat and want to take a sutta on practicing mindfulness with me. I wonder if I should use the

Mahasatipatthana Sutta (Digha Nikaya, 22) or the Anapanasati Sutta (Majjhima Nikaya, 118) or alternate the two?

If you read one sutta very, very carefully—mindfully slowly, line by
line—then that one sutta is enough. I think the Anapanasati Sutta
is a very good one if you understand it well. If you don't understand
it, you can go to the longer one, the Mahasatipatthana Sutta—that
will give you more details about breathing practice.

So, select whichever you feel comfortable with. I recommend
using only one of them. The Mahasatipatthana Sutta has a section
from the Anapanasati Sutta. The Anapanasati Sutta is a very profound, subtle discourse. If you think a detailed discussion will work
better for you, use the Mahasatipatthana Sutta.

CORE SUTTAS

Are there core Buddhist suttas you recommend that people
spend a lot of time on?

I think essential teachings can be found in the Majjhima Nikaya.
There are many wonderful discourses in other nikayas like the
Samyutta Nikaya and the Anguttara Nikaya. The Samyutta Nikaya
has special areas devoted to the teaching on Dependent Origina-
tion and the aggregates and so forth. But to start out, the Majjhima
Nikaya is full of very meaningful and practical discourses.

WHERE IS THE "I"?

Can you give practical examples of how there is no "I," "me,"
or "mine" in our perceptions, volitional formations, and
consciousness?

My practical example is this: have you ever seen longitude, latitude,
or the equator? Never. But these are conventionally accepted marks

of geography on the map. So, somehow we can go there. All are concepts, very practical concepts.

Similarly, "me," "mine," and "I" are very important practical concepts. Even though you might study anything under the sun—science, mathematics, physics, biology—and you use all the knowledge you've gained, can you see if there is something called "I"?

If you find it, please come and show me, I will definitely accept it. If you prove to me "self" is such and such, "mind" is such and such, and "I" is such and such—well, until then, don't worry about it. You can't find it.

IGNORANCE AND CRAVING

Is ignorance or craving the source of suffering?

Ignorance doesn't work by itself without the support of craving. Both have similar characteristics. When craving or greed obsesses our mind, the mind will become very dull. When we are obsessed with certain types of craving, we have a one-track mind. And the same thing happens when the mind is obsessed with ignorance. These are like twin brothers.

That is why in some places Buddha mentioned ignorance as the cause of suffering. In other places he mentioned craving as the source of suffering.

THE CHARACTERISTICS OF EXISTENCE

When we meditate, how do we observe the three characteristics of existence—impermanence, unsatisfactoriness, and nonself? Can you provide some examples?

Everything in existence is very clearly marked by these characteristics. Just look at how we enter this world. We were not born like this, for sure, as we look at our bodies today. When we were born we were like a tiny piece of meat. Our mothers and fathers had to devote their entire being to raise us, doing everything for us: feeding, clothing, educating us. So, we begin as one cell and turn into 300 trillion cells. And these cells are wearing out all the time.

We experience this impermanence in our daily lives. This morning you felt one way. Do you feel the same way now? No, you may be tired now. When you drink water, you quench your thirst. Ten hours later you're thirsty again. More impermanence. And so forth and so on. We experience impermanence every moment.

The suffering we undergo every day is the mind wishing for something permanent. We are attached to this impermanent body, its feelings, thoughts, and sensations. But no matter how hard we wish for things not to change, change occurs anyway. The mind thinks a certain way, and the body doesn't behave.

Therefore, there is a conflict: the tension between the body and mind—wishing and not getting what we wish for and getting what we don't want. That is the suffering we undergo every day.

As we see that everything is changing in our body and mind, we also can notice that there is no central agent that has control over all this change. There is no central agent that does not change. That is what is called nonself because the notion of self assumes it can control everything.

When we assume there is a self, then that self should be able to control everything. But there is no such thing in this mind and body—because everything is impermanent. So, these are the three marks of existence: impermanence, unsatisfactoriness, and selflessness. In meditation we see all three. We see things are changing, changing, changing. We see that any time we attach to impermanent things we end up with disappointment.

So, this is how we see impermanence, suffering, and selflessness in meditation, particularly in vipassana meditation.

RIGHT EFFORT

Can you say something about living your daily life with commitment to impermanence without clinging or gasping but dedicated to right effort and the Noble Eightfold Path?

This is a very good question but would require a very long answer. I must say simply that the practice is to see in our daily life impermanence, unsatisfactoriness, and selflessness, without clinging to anything pleasant and without rejecting anything unpleasant or grasping anything pleasant. Understanding that very nature of experience is a very healthy way to develop and cultivate right effort to follow the Noble Eightfold Path.

FAITH IN BUDDHISM

What is the role of faith in Buddhist practice? A common perception is that Buddhists don't really believe in faith.

In many cases, Buddha used words that had already been in use in his own time with his own interpretation. Like *kamma* and *dhamma*—these are not new words. *Kamma* is an old word in the Vedic tradition—in Sanskrit, the word *karma* is used.

Similarly, the word "faith" is used. Since we don't have a better term, we sometimes say "confidence." But that doesn't seem to give the impact, the full meaning of the word "faith." Because it is used in other religious traditions, whenever we use the word "faith," people understand the meaning. And then we have to explain what we Buddhists mean by the word. In other religious traditions faith refers to faith *in* some being—in some creator god or gods.

Actually, because of our attempt to translate the word "faith" into a Buddhist context, some people say Buddhism is a "faithless" practice. One American politician once remarked that he wanted to support "faith-based religions." Buddhism, by such a definition, is not faith-oriented. What they mean perhaps is that these religions' only base, their most important foundation and strength, is faith in their respective god. Whereas in Buddhism, faith is one of the factors, but the entire focus does not rest on faith.

We have faith in the path described by the Buddha. We have faith in his example. We are inspired by the teachings and have faith that what the Buddha said is true—if you do such and such, this will then happen. Enlightenment is possible. An end to suffering is possible.

But Buddha also said don't just believe in what I say, taking it only on faith. See for yourself if this is not true. As his final words he said, "Work out your own salvation with diligence."

The word "faith" for Buddhists is not quite so simple!

SPIRITUAL FRIENDSHIP

What does the phrase *kalyana mitta*, or spiritual friend, signify?

In order to make your life even happier, you have to have an excellent friend. In Pali it is called a *kalyana mitta*. A kalyana mitta is not just a good friend, it's an excellent friend. To have an excellent friend, you have to be excellent. You don't pick up just anybody walking on the street and say, "This is my good friend." That excellent friend is important not only to your spiritual life but in your mundane life.

In your work, when you have problems, or when you have difficulties in life or when you have a secret, you turn to an excellent friend who can keep your secrets, who can encourage you. They support you and help to sustain your self-confidence. And you've got to maintain their secrets and try to help them when they are in trouble.

This way, a kalyana mitta, an excellent friend, works in both ways. You become that person's kalyana mitta and then that person will be your excellent friend. There must be mutual trust, mutual understanding, mutual support. So, both you and the other person will be happy.

To find such a good friend you have to associate with many people, and then finally you find, "Ah! This is the one! This is the friend I need. This is the one I will support and who will be able to support me."

It all begins with you, from your own heart.

DEFINING THE SOUL

Growing up Catholic, I was taught that people have a soul, a spirit that passes out of the body upon death. The Buddha says we are soul-less. Does the concept of soul to which the Buddha refers have a different meaning than the Western meaning of soul?

What the Buddha refers to is the concept of there being any entity, any permanent entity, in this body and mind—this is what he denied. We have to understand that everything is impermanent. So, how can there be one thing that is not impermanent?

Based on this truth, we cannot find anything permanent. The Buddha does not define "soul." When you start defining something, you have to accept it first. You assume it, you presuppose there is something called a soul. If you completely reject the whole package, there is nothing to define.

That is why Buddha never defined the soul.

GENDER AND ATTACHMENT

Is it possible to say that males and females tend toward different types of attachment? If this is true, how does gender operate in the rounds of samsara? Is a being's gender generally fixed or not? Can this information help individuals let go of attachment?

Do males and females tend toward different types of attachment? I don't know. Attachment is attachment. The object may be different, but attachment is attachment. I cannot distinguish one attachment from another.

But I can distinguish one object of attachment from another object of attachment—that may be different. For instance, a woman may like to have a blouse. A man may have an attachment toward a tie. A woman may be attached to a sari. The object may be different, but the attachment is the same. We cannot distinguish attachment according to gender because attachment is attachment.

When the Buddha talked about attachment, he referred to the Five Aggregates. A man is attached to form, feeling, perception, thought, and consciousness. A woman is attached to her forms, feelings, perception, thoughts, and consciousness. And so forth. Therefore, so long as attachment is concerned, there is no difference whatsoever.

Also, existence in samsara, in the round of rebirth, as a man and a woman also is variable. For instance, a man in this life can be a woman in the next life. A woman in this life can be a man in her next life. I don't think there is much difference between the genders when it comes to attachment.

THE MEANING OF CHANDA

What is chanda?

Chanda is sometimes translated as "intention," "interest," or "a desire to act." It can be wholesome or unwholesome, depending on the mental factors that accompany it.

Wholesome chanda is *sammappadhana, iddhipada, sammappadhana vayama*, and so on. Unwholesome chanda is signified by *kama chanda, chanda agati, chanda raga*, and so on. Wholesome chanda leads to liberation, and unwholesome chanda leads to suffering.

Chanda is the root of both. Driven by ignorance, chanda becomes unwholesome, which leads us to commit unwholesome thoughts, words, and deeds. Guided by right view, chanda prompts the mind to commit wholesome thought, words, and deeds.

Books and Buddhism

Can someone develop a successful insight meditation practice without a decent grasp of Buddhism?

You know, many people who attained enlightenment in the Buddha's time were not educated people. If you learn the theory of the Buddha's teachings, it is so intriguing. You will want to read all about it in detail. And that is what most people do these days—they read and read and read and read. There are tens of thousands of pages on the Buddha's teachings. And then there are the commentaries and subcommentaries. And nowadays there are so many books about Buddhism coming out every week and so many articles and forums online. It can all be so fascinating!

But when one really deepens one's insight, the person will see the whole picture of Buddhism because insight itself shows the truth of the Dhamma. Especially the three characteristics of existence, which we can see without reading a single book: impermanence, unsatisfactoriness, and selflessness. These are very often emphasized in Buddha's teaching. You can fill in the details later on by reading Buddhist books.

When you do turn to reading, the best way is to learn Pali. It is a little difficult, but some people do it. The easier way is to read Buddha's teaching in English translation. I recommend reading *Samyutta Nikaya: The Connected Discourses of the Buddha*, which is very well translated by the American monk Bhikkhu Bodhi.

I also recommend his translation of *Majjhima Nikaya: The Middle Length Sayings of the Buddha*. The third is *Digha Nikaya: The Long Discourses of the Buddha*, translated by Maurice Walsh. The fourth is *Anguttara Nikaya: The Gradual Sayings of the Buddha.* And the fifth is the Khuddaka Nikaya.

Altogether that is thousands of pages. I recommend that you start with at least the first one: the Samyutta Nikaya. It is easy to read, as it is classified into various groups under different topics. It is a beautiful translation. As for dictionaries, there is the *Pali Text Society Dictionary,* from Pali into English. And there is an English-into-Pali dictionary by A. P. Buddhadatta Mahathera.

SECRET TEACHINGS

Some spiritual traditions have secret teachings. Even some schools of Buddhism talk about teachings that resurfaced after the Buddha's time. What is the Theravada view of such secret teachings?

According to Theravada Buddhism, Buddha did not keep any secrets. In the Mahaparinibbana Sutta (Digha Nikaya, 16) we read about when the Buddha was sick. Venerable Ananda first felt very sad. And when the Buddha recovered, Ananda went to the Buddha and said, "Venerable Sir, I was so sad when I saw you sick. Now I am so glad that you are well. When I saw you sick, I was so confused that I could not see the sun and the moon and everything was dark to me. I thought the world had come to an end."

And Buddha said, "Ananda, don't you remember that I have taught you everything without keeping any secrets? The Dhamma is there. If I die now, still the Dhamma is there."

That is why Buddha said "I have not kept secrets." That is what we have in the Theravada tradition. That is why it is said you have to use Dhamma dasa, which means using the Dhamma as a mirror to see the Buddha. When you look at the Dhamma, the Buddha is inside there, in that Dhamma. Because the words are so clear and pure and powerful, it gives an impression that the Buddha is standing right in front of us. When you see the Dhamma so clearly, in that way, Buddha said, "Yo dhammam passati so mam passati" ("One who sees the Dhamma sees me").

There is no difference between the Buddha and Dhamma. One who sees the Dhamma in this way sees the Buddha right there. Although it is a figurative expression, it is very, very true. If you really see the Dhamma in a very clear way, it is just like Buddha standing in front of you and talking to you.

In later suttas that people have composed, you don't get that kind of impression and that message. They may use all kinds of flowery language, but the message is not there. I don't actually dismiss wholesale Mahayana teaching—it contains some valuable things as well. They compose things so as to increase devotion, respect, and veneration to the Buddha, Dhamma, and Sangha. In that way they are very devotional people. When they make a commitment, they keep the commitment. The devotional aspect is very strong in Mahayana Buddhism. That part is quite admirable.

IMPROVING THE TEACHINGS

What do you think of other, later teachings in the Buddhist tradition and if they are an improvement or expansion on the Buddha's original teaching, as some claim?

Friends, one thing I must tell you—nobody on Earth or in this universe can improve on the Buddha's teaching. It is not like Microsoft Word or your Internet browser, with new, improved versions coming out all the time. You can never improve the Buddha's teachings. He perfected and marketed it. You cannot improve on it.

4

Buddhism and the Body

Limits of Sense Pleasures

What is so wrong with sense pleasures? They seem quite enjoyable.

We experience sense pleasures from sights, smells, tastes, sounds, touch, and thoughts. In order to experience these pleasures, we are dependent on external objects or passing states of mind. And they are most unreliable! These pleasures are not always readily available. And when we are ready for them, they are not ready. When they are ready, we are not ready.

Even if we gain sense pleasures, they come with strings attached. So many other conditions have to be fulfilled in order to fulfill our desire for sense pleasures. And still there is no guarantee that such pleasures will continually exist and perpetually provide us pleasure.

An object gives us pleasure one moment, and the next moment that object will not give us the same experience. You are excited to buy a new car or purchase the latest electronic device. And for a while it seems exciting to possess it. But a year later, your car has dents in it, the engine is acting up, it's a mess inside. Or your new computer won't connect to the Internet or keeps crashing for some unknown reason.

Are these objects so innately pleasurable after all? They are most unreliable. Sometimes they even betray us! My cellphone won't connect to the Internet! Or you are excited to open a box of chocolates. They are *so* delicious. But then you eat too many and you feel sick to your stomach.

External sense pleasures routinely let us down. We try to repeat the same pleasures over and over, hoping to find some lasting peace of mind, some continuous pleasurable state. But because all sense pleasures are inherently impermanent, there is no way they can afford us any lasting joy and happiness. They can't endure.

Even pleasurable states of mind are like this. Say, for instance, we look at a rainbow. It is not the rainbow itself that makes us glad or happy but the state of mind it generates in us. The same rainbow may not give us the same pleasure and joy if we are feeling distracted or upset, even though the rainbow happens in the exact same way. The colors will be the same. But depending on our own state of mind, it will not give us the same pleasure as before.

We just cannot find permanent pleasure in fundamentally impermanent things and passing states of mind, however pleasurable they may seem in the moment. If we spend our life's energy in the constant pursuit of such pleasures, we will inevitably come up short.

BODILY AWARENESS

The Satipatthana Sutta and the Four Foundations of Mindfulness start with the body. What is the significance of beginning the practice by bringing attention to the body?

People pay more attention to their body than to their feelings, their mind, and so on. Also, it is the body that is subject to various illnesses, and we frequently feel physical pain. The body doesn't seem to be changing as quickly as other things. People think things are impermanent, but day-to-day they may not notice the physical changes in the body.

But when we start practicing, mindfulness of the body is an easy place to start. Because we can easily notice our breathing, our walking, eating, drinking, sitting, lying down, and so forth.

In all of these different movements, the person can be keenly aware of the body movement and can relate to that. And again, when we talk about meditation on the body, we can meditate on the traditional thirty-two parts of the body, which begin with head hair, body hair, nails, teeth, and skin. These five things anybody can see very easily. For instance, we can see that our head hair is changing and has changed. It used to be thick and full, and as we age it becomes gray and brittle. All of these five parts of the body are prominent, and it's easy to see their changes.

Therefore, because of the importance we give to the body, we can see its changes and come to understand impermanence. And in any meditation practice, especially vipassana meditation, the main core and essence of our focus is impermanence.

MINDFUL OF THE BODY

How should we view the body mindfully?

The body is the first subject in the Four Foundations of Mindfulness. When using the body, we don't look at it as a biologist, physicist, or chemist looks at the body. We look at the body to understand what happens when we use it in various ways. What happens to us in our minds when we use the body in hundreds of different ways?

The Buddha said be mindful when you go forward—have clear understanding of going forward. What does that mean? Is it just lifting our feet and putting them down? Is that all? Is it just awareness of the sensation of touching from our movements? No. Instead, we must use movements to see what happens to the mind as we move. When we move forward we must be aware of the changes, the impermanence of those movements. Along with this awareness of impermanence, we must look at our distorted perception of "I," "me," and "mine." We must come to understand that this is not "I," this is not "myself," this is not "I am."

The notion of "I"— this is a very difficult thing for people to understand. The notion of "I" totally vanishes when we see the activities performed in going forward. The notion of "I" will disappear. What we see is a dependently arising phenomena. This is called penetrative insight.

PAIN IS NOT SUFFERING

Are pain and suffering the same thing or separate things? Can we ever live without pain?

As long as a body exists with its healthy nervous system, there will be pain. But pain itself is not suffering. Suffering is in the mind. When the mind is totally free from all defilements—the ten fetters—there is no suffering.

This means you can end suffering but not pain while in this human form. You can, though, temporarily be free from pain when you attain the cessation of perception and feeling—*sannavedayita nirodha*. You develop this state after attaining the Fourth Jhana.

Through meditative insight we can understand this relationship between pain and suffering. That is exactly what we do in vipassana meditation. We honestly look at ourselves. With no biases, no pretenses, we look at our own body, feelings, perception, volitional formations, and consciousness—the Five Aggregates.

In this way, we realize impermanence, suffering, and nonself—anicca, dukkha, anatta. This is vipassana meditation. Nobody can ultimately be free from suffering without a perfect realization of anicca, dukkha, anatta.

Dukkha Is in the Mind

What is the relationship between physical pain and our mental aversion to it? Do we create dukkha in the mind in response to pain?

Friends, feeling physical aches and pains itself does not explain dukkha.

Real dukkha is in the mind. The physical sensations will not go away even if you attain enlightenment. Arahants have pain. Even the Buddha experienced pain. But they do not suffer from their pain.

We suffer in our mind—the mind feels the pain and it remains as long as we have a body. But suffering is definitely a psychological mental state, and that is what we want to get rid of—and it can be gotten rid of.

Unpleasantness of the Body

A story is told in the Pali canon about bhikkhus misunderstanding meditation on the unpleasantness of the body, some even killing themselves out of repulsion for the body. Could you go into what the Buddha actually meant?

What the Buddha intended was for us to practice mindfulness of the impermanent nature of the body, not to cultivate negative emotional reactions to it.

Mindfulness meditation does *not* generate loathsomeness or hatred of the body. The purpose of mindfulness is never to develop negative states of mind. When you look at the body as loathsome, ugly, or repulsive, what kind of emotion arises in the mind? Hatred and rejection.

There is a beautiful sutta in Majjhima Nikaya, the last one, 152, called "Development of the Faculties," where the Buddha specifically mentions that the purpose of mindfulness practice is to cultivate equanimity. Equanimity is not something negative but is the highest altruistic, emotionally balanced state of mind.

That means an impartial attitude toward the body, too. When we are unmindful, for instance, we admire our hair. When we have good hair, healthy hair, protein-rich hair, young-looking hair, we love that. We take great pride in our hair when it is on our head— but *only* when it is on our head.

While eating, if one of those beautiful hairs falls into your bowl of soup, do you eat that soup? You are now repulsed by it! But it was your own hair a minute ago, hair you so lovingly admired in the mirror! Now it is in the soup and you throw away the whole bowl. Why?

Because you are looking at your hair unmindfully. If you looked at your hair mindfully, it wouldn't matter whether that hair is on your head or in the bowl of soup. Your attitude will be the same— an equanimous attitude. You understand that this is just hair. When it is on the head it is not different from when it is in that bowl of soup. It's just hair.

So, rather than looking at the body with either excessive repulsion or—and this is more likely—excessive attachment, we see it for what it is.

SEXUAL MISCONDUCT

Buddhist precepts speak of "sexual misconduct." Can you please define this term more specifically?

The precept actually is not only sexual misconduct, it is *sensual* misconduct. Most of this time this precept has been narrowed down only to sex. But the precept is in plural—*kamesu michacara*. Since it is said in plural, it means sensual misconduct: abusing our senses, which includes sex. I have given a whole list of things in my book *Eight Mindful Steps to Happiness* about sexual misconduct and sensual misconduct.

To be specific, sexual misconduct is sex with anybody against the person's wish or in violation of one's vows. This includes someone who is under the protection of parents, the protection of guardians, or the protection of a spouse.

Sensual misconduct is abusing one's senses: overdoing anything excessively. Seeing, hearing, smelling, tasting, and touching all can be done excessively.

Someone I know told me he never turns off his radio because he never wants to miss any news. Twenty-four hours a day he keeps his radio on. How can this fellow have any peace of mind? The more you listen to news, what do you hear? Examples of greed, hatred, and delusion across the planet. You could say that this person is abusing his hearing faculty.

Therefore, this precept has a wider connotation rather than a narrow meaning.

DESIRE AND CRAVING

Is all desire necessarily problematic for Buddhists? Is there a difference between ordinary desire, which is human, and craving, which is a source of suffering?

Desire has two aspects: wholesome desire and unwholesome desire. Unwholesome desire is the desire to perpetuate desire, to increase desire. Wholesome desire is the desire to be desireless.

So we cultivate wholesome desire to be desireless. That is a very gradual process. Don't try to eliminate it overnight in one sitting. It takes many, many years—even lifetimes—to get rid of it.

THE DANGER IN ATTACHMENT

What is so wrong with desire? It seems like a perfectly natural thing.

We must ask ourselves: "Does this desire bring me joy or pleasure? Does attachment bring me happiness?" Honestly, you must ask yourself. Don't tell me. I'm not interested in knowing your answer. Because you must ask yourself this question with 100 percent honesty. And then find the answer.

That is because you don't understand suffering. Therefore, you answer always in your favor. You never say, "This is not what I want. I want peace. Can my so-and-so give me peace? Can my such-and-such give me peace? Can 'my my my my' give me peace?"

No.

People come up with thousands of questions, such as "How can I live without such-and-such?" All these questions arise by not understanding suffering.

As soon as a pleasure arises, the mind is completely obsessed with that pleasure and completely ignores the danger. Ignoring danger is called ignorance. We dwell upon the pleasure. We forget the adinava—the danger. We forget the danger of attachment, we forget the danger of clinging. We forget the danger of suffering. We do not understand.

That is what is called ignorance.

When desire arises, at that very moment there is no room in the mind to ask the question, is this desire giving me pleasure? There is no room in the mind. Why? Because this desire has completely taken over the mind. The mind is completely obsessed. Everything is blocked out. Therefore, we can't even ask the question. We get carried away. We try to evade the truth.

Trying to evade the truth is ignorance. So ignorance is not a simple thing.

5

Rebirth

UNDERSTANDING REBIRTH

What is rebirth?

People think there is something permanent called the self or soul that separates from the body at death and heads into another body. The Buddha taught something quite different. "Rebirth" is a very close translation of the Pali word *punabbhava* for rebecoming. Whenever we use the word "becoming," there must be causes and conditions to come together to *become* something. So rebirth is a cause and a relationship. There are conditions and causes, and when they come together, something will appear.

When we die we will be reborn—not in the same way, not as exactly the same person, but also not 100 percent different. Because of this life's kammic force, another life will appear. That life will reflect the *kamma*—Pali for the more familiar Sanskrit word *karma*—we have committed in this life. And that is what we call rebirth. This rebirth is dependent upon our greed, craving, and ignorance—the karmic forces we create. These forces keep repeating themselves in various different forms of life.

Here at the Bhavana Society all of us are meditating and generating very good kamma. What we do in meditation is to make an earnest effort to purify our minds, to wash away psychic irritants—greed, hatred, delusion, and so on. So we make the mind clean.

Yet if we don't liberate ourselves completely from these psychic irritants and free ourselves from all suffering in this life, then because of our earnest efforts to cleanse the mind, when we die we'll be reborn into another life. It may be human, divine, or some form of life where we can continue our practice of meditation. This will go on until the mind becomes totally free from all the defilements and we liberate ourselves from all suffering.

Once we are liberated from all the psychic irritants, that will bring an end to this repetition of birth and death we call samsara. We break out of the loop, so to speak, of rebirth. That is when we attain final liberation from suffering.

EVIDENCE OF REBIRTH

The principles of Buddhism are evidence-based. What is the evidence for rebirth and other realms?

We have inferential evidence, not direct evidence. And evidence from our feelings. I don't know whether you have ever met someone and felt, "I know this person." You might have never seen the person in your life. But somehow you feel an affinity for that person. You come to an inferential conclusion that perhaps this is a recollection of a previous life with this person.

And then sometimes you see someone for the first time and for no reason you hate the person. You don't know why. You come home and think, "Why do I hate this person? They have done nothing to me. This is the first time I've seen that person. But I have some aversion to them." I don't know whether it is something to do with chemistry, but that sometimes happens. This is another inference we may have as evidence of rebirth.

There are some individuals who from infancy display some skill even highly educated adults cannot do. Certain children are geniuses from birth. How did they become geniuses? If you trace their family history, nobody has qualities this little child has. Some children sing opera songs or display remarkable capabilities in mathematics. And we really don't know why or how.

These sorts of things we attribute to coming from their previous life's education—we don't attribute all these things to genes. We can use these sorts of things as evidence for rebirth.

These are the only things we can find.

No Permanent Self

What makes rebirth possible?

We do not have a permanent self that links this life with the next. Things are always in flux. "Everything changes" literally means that *every* thing changes. Rebirth is possible only because there is no permanent self. Since all things are impermanent and changing all the time, we have hope we can liberate ourselves from psychic irritants and achieve freedom from suffering.

If there is something that's permanent, we're stuck. There is no way we can get out of this loop—we'll just keep circling around on the merry-go-round of existence. And it won't always be so merry.

So, while rebirth is possible, the way it happens is extremely difficult to explain. We sometimes use crude examples to explain it. I like to say it's like sending a fax. What goes from here to there? The entire message or document that you fax remains in your fax machine—not a single syllable went somewhere else. But that entire letter, every punctuation mark, appears in some other place. A carbon copy, so to say.

When we are reborn, what really goes from here to there is not some permanent, eternal soul. It is the transformation of one situation into another. The new life is not completely different from the previous one, nor is it totally identical. It's a transformation fueled by information collected from the previous life. So that new life carries a certain amount of identity forward.

We once ordained a forty-nine-year-old man here at Bhavana Society. When he was only two and a half years old, he was able to recite many, many Pali suttas. We still have these tapes of him. His Pali pronunciation was impeccable. Not even many adults could pronounce Pali in that way. Yet this child could hardly speak otherwise, let alone know his alphabet.

But he'd sit there cross-legged, reciting Buddhist suttas, and his stepfather would grab the tape recorder. He recited only when he wanted; if someone asked him to recite, he'd run away. I've known him for many years. His skill as a child is evidence of his training in using Pali in his previous life, I believe. So this kind of special ability or skill we can inherit or bring to this life from previous lives.

REBIRTH AND REINCARNATION

You say you do not use the word "reincarnation," preferring the word "rebirth." Why? What is the difference?

Reincarnation is an idea that, in reality, is alien to Buddhism. Traditional Buddhists do not even use the term. *Carne* is "flesh," *incarne* is "getting into flesh." Then, *discarne* is separating from it and *reincarne* is re-entering the flesh. That means that something first gets into the flesh, then comes out of it to re-enter the flesh. This is contradictory to the teachings of the Buddha. It implies there is a permanent, eternal substance we call self or soul, which Buddhists deny categorically.

We use a different term with a different meaning: "rebirth." The word "birth" doesn't imply something coming from something and re-entering something.

People ask, how is rebirth even possible if there is no self or soul? Rebirth is explained in terms of neither this nor that—the new life is neither totally the same nor completely different. It means that because of certain things, certain things come into existence.

Rebirth is the result of three factors: ignorance, greed, and kamma. None of these is material. Although someone with flesh and blood commits and creates all these things, what remains is the power or the kammic energy: the energy of greed, the energy of ignorance, the energy of hatred. When these things combine together they can reproduce their image in the next life.

When we die this is the force that departs from this life. It gives sort of a kick-start to the next life. It will not be exactly the same as that which left the previous life. So, in that case, we cannot say something from here went there. Nor can we say something from here did not happen for the next life to be initiated.

So we don't use the term "reincarnation" since it signifies some unchanging, immutable, permanent entity moving from one life to another. "Rebirth" does not have that meaning.

Having said all this, I must tell you, it is extremely difficult to comprehend this particular truth, this reality, until we have gained a very good understanding of the whole process of existence, from deep insight and wisdom through the practice of meditation. The Buddha himself said kamma is one of the most difficult things to explain because you need very clear insight and purity of mind to understand it completely.

HUMAN REBIRTH

It is said that the human state is the most fruitful one for attaining enlightenment. How do you live in such a manner as to be reborn a human being?

Practice dana, or generosity. Practice sila, or morality. And practice meditation. Every day keep the mind as clean as possible and live just an ordinary, honest life, always keeping the mind as clear as possible.

Then, at the moment of death, you will remember your good children, good parents, good friends who are always good to you and you are good to them. At the last moment of your mind, you desire to be one of those good human beings. You desire to be one of those good friends in your next life.

REBECOMING, NOT REINCARNATION

I have read differing opinions about what the Buddha actually said about reincarnation. I believe I am reincarnated every morning and can start my life anew and strive to live fully Buddhist principles. I have struggles with understanding life after life and why it matters. If I don't remember past lives, is reincarnation important to me in this life if my behaviors and kamma bring me a better life?

You don't have to remember reincarnation at all. The word "reincarnation" is not a Buddhist term—we talk of "rebecoming" or "rebirth." But I don't want to get into technical interpretations of the word. If you do things honestly, sincerely, paying heed to your conscience, you don't have to worry about anything.

The Buddha gave four solaces in the Kalama Sutta (Anguttara Nikaya, 3:66). One is, if there is no rebirth, if I do something wicked, vicious, unwholesome, or wrong, I suffer in this life. By law or by my conscience, I suffer. If there is rebirth, then I suffer twice. Or, if there is no rebirth and I do everything correctly, rightly, honestly, answering my own conscience, anytime I think about my life, I will be very happy, even if there is no rebirth. But if there is rebirth, then I will be happy again. Either way, I'm happy.

The Buddha said don't worry about the past, don't worry about the future. Without worrying, do what you are supposed to do as a human being. Not killing, stealing, committing sensual misconduct, lying, slandering, gossiping, becoming addicted to alcohol and drugs, murder. Don't do those things!

You can go to bed thinking, "I spent my day in a very, very honest, sincere way." The next morning you get up and think, "I'm not going to do any of those things. Today I will live exactly as I did yesterday!"

That's all. That is why we pay respect to the Buddha. Every time I think of the Buddha I realize he gave us perfect answers to our problems. If you have any doubts about reincarnation, about rebirth, there is no need to worry if you are living in a wholesome way.

SOWING AND REAPING

When I read about the great disciples of the Buddha such as Sariputta and Moggallana, I understand that their wish was to be disciples of the Buddha and they went through so many lives to accomplish this. I was wondering what you make of that type of a wish—because when we live our lives, we have all kinds of wishes. We wish to win the lottery or become famous. How do we make such a meaningful wish as Sariputta and Moggallana did? Is that any different?

Yes, there's a difference. If you make a meaningful wish, you will get what you wish. If you make a confused wish, you will get that.

There is a beautiful sutta in the Majjhima Nikaya. There were two men—one was observing a dog's practice. He would eat like a dog, bark like a dog, and sleep on the floor, following a dog's behavior. The other man was behaving like a cow. Both of them went to see the Buddha.

The man who was behaving like a cow, eating grass and so forth, asked the Buddha, "Venerable Sir, my friend's practice is practicing like a dog. What will his destination be after death?" Buddha said, "Don't ask me that."

"No, please tell me," the man said. Finally the Buddha said, "If somebody thinks like a dog, eats like a dog, acts like a dog all his life, what do you think will happen to him after death? He will be a dog."

Then the man who practiced like a dog began to cry. The Buddha said, "That is why I told you not to ask me that question." The other man asked, what happens to the man who behaves like a cow? Buddha said the same thing, "Then you will become a cow."

This is confused intention. They have made this wish. However, Buddha said, if you have saddha, viriya, sati, samadhi, and panna—faith, perseverance, mindfulness, concentration, and wisdom—these all are very noble qualities. With these noble qualities, you practice meditation. You offer dana and take care of the poor and do service to your community and your country without expecting anything in return.

You do these things with a pure heart. Then you wish, "By the power of this merit, may I be reborn as a divine being"—it is possible you can be reborn as a divine being because your mind is very pure and clean.

So, every life you live like that. Then you might wish, "Let me be reborn as a brahma." You practice jhana and then are reborn in the brahma realms because for that aspiration you have prepared. There has to be a matching preparation for the attainment. These must be compatible.

Sariputta and Moggallana had—for many lives—practiced all these noble qualities to become a noble person. So they became noble disciples. That is the very nature of kamma. You reap what you sow. The Bible says that too. Everybody—whether they are Buddhist, Hindu, Muslim, Christian, or Jew—reaps the results according to the kamma they commit.

6

Dealing with Daily Life

MEDITATION IN BUSY LIFE

On retreat I feel it is easier to meditate because that is what everyone has come to do. Yet returning home to busy, modern life, it is hard to maintain mindfulness and calm awareness. How can we bring the benefits of meditation into our daily lives?

Slowing down is a way to nourish the roots of mindfulness. We can do this wherever we are, in a monastery but also at home and in the workplace. We talk about creating world peace, but people must also be concerned with creating mental peace—making their minds healthy and calm. And a healthy mind comes from mindfulness.

When you're at work or when you are unable to sit for a longer period in a quiet place, you can also enjoy a few moments of mindfulness. I recommend that everyone take one minute every hour during the day to do this. Work hard for fifty-nine minutes, then take a one-minute break and totally focus your mind on your breathing.

Close your eyes, if you can. Or if you're at your desk in a busy office, keep your eyes open at a point in front of you. Quietly, peacefully, count out fifteen breaths—that's about a minute. Don't think about the future, don't think about anything during that one minute. Just keep your mind totally free from all those things.

When that minute is over, you have added some clarity to your mind. You have added some strength to continue on for the other fifty-nine minutes in the hour. Then vow to yourself that when another hour has passed, you'll give yourself another one-minute mindfulness break.

You can do this at your kitchen table or office desk. You can do this after you've parked your car and turned off the engine. You can do this during a restroom break. If you do this kind of one-minute meditation the whole day, then at the end of an eight-hour work period you'll have spent eight minutes in meditation. You'll be less nervous, less tense, and less exhausted at the end of the day. Plus, you'll have a more productive and healthier day, both psychologically and physically.

It is up to each person to take charge of their own mind. Each one of us must learn how to slow down. You know, *un*mindful people are always in the majority! You can easily lead yourself down that same path if you let yourself. Don't get caught in this trap!

Wherever you are—at home, at a retreat center, in your car, in line at the grocery store—mindfulness can rescue you from stressful, painful mental states. I like to call mindfulness one's emergency kit. It's like when you cut or burn yourself—you immediately reach for a first-aid kit to treat the wound. The same is true for the mind. When the mind is pained, when it is agitated and distracted, when you are suffering mentally, you really need some first aid to come back to mental health.

But if you don't take care of painful mental states, they can grow worse, just like a wound. At their worst, we slip into a depression or nervous breakdown. And our mental suffering can manifest itself in all kinds of illnesses, from stomach problems to heart disease. So many things are going on in your mind! Only when something triggers a breakdown or serious illness do you begin to look back at all the time you've spent making your life chaotic.

You must bring yourself back to mindfulness wherever you are, all the time. Along with your regular meditation practice, add practices such as this one-minute meditation into your daily life. Train yourself in this way—as soon as some psychic irritation arises, stop and take care of it before you proceed with other activities in your day.

MEDITATION AND SLEEP

Why when I meditate long hours do I sleep less? Also, my sleep is different, as if I were alert in sleep.

When you meditate long hours, you gain sufficient rest for your neurons. That is equivalent to your sleeping state. The difference is that in the sleeping state you are not aware. But in a meditative state you are aware, so you get enough rest during meditation. Therefore, you don't need as much sleep.

That is why even the Buddha recommended we train ourselves to stay awake and alert at night. Normally in regular society people seek to sleep eight hours. If you meditate you don't need eight hours of sleep. If you meditate you replace the rest you get from sleeping with meditation.

So, don't worry about it. This is a very usual thing. All the things that are to be repaired in our body through sleep, the brain will repair them during meditation and you'll feel refreshed.

ANTIDEPRESSANTS AND MEDITATION

Can those with depression, anxiety, and such syndromes as attention-deficit disorder use antidepressants, anti-anxiety drugs, or stimulants to support them while they practice? Does it violate the Fifth Precept against using intoxicants?

If these medications help them to correct such mental problems and the mind remains steady, calm, without having any other side effects, and so forth, I think they can use such means. It is not violating the precepts because they have to take care of their health.

Good health, physical and mental, is absolutely necessary to practice meditation. Meditation alone cannot correct all of the mental problems that sometimes arise from birth. There has to be some kind of way they can correct such issues so they can get back to the mainstream of life and practice meditation.

RESPECTING OTHERS

You have said respecting others is an important trait. Why is that?

When you respect others, that's what you get—respect. If you don't respect others, that's what you get. People who respect others, who deserve their respect, they will become humble, and people will love such people as they learn to respect others.

Therefore, in this life when they respect others everybody appreciates them. Even after death they will be born in a state where they will receive respect from others. In the next life they will be respected by others because they have respected others in this life.

So respecting each other is a very wonderful practice. We don't lose anything. We always gain something spiritually. Therefore, the Buddha gave us this advice to practice. It is very practical advice.

HATE AND VIOLENCE IN THE WORLD

The world seems so full of hatred, violence, and pain. How is it possible to pursue joy and also have compassion for those who commit such cruelties?

It is very difficult to imagine how cruel human beings can be. We cannot even say "bestial" since wild beasts don't commit the kinds of heinous crimes people do. When wild beasts kill, it's to eat. When full, they don't bother to kill other animals. So beasts often behave much better than human beings!

Fortunately, not all human beings are violent and cruel. There are many kind, compassionate, and good people. In fact, they are in the majority when we think about it. Yet only a small minority makes the news—the ones whose cruel-hearted, violent actions can shake up the whole world.

So we have to cultivate loving-friendliness—metta—for them along with all others. They commit crimes since they themselves are suffering. As a result, they are totally confused. I don't think any right-minded person, one who thinks and sees clearly, would commit such violence. People have to be very, very confused to be worse than beasts. We should not give up on them—we must try to share loving-friendliness with them. They need a lot of metta.

By sending our metta they will not, of course, suddenly change. Sometimes a person's kamma is so strong, they cannot see the pain they're causing others or they don't care. So they commit more bad kamma and suffer yet more.

We can at least have metta toward them. We can try to understand how much they must suffer to have become so violent and indifferent to other people's lives.

Please keep practicing metta for yourself and share your metta with all: criminals, the victims of criminals, their bereaved relatives. All deserve our metta. I can send my metta to all of them. May all learn to live in peace and harmony.

OVERTURNED BOWLS

What if a government or government leader is doing bad things and is hurting people and they go and give to the sangha of monastics. What is the right response?

In some places, when they know that governmental leaders are suppressing people and doing all kinds of wrong things and the monks feel very bad about it, in order to teach these leaders a lesson, they go in front of the leader's house and turn their bowls upside down. A monastic can do that to a layperson if the monastic knows this layperson has done something very, very wrong.

BUDDHISM AND WESTERN PSYCHOLOGY

Is Buddhism compatible with Western psychology?

Certain aspects of Buddhism don't conflict with Western psychology. Other aspects like kamma and rebirth would not be easy to explain. But I don't think Buddhism in general contradicts Western psychology in its approach to the problem of suffering.

That is, there is a very evident, irrefutable problem: suffering. This suffering, this problem, this sickness must have a cause. In order to be cured, to be free from the suffering, the cause must be addressed—so long as the root cause remains, you cannot cure the patient. We all recognize this.

And to be free from the suffering, there must be a method, a system, a cure. Guidance is given and certain prescriptions are suggested. So, this is the system that Buddhism follows. Western psychology also offers insight into how the past may have affected your current mental state—and how healing the mind and spirit can create a more wholesome, happy life. This is very much in the spirit of Buddhist teachings.

Yet Western psychology is also very often based on treating this suffering neurologically: addressing the chemistry of the brain through medicine. Buddhism is based not only on physical things—it deals directly with mental states, which are not always physical.

There's a physical base to the mind, and yet the mind is not just something physical. Western psychology does offer guidance in how we may better understand the sources of our own suffering and cope with it. Yet Buddhism takes this approach far deeper and more systemically. The Four Noble Truths, after all, talk about the method and the path that will lead to suffering's final end.

THE MIDDLE WAY

Buddhism speaks of the Middle Way between extremes. Couldn't this also apply to activities like drinking alcohol and telling the truth all the time?

The Buddha referred to the Middle Way as the path between extremes of behavior. Between asceticism and hedonism, between self-mortification and self-indulgence. Yet people can mistranslate or misuse the phrase "Middle Way" to justify compromises between unwholesome and wholesome actions, between good and evil.

If you hear someone lying, you may say, "No, it's not right to lie." The person may justify it by saying, "It's OK to tell white lies. You just don't go to extremes—this is the Middle Way." If someone drinks and you advise them not to drink, the person may say, "Oh, come now, I follow the Middle Way when it comes to drinking." For this reason, sometimes we hesitate to use the phrase "Middle Way" in a loose sense.

STAY COOL

"Coolness" is seen as an admirable virtue in Buddhist teachings, but that is such a radical critique of our usual value system, especially in the West because we value stimulation, excitement, and passion. It seems this notion of cool and calmness runs counter to the culture. Do you agree?

You know, you destroy the very thing you are fighting for if you are agitated and excited. You can bring peace to others only by being peaceful. When you move quietly, calmly, and peacefully, you have enormous energy.

When there is a big flood and water rushes by, how long does it do that? Only for a short period of time. Yet if water flows slowly, gently, over a long period of time, it can cut through mountains because slowly and steadily it moves, never stopping.

The Buddha advised monks and nuns to behave in a way that arouses faith in those who don't have faith in the Buddha, Dhamma, and Sangha, and to increase the faith of those who already have faith in the Triple Gem. Two episodes illustrate how cool and calm behavior affect very devotional people.

Venerable Assaji was one of the first five disciples of the Buddha. One day soon after his enlightenment he was going on his alms round in Rajagaha. At that time, Upatissa was traveling, looking for an enlightened teacher.

Seeing Venerable Assaji's calm, serene composure, he thought, "Never before have I seen an ascetic like this. Surely he must be one of those who have attained arahantship or one who is treading the path leading to arahantship. What if I were to approach him and ask, 'For whose sake, Venerable Sir, have you retired from the world? Who is your teacher? Whose doctrine do you profess?'"

But he waited until Venerable Assaji ended his alms round. When he sat down to eat, Upatissa served him with water. After Venerable Assaji washed his hands, Upatissa asked him who his teacher was. He said that his teacher was the Buddha. Upatissa asked him, what did he teach? Venerable Assaji was an extremely humble arahant and so he said, "I am still a novice in the Order, brother. I am not able to expound the Dhamma to you at length."

"I am Upatissa, Venerable Sir. Say much or little according to your ability, and it is left to me to understand it in a hundred or a thousand ways."

So, Venerable Assaji said:

Of things that proceed from a cause
Their cause the Tathagata has told,
And also their cessation:
Thus teaches the Great Ascetic.

Listening to this utterance, Upatissa attained stream entry.

At another time King Asoka maintained the custom of offering alms to ascetics, a practice instituted by his father. But soon he was disappointed in the recipients. He began looking for holy men.

At this time a novice monk known as Nigrodha was walking calmly, slowly, and mindfully by King Asoka's palace. His demeanor was very peaceful, serene, and composed. Noticing the young novice, Asoka was at once drawn to him and invited him into the palace. The king offered him his own throne on which to sit and asked him to give a sermon.

Nigrodha gave him a sermon on mindfulness, which greatly pleased the king. Immediately the king started following the Buddha, Dhamma, and Sangha and donated a large amount of wealth. He asked the novice Nigrodha to use it for spreading the Dhamma and to support the community of the Sangha. In addition, he sent sets of robes each day. Nigrodha gave these robes to other monks.

So, you can see that a cool approach is a wise approach. You take your time and do not lose your energy.

I remember being in Bhutan, which has these very steep mountains to climb. Visitors arrive with big pieces of luggage. Now, the Bhutanese people are not as huge as Americans, but these small people carry tourists' luggage.

The visitors arrive in boots and socks and gloves and overcoats and caps and so forth. The natives may have on only a pair of sandals and not too many clothes, not even a hat. Up the steep mountains they carry all this luggage as they methodically keep walking, walking, walking, slowly and steadily, until they reach the top.

But the visitors are so enthusiastic, they run up the mountainside and then have to stop for breath. Even though the natives and tourists started out together, an observer might think the visitor is going to beat the native to the top because he is going very fast. But the native takes it step by step and reaches the top maybe an hour earlier than the visitor. He knows! He has experience, he has wisdom that if he runs very quickly at the beginning, he cannot run too far. He conserves his energy and gives the body time to rest.

So coolness, not rushing, does run counter to modern life.

Even we monks are advised to slow down when teaching! Buddha said, when you give a Dhamma talk, don't rush. Don't speak quickly because you will get tired and you will become confused.

This approach, taking things with a cool attitude, can last longer and be more effective in many regards.

IMPERMANENCE AND SADNESS

I'm very attached to my loved ones, including a loyal, loving dog. I try to stay in the present to be grateful and remember impermanence. Still, when one of my beloved family members or pets is very ill or dies, my heart breaks. What more should I do?

We had a wonderful dog at the Bhavana Society for many years. We all know how beautiful, friendly, and faithful dogs are. Every person's dog is a wonderful dog. My dog stayed here for seventeen years. And he died. It was very sad. So I decided never to raise dogs again. I think your sorrow or lamentation, the grief over a beloved pet or loved one passing away or becoming sick, will stay there until you attain full enlightenment.

Practicing mindfulness of impermanence is a very good temporary measure. We practice it every day—noting the impermanence of ourselves and everything else around us, including our friends and relatives, your loving, friendly dog and friendly cat. All are impermanent.

When you keep practicing, practicing, practicing, your mind will become very strong. Sometimes even then you still have some sor-

row when a loving pet or person dies. I know this from my personal experience when my brother died, my father died, my mother
died. I felt very sad and even cried in spite of all my knowledge
of Dhamma, all my practice of meditation. That hasn't happened
recently. If it happened now I could control my emotions. But in
those days, I couldn't—I cried.

So this happens to everybody. As we grow and mature and
understand impermanence better, then our sorrow and grief slowly
fade away.

LETTING GO

**Sometimes I look at Buddhist magazine ads filled with beauti-
ful people in beautiful clothes, seated on beautiful cushions,
and think that many of us don't have beautiful, perfect lives
and how can I live up to this image?**

This is how marketing techniques work. They keep repeating the
same ad, the same commercial again and again and again. And one
day you think, "Gee, let me try this," until you have completely sur-
rendered yourself to the ad.

Therefore, the wise, mindful person must think, "Do I need all these
things they advertise? How many things do I really use in my everyday
life?" There are those immediate things we use and need, but, really,
there is just a small number of very absolute necessary things.

You know, when people practice the second step of the Noble
Eightfold Path—samma sankappa, or Right Thinking—the
number-one thing is letting go. This sounds very big and somehow
overwhelming and intimidating!

But they must ask themselves, "What should I give up first?"
There are so many things we collect in our lives. People end up
having huge collections of things. What do you do with them? You
buy a glass showcase and say, "Oh, I got this from Korea, this is
from South Africa, this is from Russia, this is from China . . ." But

it is just boosting your ego, increasing your greed. Of course, giving up things we cherish is difficult. But we must learn to let go of unnecessary things first.

Then, you take stock and see other things you don't use. There's something in the closet you have not used for ten years? Get rid of it! There's another set of things you haven't used for five years? Get rid of it! Those are the things we must let go of first.

We reduce and reduce and reduce until we keep only a bare minimum of the things we need for our daily use.

LOOK TO YOURSELF

How do we master the task of generating happiness within ourselves instead of searching for it in other people and depending on them?

When you want to practice anything, you have to do it by yourself. When you are hungry, if you think of other people eating and let others eat for you, can you satisfy your hunger? When you are sleepy, you go to sleep. When you are thirsty, you drink.

Similarly, if you really want to find happiness, you've got to look to yourself. Not even your mother, your father, or any other relative or friend can do so much good for you as your own well-directed mind can do for you.

Happiness for yourself comes from your own personal, diligent, independent practice. Keep thinking about it: "I must practice in order to make myself happy." Others can help to some extent. A kalyana mitta, a good spiritual friend, can give some tips that encourage you to practice. But we have to do it by ourselves.

SPIRITUAL PRACTICE IN LAY LIFE

Sometimes I feel the Dhamma is so profound, I should take steps to become a monk. But to be honest, at present I would

really like to lead a lay life guided by the Eightfold Path. I'm worried that in lay life I might be more prone to stay in samsara and the endless round of rebirth. Is there a way to choose the lay life and still take the best approach to attaining Nibbana?

Even in the time of the Buddha, everyone did not become a monk or nun among his followers. There were many laypeople practicing who attained full enlightenment. But you have to be very serious while living a lay life. You have to work a little harder to practice the Noble Eightfold Path.

Since this is a path for both laypeople and monastics, if you undertake that path very seriously and do your practice very consistently, you certainly can attain stages of enlightenment, such as the first stage of enlightenment: stream entry, or the Sotapanna stage. There are many people in the time of the Buddha who as laypeople practiced and attained enlightenment.

So don't hesitate. You will have fear of samsara, this interminable cycle of rebirths, if you do not practice. If you practice, you will have no reason to fear samsara. Whether you are a monastic or a layperson, we follow the same path.

Monastics have more rules and regulations. It's very strict—laypeople do not have that many. Monastic commitments are more serious because a monastic has undertaken special precepts. Laypeople's practice is easier in a way because they don't observe so many precepts.

But both laypeople and monastics must very diligently and sincerely follow the Noble Eightfold Path.

WHOLESOME DIRECTIONS

In your book *Eight Mindful Steps to Happiness* you write that loving-friendliness is not love as we ordinarily understand it. It is not conditioned by the behavior or qualities of a person. Loving-friendliness motivates us to be kind to everyone. But what did the Buddha have to say about personal love? Do personal love relationships and loyalties as we normally understand them have a value in spiritual life? Do they play a part in bringing us closer to enlightenment?

What did the Buddha have to say about personal love? Personal love, of course, is important for people's relationships. We wish to be together, to support each other emotionally, and to maintain a sense of security and to make people's lives harmonious.

Personal love is important. And if people live that life with 100 percent honesty, sincerity, and faithfulness to each other, then that is an ideal life for laypeople. It is sometimes possible. Some people live like that.

But the problem always arises when there is friction, misunderstanding, distrust, unfaithfulness, ungratefulness, anger, hatred, jealousy, fear, rivalry. When these things come into play, then this relationship can become very difficult.

So the Buddha gave a special discourse to laypeople in the Digha Nikaya called the Sigalovada Sutta, a discourse delivered to a person called Sigala. In this sutta he gives instructions about how to live together: spouses, partners, children, parents, brothers, sisters, teachers, students, masters and workers, rulers and their subjects. There is a long list of duties and responsibilities to each other. This whole discourse is called the Layman's Code of Discipline.

Plus, there are many other suttas in the Digha Nikaya, Majjhima Nikaya, Anguttara Nikaya, Samyutta Nikaya, and Khuddaka Nikaya that the Buddha delivered especially for laypeople on how to live their householder lives. The Buddha always praised good and noble relationships between spouses and their partners. If they live that kind of life, observing the Five Precepts, even they can obtain full enlightenment.

So people must learn how to live a balanced lay life. There are many people who are 100 percent honest and sincere, and it's quite possible for them to obtain enlightenment.

Sincerity is the number-one qualification along with honesty—honesty toward oneself and with others so that the mind always remains very steady, powerful, and clean. As soon as the person sits to meditate they gain concentration quickly. Why? The person is honest and sincere.

Say, for instance, a person has wealth and they are secure in knowing they earned their wealth honestly and by noble means. Then that realization is a source of happiness. Having wealth is a blessing in that case.

This life itself is neither good nor bad. Money is neither good nor bad. Having a body is neither good nor bad. But how we use the body, how we use that money, makes all the difference. Something very neutral can be made into something very unwholesome.

So it all depends on how we use our body and mind. They are neither moral nor immoral. If we understand this and live honestly and sincerely, then our personal relationships, our wealth, and so forth will lead us in a wholesome direction.

CLINGING AND RELATIONSHIPS

How do you differentiate between a clinging relationship and a genuinely close one?

Clinging relationships bring more pain and suffering than a healthy and close relationship. But we must also understand that any relationship is impermanent, no matter whether it is a clinging one or a nonclinging one. This law of impermanence doesn't spare anything.

A PREGNANT BLESSING

What kind of blessing or wisdom do you tell a woman soon to experience childbirth?

We have a special blessing, which comes from the Angulimala Sutta (Majjhima Nikaya, 86). Angulimala was a very famous criminal, and so this sutta is named after that criminal. He had killed 999 people according to the sutta. When he was going to kill the Buddha, instead, Buddha converted him and he became an ordained monk, a bhikkhu. Soon after that he attained full enlightenment.

One day when he was going on his alms round, he was standing in front of a house and heard a woman crying out from her labor pains. His heart melted. Before he met the Buddha, this person didn't have any compassion—he simply killed. Now he was filled with compassion. He went to the Buddha and reported on his experience of hearing the woman in pain from childbirth. The Buddha said, "Angulimala, go and tell this woman: 'Since I was born, I have never killed any living beings. By the power of this truth may you deliver the baby without pain.'"

Angulimala said, "But Venerable Sir, how can I say this? I have killed with my own hand 999 people. Now you go and tell me to tell a lie?"

Buddha said, "You must remember, Angulimala, since you became a monk and attained enlightenment, you have never killed any living being. Use that truth as a power to give a blessing to this woman."

Bolstered by the Buddha's words, he went back to the house and standing outside, he said, "Sister, since I was born in the Ariyan Clan [became a Bhikkhu] I have never killed any living beings. By this truth, by this power, may you have a safe delivery."

As soon as he recited these words the woman safely delivered her baby. Since then, this has become a sutta to recite for pregnant women just before they give birth. For some reason, it seems to work. Many women thank us for reciting this. So this is what we do.

TEACHINGS ON THE FAMILY

Are there teachings on the family? Is having children a holy duty or a selfish act?

Buddhism doesn't talk about reproduction because Buddhism assumes that all living beings have an inborn desire to reproduce. So they don't need any special teaching for that.

What Buddhism says is that once born, then there are certain things one has to do in regards to family life—these things the Buddha recommended. The Sigalovada Sutta in the Digha Nikaya, also known as the Layman's Code of Discipline, outlines the entire structure of family responsibilities and duties.

Besides that, there are many discourses for laypeople to follow. None of them talks about family planning or reproduction and so forth. And it is selfish definitely, you might say, if you want to see yourself reflected in a child: "That is my boy! That is my girl! My boy is such and such and such!" Don't get offended when I say this.

MEDITATION AND TRAUMA

Do you think meditation can heal trauma? For example, can it heal the memories of traumatic feelings and experiences stored in the body?

Suppose somebody has never meditated. And then after some traumatic experience, if the person tries to meditate to overcome trauma, it might not be very easy.

But if somebody who has been meditating encounters that traumatic experience during meditation, then they can use their meditation experience to overcome or sit with the trauma.

CRIME AND COMPASSION

How should we react to atrocities such as terrorist bombings that kill people indiscriminately?

We feel sad, certainly, out of compassion. The underlying principle even there is how to bring happiness. We feel these things are unacceptable. How to help? Not only the victim but even the criminals need help. We often seek to help the victims, but the one who caused the crime or atrocity also has been suffering from psychological issues. We ought to find a way to help even that person.

Of course, sometimes we hear of these things and feel helpless. But the real motive in responding should be to bring happiness to everybody. Sometimes we get sad and angry. Why? Because this person took away other people's happiness, their health, their lives.

However, we also must think, "Why do these people do this?" Because they themselves have problems. We cannot solve all such problems, but we must consider how to help these people who have caused them. So inwardly what we really have is compassion and the intention to bring true peace and happiness.

We know that we cannot solve all the problems in the world. But in the smallest ways we try to train our children to live in peace and harmony. We cannot do anything about what has already happened. We must consider and learn ways to encourage peace and harmony in the present and the future.

LITTLE WHITE LIES

Is it OK for parents to tell a white lie to their children? Such as, if a small child asks where babies come from?

I think parents always must train themselves to tell the truth—not even white lies. Children are like a sponge and absorb everything. "Mom said it was like this!" They always quote their parents as the authority. Therefore, the parents are the ones who should follow the principle or precept of telling the truth.

One time an eight-year-old girl came with her parents and grandparents to our monastery. We were sitting on the porch in West Virginia. In front of all these people, the girl said, "Venerable Bhante, we children don't kill, steal, commit sensual misconduct, we don't lie, we don't drink. But our parents don't observe any of these things." The parents blushed. The grandparents blushed. They were so embarrassed. See the way children observe?

Don't underestimate children. They're always observing. Therefore, parents must learn to tell the truth to children.

So, what should you do if a small child asks you where babies come from? You tell her, "Darling, you are too young to understand this. I will tell you when you are a little older."

This is better than telling white lies such as, "Oh, my dear, I went to the hospital and came back with you." You will just make her even more confused. When you tell her, "I'll tell you when you are ready. You are too young to understand," then you are telling the truth.

FITTING IN MEDITATION

How do we as laypeople fit meditation into our busy daily lives?

I encourage people to set up time at home to meditate at least twice a day, once in the morning and once in the evening, so you can deepen your practice. Then, when you are able, you can go on a retreat.

Build meditation into your day amid all of your household activities. Anyone can meditate at home if they make a proper schedule. Then you can incorporate mindfulness into all the activities of your daily life.

Plus, we try to see impermanence in all things and at all times. We can do this anytime, whether we are meditating at a center or at home while eating, drinking, talking. At any time we can at least notice how things are changing.

Our feelings change, our perceptions, thoughts, and ideas all change. Try to pay attention to these changes anytime during the day or night, wherever you are.

At that time, you are meditating.

STRONG EMOTIONAL STATES

In meditation sometimes I encounter strong emotional states such as anxiety and fear. How do you advise dealing with such strong emotional states?

That depends on the kind of emotion. I would advise the person not to think of the things that caused the emotions. Just let them go. That is difficult, but that is a very practical way of dealing with them.

That is why the Buddha said, those Dhammas that are not supposed to be remembered, don't remember them! Because when you think of those things, many other defilements related to them will appear in the mind and you will get all muddled. This is also called proliferation—conceptual proliferation, or papanca. When you start thinking of one thing, then a host of other things comes along with it.

It is helpful to recall the Buddha's teachings on mindfulness. The number-one thing is to not let fearful or agitated states appear in the mind in the first place. But once they do appear, then we are mindful that the things that caused these states have passed. There is no substance except for this concept, this memory, this feeling. These do not serve any purpose now—what is more important is what is happening now.

The Buddha said one who does not think of such things shines like the moon free from clouds. Do not let them arise and cloud the mind. At the same time, when such states do arise in the mind, one has to be very mindful of impermanence. These states are all appearing and disappearing depending on the causes and conditions they arose. All the causes and condition are no longer there, so this is just a mere memory.

So if the person keeps thinking of positive and wholesome things again and again and again, then negative things will slowly fade away and disappear from the mind.

There is the Buddha's simile of the salt crystal. If there is a small cup of water and you put a lump of salt in it, the water will be very salty. If you take a similar lump of salt and put it into a large river, the river would not become salty.

Similarly, when we keep cultivating wholesome thoughts again and again and again, then when unwholesome thoughts occasionally arise, they will not affect the mind. Because we are repeating wholesome things, the mind is fully charged with wholesomeness. And there will not be enough room for unwholesome things to arise in the mind. That is the meaning of the simile of the salt crystal.

Another simile from the Buddha's teachings is the simile of the conch blower, as in the Sankha Sutta (Samyutta Nikaya, 42.8). The conch blower develops and cultivates metta. He charges the mind with metta—whichever direction the person focuses his mind on, they can send metta in that direction.

And so they can send metta to all ten directions—north, northeast, east, southeast, and so on. Then that person forgets himself in this practice of sharing metta in all directions. Eventually all these negative things in the mind will go away as a result of that metta practice.

These are the things we need to remember when emotional or difficult states arise in meditation or at any time in our daily life.

BREEZY INSIGHT

What is the role of attitude in our practice? As I sit outside, I am aware of the breeze, the temperature, the changing nature of conditions. One time the breeze may feel cold and I want to get away from it. Another time the breeze may be pleasant when the sun is on me. And a third time in the heat of the day, I may long or crave for a breeze. The difference is not in the breeze but in my attitude toward the breeze. If I hold on to any of these attitudes, then I suffer. If I don't attach to the attitude, then as the breeze comes or goes I do not suffer.

That is very true. When our attitude is healthy, strong, and mindful, we remain equanimous. It doesn't matter what the other conditions are.

So a breeze is just a breeze, whether we are in the sun or in a cool place. We feel the cold when the cold breeze flows, but we are not averse to the breeze. We accept it and understand the feeling.

VEGETARIANISM

One of my greatest wishes is to be compassionate and refrain from causing suffering to other beings. However, I am conflicted. I also want to have good health and be good to my body. What does the Dhamma have to say about the consumption of animals? I go back and forth about being vegetarian. But I hear all these things about how we need to eat meat to stay healthy.

It is a wonderful wish. How I translate *metta* into English is "loving-friendliness." Many call it loving-kindness. We try to practice loving-friendliness for all living beings. We should strive to practice compassion, or karuna, the second of the Four Sublime States. One seeks to live a compassionate life by not hurting any living being in thoughts, words, and deed.

And so we act with mindfulness, with loving-friendliness and compassion. We think and speak and act with this attitude. In order to act with this attitude, we must always keep this in mind, even to the level of our eating and drinking and daily behavior.

It is a meaningful and wholesome practice to be a vegetarian, to address your conscience about the treatment of animals, because you might feel you are contributing to killing indirectly if you consume meat. But that is controversial.

That is because restraining from eating meat is not necessarily automatically contributing to compassion. You are not going to be compassionate just by not eating meat. Look at Hitler. He was a vegetarian. So being a vegetarian itself is not a guarantee of practicing compassion.

It is not what we eat that makes us compassionate but how we think, act, and speak. Even a monk may not necessarily be a vegetarian because when he takes his alms bowl and goes from house to house, people offer whatever they have in their house. He is supposed to accept what people offer. Whether he eats that or not is a different question.

So to be a vegan or vegetarian is not a necessary condition to being a compassionate person. It is true that one should not be directly involved in killing, supporting killing, or promoting killing. One should stay away from all that while practicing compassion in thoughts, words, and deeds.

ASSISTED SUICIDE

If someone is suffering and thinking about ending their life because of a terminal illness, is assisted suicide a permissible act of loving-kindness? Or is it killing?

From a Dhamma point of view, it is killing. You know, there was the case of an individual who had taken part in an assisted suicide. It ended up in court and the verdict was that the person was found not guilty. That may be the way the judge interprets the law, but this was a secular situation.

If someone suffers from an incurable disease, we must do whatever we can as human beings to help the person to reduce their pain. But we have no right to take anybody's life or to assist or advise somebody to kill oneself.

ANIMAL EXPERIMENTATION

I am concerned about the many animals sacrificed for exper-imental use in the name of improving human health and pro-ducing drugs and other products. Can Buddhist philosophy offer an alternative perspective to improve such real-world problems?

Actually, hurting animals in any form for any purpose is not com-patible with metta practice. People argue that human life is more valuable than an animal's life, so then let us use animals for human benefit. But technology can perform miracles in this age. With that powerful technology, scientists should be able to conduct experi-ments without using animals. That is my personal belief.

BUDDHISM AND POLITICS

Buddhism has a reputation of not engaging in the politics of the world, yet we have some clear examples in contemporary politics of Buddhist governments and monks taking part in sur-prising acts of hostility and violence. What are your thoughts about such behavior?

In the history of Buddhism, whenever people become overly nation-alistic, there is the danger of fanaticism. They forget religion. They forget Dhamma. A country can be a Buddhist country, but killing and chasing people who are not Buddhist out of the country and depriving them of all human rights is not Buddhist practice. They simply became fanatics. That has happened to Hinduism and Islam and religions of all kinds.

When we become ultra-nationalistic, we forget the basic fundamental truth or principle of the founder of our religion. Buddhism is known for its wisdom and compassion. Where is the wisdom in discriminating against people? Where is the compassion in discriminating against others?

If I had power, what would I do? I would try to live with non-Buddhists in peace. If you commit crimes you will be treated exactly like anybody else, therefore, don't commit any crimes. And you can follow your principles, you can follow your religions. We are not going to change that. But don't commit any crimes. And there are also very peaceful ways of dealing with crimes.

For monks and Buddhist leaders to discriminate against whole populations, this is lawlessness. Everybody is taking the law into their own hands. I completely condemn such behavior. I would never support it. Never.

Therefore, it is not Buddhism! This is not Buddhism. If they really practice Buddhism, in spite of all these differences among different people, they should practice metta or loving-friendliness.

7

Enlightenment

THE POSSIBILITY OF ENLIGHTENMENT

How can we have faith that enlightenment is possible in this very life?

When you understand the Dhamma, you will have a very strong faith in the possibility of realizing enlightenment because the path of the Dhamma is clear and straightforward.

Depending on our comprehension and the effort and time we put into the practice, that attainment can take place. If we are not confused, if we diligently and honestly practice the Dhamma without hesitation, fear, and doubt, then we can attain the stages of enlightenment.

I sincerely and strongly urge you all to have this faith: that you can attain at least one level of enlightenment—if not all the stages of enlightenment—in this very life.

WHY NIBBANA?

If everything is impermanent, what is the point of trying to get enlightened?

The point of trying to gain enlightenment is Nibbana. That is why we want to strive hard to obtain that state. We have to go beyond all of these impermanent things to reach that permanent state.

THE ONLY PERMANENT STATE

Is Nibbana permanent?

Yes, it is the only permanent state. That is why it is said, when one sees with wisdom all conditioned things are impermanent, that is the path to liberation. This means that everything that we can think, everything that our mind can conceive or perceive, whatever exists in the universe is impermanent.

Now, Nibbana is not something that exists just like an object. It takes place in our own mind when the mind is 100 percent pure and clean of all the defilements and even wholesome states. What appears then is Nibbana—which is not impermanent. It is the only permanent state. That is why we want to strive to obtain that state.

SPIRITUAL ATTAINMENTS

Is it permitted in the Buddha's teaching to declare one's spiritual attainment?

The Buddha said in several places that there are seven qualities of a noble individual—to abstain from killing, stealing, sexual misconduct, telling lies, divisive talk, harsh speech, and useless talk. And four desirable states—faith in the Buddha, the Dhamma, and the Sangha, and maintaining sila, or having high moral standards.

When a noble disciple possesses these seven good qualities and these four desirable states and has attained the first stage of enlightenment, or stream entry, if he wishes, he could declare, "I am one finished with hell, finished with the animal realm, finished with the domain of ghosts, finished with the plane of misery, the bad destinations, the nether world. I am a stream-enterer, no longer bound to the nether world, fixed in destiny, with enlightenment as my destination."

A SOTAPANNA

What is a Sotapanna?

A Sotapanna is one who has attained the first stage of enlightenment, also referred to as a stream-enterer. Once, the Buddha said to Venerable Sariputta:

"Sariputta, this is said, 'The Stream, the stream.' What now, Sariputta, is the stream?"

"One who possesses this Noble Eightfold Path, Venerable Sir, is called a stream-enterer. This Noble Eightfold Path, Venerable Sir, is the stream. That is, Right View, Right Intention, Right Speech, Right Action, Right Livelihood, Right Effort, Right Mindfulness, and Right Concentration."

"Good, good, Sariputta! This Noble Eightfold Path is the stream . . ."

QUALITIES OF STREAM ENTRY

I would like to know what it really feels like when someone experiences stream entry, the first stage of enlightenment. What comes to the mind and what do you see? Afterward, what qualities does he or she have?

When one enters the Sotapanna level, that person feels free from the fear of taking rebirth in lower realms of existence, such as the animal kingdom, ghostly realm, hell realms, and the asura realm. Also, that person is endowed with the four factors of stream entry—*cattari sotapattiyangani*. These are unwavering confidence in the Buddha, the Dhamma, and the Sangha, and the virtuous behavior dear to the noble ones.

But strong joy can arise without attaining the Sotapanna state. When one attains jhanas, one will have joy and happiness. When all the defilements are completely eradicated from the mind, a very bright light arises in the mind. This is what happened to the Buddha when he attained full enlightenment. He said, "Light arose in me—*aloko udapadi.*"

How Can One Achieve Nibbana?

Sometimes I become disillusioned by the large amount of work I have to do to become enlightened. How can one ever achieve Nibbana? It seems like such an impossible goal!

The simplest way to attain enlightenment is just to get rid of your greed, hatred, and delusion. That's all! You don't have to do anything else!

It's true that enlightenment appears to be very difficult. I have to say, though, that this question stems from our most basic ignorance. Please don't get offended when I use the word "ignorance." We all have ignorance. Some people have more, some less. But until we eradicate this ignorance, then enlightenment appears to be impossible. As we learn to eradicate ignorance, then enlightenment seems more and more possible.

Sometimes when we use the term "enlightenment" it sounds like some mind-boggling, far-out, impossible concept. You may think, "I have so many problems in my life. I have so many faults. I can't even balance my checkbook at the end of the month much less achieve Nibbana!"

Or some Westerners may think, "Oh, enlightenment, that's something for Asians. All the enlightenment is over there." So they decide, "Let's go to Asia and get ourselves some of that enlightenment!"

Westerners read lots of Buddhist books that talk about so many beautiful things. Straightaway, they read about Nibbana and it sounds so peaceful, so calm, so quiet. No worries! No fears! So they head to Eastern countries with the belief that every one of those millions of nuns, monks, and laypeople there are sitting under trees, meditating, and they are well on their way to Nibbana. "That must be why they are poor. They never work, they're always meditating."

But when you go to Asia, you hardly see anybody sitting anywhere except perhaps alongside the road waiting for the bus. So it's a completely wrong notion! Enlightenment is not there. Enlightenment is, in fact, *anywhere* we are.

It all begins with the way we train our mind. Don't worry about enlightenment right now. What we have to do is take first things first. Just take one step at a time. Just begin.

Unfortunately, there is no shortcut. You must commit to the process and stick with it. As you begin, as your practice and experience deepen, you will start to see it taking shape in what the Buddha called the Seven Factors of Enlightenment. They are sati, mindfulness; Dhamma vicaya, investigation; viriya, energy; piti, joy or rapture; passadhi, relaxation or tranquility; samadhi, concentration; and upekkha, equanimity.

Each of these Factors of Enlightenment links up and connects with the following one. You begin with mindfulness, which leads to investigation, which leads to energy, which leads to joy, and that leads to tranquility, then concentration, then equanimity.

With an honest commitment, we can at least have a glimpse of all these things in our meditation practice. As our practice deepens, so will our understanding. The important thing is to just begin and then to stick with it.

A RARE COMMODITY

I wonder if it was easier for people to attain enlightenment in the Buddha's day than today, at a time in the monastic order when there were fewer rules.

In the past you had very few rules and regulations, but more people attained enlightenment. Now we have more rules and regulations, and less people attain enlightenment.

In those days people who renounced household life and entered monastic life were like a dry desert where there is no water. The earth is cracked because of a lack of water, and when a rain comes, every drop is absorbed. Similarly, those who entered the order in early days were so thirsty for Dhamma! They were so sincere and honest, they would do anything to absorb the practice.

Throughout the centuries as more people have undertaken practice with various motivations, not all of them had that same sincerity and honesty. Now, 2,600 years later, practice has become weak, diluted, and complacent. Not only among common people—even among monastics, there are those who are not practicing that seriously.

Therefore, attainment has become a very rare commodity. And that has been going on for centuries. The practice slowly, slowly disappears—that is what is happening.

The more that people become materialistic and less spiritual, you can expect all kinds of things. Therefore, I am so happy to see a place like this meditation retreat center and to find people who try to taste the truth of Dhamma in their own personal life.

The Buddha said this Dhamma is personally realizable. This is not a Dhamma we accept through belief. This is Dhamma we realize within ourselves. So we need a time and a place to practice to realize the Dhamma that we have in us.

Awakening to Awakening

What are the characteristics of the experience of path and fruition? Or in other words, how may we know whether we have attained a stage of awakening?

The experience of path and fruition is not very clearly explained or defined in many places. In the suttas, we find that our fetters subside at a certain level at the path stage and at a certain level at the fruition stage.

For instance, when you attain the first level of supramundane attainment, that is called stream entry. You abandon your belief in the notions of an unchanging or permanent self or soul, including ideas you have had about your form, feelings, perceptions, and consciousness—that form is in the self, self is in the form. In these ways, you normally think there is a self.

But when you keep practicing mindfulness meditation, one central factor is impermanence. You see impermanence in everything. Everything is permanently impermanent. You see this over and over, again and again. That is the beginning of the attainment of stream entry. You see and understand with wisdom that everything is impermanent.

This is not just from the viewpoint of chemistry or physics, which is an external theoretical understanding. Understanding from a scientific viewpoint is important. But when you understand impermanence yourself—that in you there is no permanent self—you realize it, experience it, and comprehend it very clearly. At that moment, there is no question after that. You are on the path of stream entry.

So you keep practicing—again and again and again—mindfulness meditation. Not only samatha, or concentration meditation. Mindfulness meditation is absolutely necessary for the attainment of liberation.

You keep practicing with more vigor, more courage, more effort. You keep practicing. Then your doubt about the Buddha, Dhamma, and Sangha will fade away. You have not a scrap of doubt about the Buddha's teaching because you have experienced it, you have seen it. It is undeniable truth. And so you will have perfect wisdom and faith in the Buddha. That is called *aveca pasada*. *Aveca* means realization or understanding. *Pasada* means clarity.

Still, you are on the stream-entry path. You keep practicing mindfulness meditation, you keep practicing, practicing, practicing, practicing. Then one day you realize, "All these rituals I have been following all these years, thinking they would help me attain liberation, are completely useless and meaningless. There is no way they can lead me to attain liberation."

When you come to that level, that understanding, you are at the stream-entry fruition stage. This is how I understand it. Buddha has very clearly laid out the eight kinds of individuals in the order of the Sangha. One who is on the stream-entry path, another attains stream-entry fruition. The second is the once-returner, on the path and at fruition. Then there is the never-returner, at the path and fruition stages. And the arahant path and arahant fruition stage.

Anyway, you know when you attain stream entry. You will not need to ask, "Am I a stream-enterer?" It is like you are having a headache. Do you ask, "Do I have a headache?" You know.

MEAT AND ALCOHOL

What about eating meat and drinking alcohol? Is it possible to obtain enlightenment without renunciation of such things?

Eating meat is not an impediment to the obtainment of liberation, provided you don't go out and kill and raise animals for slaughter. And when there is an animal product in their medicine, people can take it and get cured.

What about being served meat? Suppose one is invited to somebody's house and they happen to serve meat or fish and they are not a part of the killing of that food directly. In order to avoid embarrassment, to avoid disappointing the host, if you very mindfully eat what you receive, that is all right.

For Buddhist monks and nuns who go out collecting food into their alms bowls, they do not choose. They are sort of beggars— and beggars can't be choosers! They eat whatever they receive.

But alcohol, by all means, we must avoid. It is not going to help us anyway. It confuses the mind and can lead to lots of problems.

Everybody who practices meditation—whether laypeople or monastics—practices renunciation in the widest sense of the term. Generally, the word "renunciation" is used for people leaving homes and going to monasteries. But in the very strictest sense, the word "renunciation" means letting go of our greed, our hatred, and our ignorance. Even as a layperson, you must learn to let go of greed.

Letting go of greed is renunciation. In the Noble Eightfold Path that is Right Intention—and a key element of Right Intention is renunciation. Letting go of our greed at any level and any degree is renunciation. That is what we have to practice.

ARAHANTS IN MODERN LIFE

Is it true there are no arahants—or fully enlightened beings—in the world today? If not, why not?

I don't say there are no arahants. There may be arahants, because there are so many wonderful individuals living in solitary. So it is not right for us to think there are none.

The other thing is, as the Buddha said in the Mahaparinibbana Sutta (Digha Nikaya, 16), as long as the Four Noble Truths exist, arahants can exist. The Four Noble Truths still exist. So it is quite likely that there are individuals who have realized these truths exactly as the Buddha taught. Therefore, it is possible for arahants to exist even today, in this very life.

Actually, it is impossible to recognize an arahant through a casual visit. Even if we associate with somebody, unless you are very mindful, unless you know how an arahant is, unless you are an arahant yourself, it is not possible for you to know who may be an arahant.

Yet even today there can be arahants. But we don't know. Normally, if a person is an arahant, they would not come and declare to the world that they are an arahant. Arahants don't do this. If somebody made a claim of being an arahant, then it might be safe to say for that reason that they are not an arahant. Therefore, it is not possible for us to know who an arahant is.

However, if you associate with an arahant, and you have come to deeply know this person's behavior, you may come to know this person is something different. This person talks and acts without greed, hatred, and delusion. Then you can conclude this is an arahant. But without associating with such a person for a long period of time, it would not be possible for you to know.

After Enlightenment

Why did the Buddha continue to meditate after attaining full enlightenment? One cannot perfect perfection. Was it to motivate his disciples?

Yes. To motivate his disciples, to encourage his disciples. Plus, whenever the Buddha was tired physically he meditated—he was said to have slept only two hours a day, so twenty-two hours he was awake, attending to various things out of compassion for all of us.

So when he was tired he sought to refresh his mind and body, and at that time he entered what is called the attainment of the Bliss of Emancipation. He stayed always mindful. Sometimes, in between Dhamma talks, he meditated. He spent his time in meditation to keep his mind fresh and his body always relaxed.

After all, after attaining enlightenment he could completely enjoy the attainment of liberation. I use the word "enjoy" in a conventional sense, but it is much more than that. This was not the bliss we talk about in day-to-day conversation. This was a very altruistic bliss.

Also, he sought to motivate his disciples. We look at his example and think, "If he continued to meditate after enlightenment, why don't I meditate?" For these reasons he continued to meditate.

WHERE DO THEY GO?

An Anagami is called a nonreturner—one who will not be reborn. Since they are not coming back, do we know where they go? Where did the Buddha go? It is helpful to know about this because I know it will help me to let go easier—for otherwise, enlightenment sounds like "Poof!" One is gone and disappears from all existence.

Actually, I don't blame you for raising questions like this. That is a normal thing. It is also important to know the answer although we cannot give you a full answer.

When we attain Nibbana we end this cycle of birth and death. When we end the cycle of birth and death, if one were to ask about when the cycle ends—then what? Sometimes people ask, if everybody attains full enlightenment, then what happens to the world?

Who cares?

So long as we are here, we care for each other because each of us has problems, pain, and suffering. But if everyone were to be free from pain and suffering, why should we worry? When we attain full enlightenment what we will simply have is peaceful, eternal bliss. Do you want something less than that? When you have full enlightenment—full bliss forever—what else do you need? So that is what happens when one attains enlightenment, or Nibbana.

A never-returner still has some existence in a state called a Pure Abode—there are five Pure Abodes. They stay there until they attain full enlightenment. The Buddha and the arahants—once they attain full enlightenment—are in a phenomenon called the Bliss of Emancipation.

Buddha said that there is a state called Nibbana. In the Udana he has very clearly stated Nibbana is only in the present. And Buddha said there is such a state where there are no elements or beings, no ups and downs and past and future and changes. None of those things exists.

Therefore, once a person attains enlightenment, eternal bliss pervades forever. That is called Nibbana.

Lay Attainment

What meditative attainment can a layperson attain if they practice with dedication and a sincere heart? Can a layperson aspire to stream entry in this life?

Definitely. There is no magic in meditation. But it is hard work. Yet it is good work! If you work hard, following the instructions exactly as they are given, you can attain stream entry—the first stage of enlightenment—in this life.

What do you have to do to attain stream entry? Keep practicing the Noble Eightfold Path. That is the only path and it's a straight and direct path. Keep practicing, practicing, practicing. Sincerely. Honestly. Every day. Every step of the Noble Eightfold Path. Not just one! Not picking and choosing. Every step: Right View, Right Intention, Right Speech, Right Action, Right Livelihood, Right Effort, Right Mindfulness, and Right Concentration.

Then one day you will see that all the rituals you have been following have proven useless. Futile. They have no meaning. So your mind will let go of all rituals. And then all the doubts you have about the Buddha, Dhamma, and Sangha will disappear. That's because you see the Dhamma very clearly by following the Noble Eightfold Path. Dhamma is in the Noble Eightfold Path.

One day you will realize anicca—impermanence. Suffering arises because of attachment to impermanent things. You will see this 100 percent clearly. And so on, with every step on the path. Then your doubt will vanish from your mind.

So these are three things that you will get rid of in attaining stream entry. One is attachment to needless rules and rituals. And then doubt. And the third comes when you see there is no permanent entity called self. Self is a notion we fabricate in our mind. That will vanish when you see impermanence. When these three things vanish completely, never to return again, you have attained stream entry.

Any layperson can do that.

8

Working with Thoughts and Speech

CAKE OR MEDITATE?

Is there a particular pattern to the way the hindrances arise?

Hindrances don't arise in a particular order. Nobody can guarantee that the hindrances will arise in the way they are listed: sensory desire, *kamacchanda*; ill will, *vyapada*; sloth and torpor, *thina-middha*; restlessness and worry, *uddhacca-kukkucca*; and doubt, *vicikiccha*.

The list is one thing, but practical experience is quite another. You will see this in your meditation.

Perhaps greed arises—a sensory desire. For example, when you are meditating, suddenly you remember, "Oh, I left a delicious piece of cake in the refrigerator!" As soon as that image arises, your mouth begins to water. Your mind goes haywire and you cannot meditate, your desire is so strong. You cannot proceed with the practice when such strong greed arises.

So you get up and go to the refrigerator and get this piece of cake and eat it. Listen, I have a name for that person. That person is called a "fridgeterian." You have vegetarians? Suddenly you become a fridgeterian. After eating that rich piece of cake, can you meditate? No! You've put a lot of sugar into your body and you become even more hyperactive.

Therefore, when greed arises you've got to be very mindful and talk to yourself mindfully. Tell yourself, "I have eaten cake thousands of times in my life, from my childhood until this day. This is not something unusual. This is not heavenly cake. I can bake an even better cake next time. Or I can buy a brand new, different kind of cake made in Japan. And this cake will not disappear. I will lock my doors. Nobody will come in and steal my cake. It will still be there!

"But this moment of meditation? I was looking forward to this, I built up momentum to meditate. This is a very rare occasion. I might not live through to the next minute. Therefore, I will let go of thoughts of this cake, I will let go of this desire, this greed. I will not die if I don't eat this piece of cake. But this opportunity to meditate, once it is passed, I will never get it back. The cake will remain. But I may not find the same meditative mood."

This is how you have to talk to yourself.

Resistance to Meditation

Could you explain how to deal with resistance to meditation when it arises?

Sometimes people face stumbling blocks in proceeding with their practice. To break through this resistance, they must arouse what we call spiritual urgency. Think of how valuable and short this life is! It appears to us to be long, but life is really very short. During this short life, how much time have we spent in eating, drinking, and merrymaking? And how little time do we have to gain real peace, real happiness, and true comfort?

We arouse our devotion and faith in the Buddha, Dhamma, and Sangha. Friends, Buddha never deceived us or sold us a bill of goods! He was 100 percent honest and sincere and spoke to us with the utmost compassion and wisdom. He saw how we can liberate ourselves from suffering and pointed out the path to follow. He went out of his way to help us.

You know, Buddha slept only two hours a day—even at the age of eighty, he was full of energy. He didn't have to work like this. He was not paid a penny. He didn't work for praise or gain. He devoted his life to teaching purely because he wanted us to understand suffering.

In essence, he said, "Liberate yourself from suffering." We must understand how much compassion the Buddha had. Out of that compassion, he said, "If you want to respect me, liberate yourself from suffering! Don't suffer. That is the favor you do for me."

How can you find any better, more compassionate statement than that?

So, we are following the Buddha's advice through his teaching. There is no cause for us to be lazy. We must do everything we can to follow in his footsteps. We do this for ourselves—we are not doing it for anyone else. But someone else will benefit through our example and through our behavior.

PAPANCA OR MENTAL PROLIFERATION

What does the term *papanca*, or proliferation of thoughts, signify?

Perpetuating streams of thoughts is called *papanca*. That's what we find described in the Madhupindika Sutta (Majjhima Nikaya, 18).

Many scholars, writers, and teachers have given different interpretations and meanings of conceptual proliferation. The Pali word is *papanca*. There's a book written by Venerable Nanananda in Sri Lanka called *Concept and Reality* devoted entirely to explaining this profound word.

So what does it mean? To put it into simple language, I look at it this way: papanca is any thought that delays your attainment of enlightenment. You are going in one direction and so many things are coming your way.

It is like a child whose mother is having a headache. She sends him to the nearest drugstore to get some aspirin. Along the way the child sees a butterfly and sits down to watch it. Then he sees a kitten and picks it up to hug and kiss it. Then he sees a puppy and plays with that. Then he finds some children and goes and plays with them.

By the time he gets to the drugstore, hours have passed. The mother wanted to get the aspirin very quickly. But this child—not knowing the importance of his mother's request—takes his own sweet time and delays getting the medicine. When he comes home, the mother has a terrible headache and is crying.

This is how we travel in samsara, this cyclic round of rebirths. This is why we don't make quick progress. The Buddha used a very beautiful term: *Dhamma samvega*. *Vega* means speed. *Samvega* means additional speed. You go with additional speed to liberate yourself. Samvega means that seeing our suffering, being alarmed by it, you accelerate your practice to attain liberation. And whatever comes in your way to delay your progress is called papanca.

This is how I understand it and explain it. It has a very deep meaning. Although the meaning is very deep, we don't have to go to scholars to understand it.

Say you become engrossed in some comment you perceive as an insult. "Yesterday he did that! Last week he did that! The week before last he said that, and last month he said that . . ."

You keep building, building, building things up regarding the past event. Then you think about how you feel right now. "I didn't do anything to him! He triggered my anger! Why does he want to do this? He's a nasty fellow!" And then you think, "Tomorrow he'll be just as bad. The day after tomorrow as well!" This kind of endless succession of thinking is called conceptual proliferation.

In biology you learn about how a tiny cell is conceived, and then the cell keeps multiplying, multiplying, multiplying. Thoughts are like that when we get caught up and lost in conceptual proliferation.

Mindfulness is the buffer to prevent this sort of thing from happening. As soon as that kind of mental state takes hold, you immediately understand that this is impermanent. This is not going to last forever.

Look at the particular emotion that might be driving the proliferation of thoughts. And as you are watching, take some deep breaths. Looking at it, breathe out deeply—looking at it, breathe in deeply. You will see it disappearing. Mindfulness comes to rescue us from getting carried away with runaway thoughts, to offer support to increase wholesome mental states. Mindfulness works in both ways—one is to address negative states that have arisen. The other is to encourage us to direct the mind into more wholesome pathways.

RIGHT SPEECH

In the Rahulovada Sutta the Buddha spoke to his son about good behavior, including Right Speech. Does Right Speech include even less overt levels of speech, such as making a joke at someone's expense or being sarcastic as is so common in Western society?

Even that is included. Somebody who is strictly and diligently following the path to liberate oneself should be very mindful when they speak. So even as a joke one should not lie because eventually people will not take our words very seriously if we just keep lying and making jokes.

That is what Buddha advised Rahula—not to lie even for a joke because Buddha wanted to make him a perfectly moral, ethical, decent monk. So he gave him this advice.

Rahula was so obedient and so faithful in wanting to observe ethical principles diligently that every morning he took a handful of sand and threw it in the air and said, "Let me receive as much advice today as there are grains in the air."

In daily life, somebody who is very serious in the practice should avoid such speech. That's not easy when somebody is not taking things seriously and is not mindful.

In the Dvedhavitakka Sutta, called "Two Sorts of Thinking" (Majjhima Nikaya, 19), Buddha said that whatever thought we repeatedly cultivate, that becomes a habit. If somebody uses sarcastic remarks often, it becomes so strong a habit, they cannot help it. It comes automatically, often at the wrong time in front of people in society. Such sarcastic remarks may come out of that person's mouth at any time because the habit has already formed and been established.

By not cultivating this habit, we cultivate mindfulness. That means we check our mind very quickly. As soon as the thought arises in our mind to say something sarcastic or mean, we say, "No! I'm not going to gain anything by saying this. Nor will I lose anything by not saying anything."

This takes effort. After all, the teaching is one thing. Putting the teaching into practice is quite another!

WISE REFLECTION

I do metta, anapanasati, and vipassana meditation every day for about two or three hours. But it appears to me that the latent tendencies—the anusayas—in my mind do not go away. For example, when I see a pretty face on TV, I am automatically attracted to it. Is there a way these tendencies can be subdued little by little?

It is quite normal for the unenlightened person's mind to be attracted to beautiful objects. This, as you have recognized, is due to the presence of underlying tendencies. They will disappear only when one attains full enlightenment. An Anagami—one who attains the third of the four stages of enlightenment—will not have the desire for sensual pleasure as an underlying tendency. Until such time, one must work very hard to overcome such tendencies.

One effective way to do this is to deepen your understanding of impermanence and unsatisfactoriness. I would not suggest that you meditate on the impurities of the body without any understanding.

Sometimes it does not work. Rather, it can arouse either lust or hatred of the body.

We don't meditate to hate our bodies or other bodies. Unsatisfactoriness depends on clinging to impermanent objects. A mindful meditator should remind himself or herself that an attractive object has triggered sense desire. One should then develop wise reflection or mindful reflection.

The Buddha gave a very meaningful simile to underscore the meaning of mindful reflection, or *yoniso manasikara*. Suppose you throw a stick to a dog. The dog runs after the stick and bites on it or brings it back to you. But if you throw a stick to a lion, he does not run after the stick. He runs after you! He wants to know where the stick came from. That lion wants to go to the root.

Similarly, mindful reflection goes to the root. We have six roots. They are greed, hatred, and ignorance on the unwholesome side. And nongreed, nonhatred, and nondelusion on the wholesome side. When an unwholesome emotional state arises, we should be mindful enough to go to its roots and mindfully reflect that it is impermanent, unsatisfactory, and without self.

In the Dvedhavitakka Sutta the Buddha said he divided his thoughts into two classes—unwholesome and wholesome. And when unwholesome thoughts arose in his mind, he reflected mindfully. Then he saw danger in them and determined to abandon such thoughts. When a wholesome thought arose in him, then he saw its benefit and he cultivated it mindfully.

In the Vitakkasanthana Sutta (Majjhima Nikaya, 20) he gave five methods of getting rid of unwholesome thoughts. And in the Sabbasava Sutta (Majjhima Nikaya, 2) he gave further instructions on how to deal with unwholesome thoughts. He did all this before he attained enlightenment.

Buddha did not attain enlightenment by simply sitting under the Bodhi tree one evening and the next morning standing up as an enlightened person. He explored and went through everything in his experience.

From his own personal experience he learned how to deal with various troublesome mental states. And so from his own personal experience he taught us the Dhamma.

We must learn the Dhamma and use the teachings exactly as he used them. Use your knowledge of Dhamma to deal with every defilement that bothers you during meditation and daily life.

We learn Dhamma not to debate and win an argument. We learn Dhamma not to show off or to be proud of our knowledge or our ability to instruct others. We learn Dhamma to use it in dealing with our own mental states. Teaching others is secondary. Go through the suttas that you have learned all these years and use the instructions given there to overcome your own underlying tendencies.

This reminds me of two wonderful stanzas in the Dhammapada. When I was learning them as a young novice monk, I never appreciated their meaning as I do now. Here they are as a reminder for when you confront any problem and as a spur to living according to the Buddha's teachings:

> One who recites many teachings
> But, being negligent, doesn't act accordingly,
> Like a cowherd counting other's cows,
> Does not attain the benefits of the contemplative life,
> One who recites but few teachings,
> Yet lives according to the Dhamma,
> Abandoning passion, ill will, and delusion,
> Aware and with mind well freed,
> Not clinging in this life or the next,
> Attains the benefits of the contemplative life.

9

Negative Emotions

NEUTRALIZING FRUSTRATION

Sometimes I feel such frustration in practicing meditation and maintaining mindfulness in the middle of the day. Can you give me some advice on working with frustration?

Frustration arises from three unwholesome roots: greed, hatred, and delusion. We have to make our mind clear. How do we make our mind clear? Meditation. When you meditate your mind becomes very clear. Then you will see that when unwholesome tendencies arise in our mind, we immediately become mindful and try not to cultivate them and work to abandon them.

We try not to get carried away with unwholesome tendencies. We immediately switch to wholesome mental states. We can do this through the practice of meditation, particularly mindfulness meditation.

Normally we focus our mind, ears, nose, tongue, and so forth on outside forms, sounds, smells, tastes, touch, and thought. We do not focus on our own feelings, perceptions, thoughts, and consciousness. So long as our senses are always extroverted, we bring unwholesome things into our mind. When we train our mind to look at things introspectively, to look inside, then we can see where we go wrong and we can make the adjustment.

Unwholesome roots are not outside of us. Greed, hatred, and delusion or confusion are not coming from the outside world. They all come from within, in our own minds. So when we meditate we can see how greed arises in us, how hatred and confusion arise in us. And then immediately we try not to cultivate them, we don't get carried away by such states of mind. We abandon them and replace them with wholesome states of mind.

We can prevent them from arising. Or we can see in our unmindful moments these mental states arise and then immediately try to nip them in the bud.

For instance, when greed takes over, there is a space in our mind to cultivate generosity—letting go of greed. When hatred fades away there is room in our mind to generate loving-friendliness—metta. When delusion fades away there is room in our mind to develop wisdom.

So we will be able to remove these things a tiny little bit at a time, not the whole lot. But slowly and gradually they become weaker and eventually they will fade away. And this is how we learn to neutralize frustration and eventually get rid of it.

There are thousands of occasions and moments every single day to become frustrated. Therefore, it may appear to be very difficult to work with these states of mind. But through constant, persistent, diligent practice, it becomes easy.

It is indeed possible to neutralize our frustration.

STRONG EMOTIONS

When strong negative emotions arise, how do we prevent them from taking over the mind and then committing unwholesome actions based on those emotions?

That is why we need mindfulness. Mindfulness is the buffer to prevent these sorts of things from happening. As soon as that kind of emotion arises, you immediately understand, "This is impermanent, this is not going to last forever." And while saying that in your mind, you look at that emotion—not just repeating the word—look at that particular emotion. And as you are watching it, taking deep breaths and looking at it, breathing out deeply, looking at it, you will see it disappearing.

Mindfulness comes in to rescue us from getting carried away with creating unwholesome kamma. We use our mindfulness to guard our senses and stop the creation of such kamma.

However, when a wholesome emotion arises, then we use mindfulness again to cultivate it, to develop it, to make more effort and remember how it happened. Mindfulness immediately comes to give additional support to perpetuate and increase that wholesome mental state.

So mindfulness works in both ways—one is to buffer negative things and the other, to encourage us to do the wholesome thing.

TUG OF WAR

Are greed, anger, and delusion of equal strength as nongreed, nonhatred, and nondelusion?

Greed, anger, and delusion are extremely forceful in binding us to samsara, this endless round of rebirths. Nongreed, nonhatred, and nondelusion—meaning generosity, metta, and wisdom—these wholesome roots are as strong or stronger than these unwholesome roots.

In reality these wholesome roots must be stronger than unwholesome roots in order to destroy them and to get anywhere in our practice.

Otherwise, if they both are equally strong, then there will always be a tug of war between them. So the wholesome roots must be stronger than the unwholesome ones if we are to make headway on the path.

SKILLFUL NEGATIVITY?

Are negative emotions ever skillful? Should we feel sad when a loved one dies or when we lose something we care about?

Negative emotions are not skillful. But you can use negative emotions skillfully. You mention sadness—when you are skillful you can use sadness as an object of meditation, asking the question, "Why am I sad? I'm sad because I lost someone or I lost something." You are sad when you lose somebody because you are attached to that person, to that situation, or to that thing that was lost. You realize, "I was attached to it and because of my attachment I experience sadness."

Should you feel sad when a loved one dies? People are sad when a loved one dies because of attachment. Why should I attach to something? Because I am ignorant. I have not trained my mind to understand impermanence. If I have trained myself to understand impermanence, then when these things I love and lose disappear, I won't be upset and sad. You use your skill when negative emotions arise to deal with those negative emotions.

DEALING WITH FEAR

How do I deal with fear? Can fear be handled with meditation?

Generally, there are two kinds of fears. One is wholesome, the other is unwholesome. People know of unwholesome fear. Fear necessarily arises from desire, craving, clinging, greed.

Suppose you have fear of darkness. Why? Does the darkness eat you up? Is darkness a person? How can darkness hurt you? Darkness in itself cannot do anything. But you have fear that something will happen to you in the dark. There may be some ghost, goblin, thief, robber, a cesspool. You may imagine something exists in the dark. Yet even if these things exist in the dark, why should you be afraid of them?

Because you love your life. You cling to your life, you cling to your mind, you cling to your feelings and perceptions. You cling to something and you don't want to lose whatever you are clinging to.

Therefore, since we cling to our life whenever there is darkness, we are afraid of darkness, thinking something might happen to me in the dark.

You buy insurance. Why do you buy insurance? There is an impending danger. So we insure ourselves against this fear. But the best insurance policy in the world cannot save you from growing old. When I turned sixty-five, many insurance companies telephoned me. They asked me to buy funeral insurance. Can insurance protect me from dying? Can insurance protect me from growing old and turning sixty-five? I have lived another twenty-one years [in 2013], and nothing could stop my aging process!

Fear is always lurking and sneaking into our lives. Fear arises from our clinging and our craving and attachment to something. How to handle that? Can fear be handled through meditation?

Definitely!

Consider the story of the Buddha before he became the Buddha. He was in the forest on a new-moon night when it was pitch dark. People are very much afraid to be in the jungle in the dark. Siddhartha wanted to spend time in the jungle on a new-moon night. He heard something very loud! He listened very carefully. When a loud sound comes from somewhere, many people run away from it to save their lives. But the Bodhisatta walked into that area to see what the sound was. Instead of running away from it, he ran into it.

All of a sudden, he encountered a peacock that had been sitting on a dead branch that broke and the peacock fell on the ground making a noise. He found the source of his fear.

You will see, fear always arises from attachment to something. We learn through mindfulness and meditation practice every day—not superficially, but deeply—that we will be able to let go of our clinging to various things and live without any fear.

THE ORIGIN OF SUFFERING

Where does suffering come from?

Suffering arises dependent on feeling, dependent on craving, dependent on contact, and so forth. When we analyze all of them, one by one, there is no single source. When all of them come together, suffering exists.

There are four rings: one is a finger ring, one is an earring, then there is an engagement ring, and finally there is our suffer-ring. Other things you can separate. But suffering cannot be separated. It is there along with everything else.

A SMILING FACE

Is it wrong if sometimes when we are not happy inside, we try to make ourselves happy by smiling? Or if we are feeling bad but force a smile on our faces?

I think it is all right to have a very smiley face. There's nothing wrong with that! I would not encourage you to smile sarcastically but with honesty and sincerity. So actually you are doing a very good thing for the other person who sees your smile. And you also feel very good because when you smile the other person also smiles. And you feel very comfortable and are relaxed. That's a very good thing.

Shame and Buddhism

It appears that shame is a cultural epidemic in this country. What does the Buddha say about this and how does Buddhism address this problem?

Actually, shame is not a problem. Shame is a safety net. Hiri and otappa control the whole universe. *Hiri* means the shame we feel in doing wrong things. *Otappa* means the fear of the results of doing wrong things. Shame protects us from doing wrong things. Our fear of the results of committing unwholesome actions protects us from doing wrong things.

When we are protected from doing wrong things by shame and fear, the whole world is protected from trouble. Therefore, that is a real safety net for all of us to live very decent, respectable, sincere, honest lives. Buddhism talks very highly of these two aspects.

If we remain mindful we can prevent ourselves from committing wrong things. So, shame actually protects us.

Self-Centered Actions

I feel bad at having hurt loved ones through self-centered actions. But I cannot change this past. Do I bring my attention to the present with forgiveness and compassion and acceptance and let it go, vowing to practice more deeply?

If you still associate with the person you hurt, it would be good to apologize for hurting them. That would be a very good thing to do. It is much like confession. Having apologized, you commit to your mindfulness practice and tell yourself, "From now on, I must pay more attention to what I say and do and to think before I speak." Because once an action is released from your body, then it is not possible to bring it back or undo what is done. Therefore, as a precaution, be more mindful and don't abruptly say or do things.

The Buddha gave this advice to Venerable Rahula, his son. He told him that before you say or do something, think. Will this action be for the long-term benefit of myself and others? If not, don't do it. While you are doing or saying something, think again and ask the same question. After saying or doing something, think again, ask the same question again. If you have done something wrong, you think about it. If you have done or said something to cause harm, then talk to the offended person and apologize. And so you learn and you do not do that action again.

SELF-FORGIVENESS

How does one forgive oneself after acting unmindfully?

At unmindful moments, we do things that cause harm to ourselves or to others. But when you are mindful again, you forgive this unmindfulness. To be mindful of unmindfulness *is* mindfulness.

So we think, "Well, when I was unmindful I did such and such . . . From now on I must maintain my mindfulness." That is how you forgive yourself and correct yourself.

THE ROOTS OF WORRY

How do you suggest we stop worry in its tracks?

You worry because of fear that something has happened and you will get into trouble. Or you worry about the past and something you have done incorrectly. So, you worry. This worry arises from fear. Fear arises from greed. The Buddha said from craving arises sorrow—from fear arises worry.

And therefore, Buddha's advice for overcoming fear is to get rid of our greed and anger. To get rid of our greed we look inside mindfully—we look at the reality we experience every day, every moment. We have so many things we recall from the past. Because of this uncertainty and fear, you have worries.

Buddha advises that we look at reality and don't have any fear. When you encounter fear, you have nothing to worry about. You may have fear of losing something you attach to. When you don't have attachments, you don't have that fear because you are not going to lose anything.

THE ROOT OF FEAR

What is the root cause of all the fear we experience in life?

Your fear arises from becoming attached to something you like. If you don't have any clinging, craving, or attachment to life, you have no fear. The very reason you protect something implies you are attached to it. When you fight to gain something, you want to protect what you gain because you are attached to it.

When you attain jhana you get rid of five hindrances—one of them is greed. When you let go of greed, you attain the jhana. Once you gain it, don't stay there. Don't become attached to it. If you stay in one jhana, you cannot go on to the next one.

This is like when you climb a ladder. You step on a rung. To climb the ladder you have to go to the second rung.

In order to make progress you have to let go of whatever you have. When we do that, fear will not arise in us. This is a very profound teaching.

TRAUMA AND PRACTICE

I had a traumatic childhood full of anger and hate. These emotions are still with me and make it hard to meditate and practice loving-friendliness. What is the surest and quickest way for me to overcome these hindrances?

There is no "quickest" method—but the surest method? Well, that I can tell you about. It is not very quick. Like when you take medicine to get rid of the root or cause of sickness, it can take a very long time. You have to take a lot of medicine for a long period of time.

Similarly, this emotion that you had in your childhood from your traumatic experiences has cut grooves in your brain, so to say. It has left very deep emotional scars in your life. Therefore, you need a lot of treatment with mindfulness and metta. Mindfulness, metta, forgiveness, patience—you have to combine all these in order to cure this deeply rooted emotional state.

That is the surest way. But not the quickest.

WHEN THE WILL IS ILL

Can you talk about working with ill will?

The last of the hindrances is hatred. In English we call it ill will. It is called ill will when your will is ill. This is a very beautiful English phrase.

The Buddha compared a person full of ill will to someone who is sick. When you are sick you cannot appreciate any food because your taste buds are so badly affected. When we are sick we cannot enjoy anything in the world. The same with ill will. We are cranky and upset and hateful toward others in the world.

Therefore, we need to counter this with good will—metta. I translate this word into English as "loving-friendliness" and for good reason. The word *metta* comes from the root *mitta*. And *mitta* means friend. In Sinhalese, we say *mitra*. It means friend. Mitta's nature is metta. Therefore, the phrase should be "loving-friendliness," not "loving-kindness."

In order to overcome hatred, in order to counter feelings of ill will, we cultivate loving-friendliness. When we are friendly we become calm, relaxed, and peaceful. Then, as a result of this feeling of loving-friendliness, we gain concentration because the mind is calm, relaxed, and peaceful.

10

Cultivating Metta or Loving-Friendliness

SELFLESS SERVICE

Can you explain more about what you feel the proper focus of metta should be?

This is where metta interpretation has gone wrong. If you begin to focus on yourself, then you boost your ego. You always are thinking, "I, I, I . . ." Therefore, when we practice metta, we must forget ourselves.

There are many people who do selfless service. Some people serve others without thinking about themselves. They go through very difficult situations like helping people after a tsunami, or firefighters racing into a burning building. Or doctors treating outbreaks of infectious diseases. Or aid workers helping people devastated by bombing in a war zone. People go there and they just help.

In all these situations, whether they say it or not, they practice metta. They practice compassion. When we really develop compassion within ourselves, we act spontaneously without thinking about ourselves.

143

METTA AND MEDITATION

Do you recommend repeating the Metta Sutta at the beginning and end of each meditation session?

I think it is very good if you have time to do it, especially in your own practice at home. That would be very good. But instead of saying a long passage of many sentences, we may recite at the end of each meditation session "May all beings be well, happy, and peaceful." This one sentence itself is enough for metta practice.

MOTHERLY METTA

In the metta meditation we chanted this morning, it says, "As a mother would risk her own life to protect her only child, even so toward all beings one should cultivate a boundless heart." If I am not a mother, how can I generate such metta?

You don't have to be a mother to have this feeling. You just cultivate it in your heart. If a man can take care of a child just like a woman takes care of her child, then that man can develop the same mental state as a woman. So there is no gender distinction in the impact of metta or loving-friendliness. We have to cultivate this thought of metta irrespective of our gender.

When we practice metta, the metta thought must be like a mother protecting her child. Practice your metta for all living beings just like a mother protects her child. Try to understand the mother's connection with the child—exactly like that.

We make our metta a very powerful, tangible strong practice. That is what it really means. We generate this loving-friendliness on behalf of all living beings. You may view your metta as your child. Just as a mother protects her only child, you protect your metta practice.

SHARING MERIT

What is the difference between metta and sharing merit?

Actually, metta and sharing merit are almost synonymous. Why? Because when we share merits we wish others to be happy. And when we share our happiness with others we practice metta or loving-friendliness.

You may notice before we eat here at the monastery that all the monastics and laypeople share merits with the people who made the food. And we wish them peace, prosperity, and happiness, wishing them well. We incorporate metta with sharing merit. And sharing merit is itself part of metta practice.

METTA TOWARD ALL

How do we work to develop loving-friendliness or metta for so many other living beings?

We practice metta in three ways. One is verbal, the other is in our thoughts, the other is feelings. When we say "May all beings be well and happy," even if we only say this much, we must mean what we say. Repeat it many, many times: "May all beings be well and happy, may all beings be well and happy, may all beings be well and happy . . ."

We come to understand the meaning of it. In all directions, there are living beings. We focus our mind on this thought. We develop this metta toward all these living beings.

Then we feel metta within ourselves. Without any reservation, without any question, our minds, our hearts open to sharing our thoughts of metta with all living beings. And that is what we do in metta practice.

Eventually it becomes an integral part of our way of thinking. Once we start repeating this every day, it becomes a part of our life.

In every thought, in every act and word that we utter, this training and this conditioning will retrain our mind. And so our resentment and anger fade away. We will be able to talk in a friendly way, really manifesting our friendliness.

We can do things in daily life in the same way. For instance, you sweep this floor. Not just as a duty! You sweep the floor, thinking, "May whoever comes here feel comfortable, seeing a clean floor." That person will be pleased.

Say you go to a public toilet. When you leave, clean the toilet seat. If water spills on the floor, wipe it up. Why do you do that? So that when the next person comes they will be glad to see a clean floor and clean toilet seat. So the next person doesn't slip on that water on the floor. Nobody knows that you did it. Only you know that you cleaned it because you want others to be happy. So they feel glad and not uncomfortable.

There are many ways of practicing metta once we start cultivating this thought in our mind.

DEALING WITH BULLIES

Knowing that only love can overcome hate, what is the best way to deal with a bully? A bully sees love and kindness as a weakness.

Practicing loving-friendliness is not just surrendering yourself to any unjust situation. If somebody is a bully, you have to do something instead of just letting that person bully you all the time.

But you have to act with understanding, compassion, and love. You have every right to complain to someone who is in authority to take care of the bully, if you yourself cannot take care of that person, if you are the weaker or smaller person or are not a very assertive person. Then you can seek the help of somebody who can take care of the bully.

That is not against the practice of loving-friendliness.

THE SEED OF METTA

Is metta generated by directing thoughts and the imagination in a particular manner?

When you find the seed of metta within yourself, it doesn't automatically do anything. You've got to cultivate it, develop it, practice it. Once you've found the seed, the potential within yourself, then cultivate it.

When you are relaxed and don't have hatred toward any particular being or person or situation, then you will find metta within yourself. Keep cultivating it. You may not be able to cultivate it fully at once. But slowly, gradually, you cultivate it.

As you are cultivating metta, you experience peace in the moment—not before, not after. Remember what the Buddha said in the first stanza of the Dhammapada—when we think, say, or do things with a pure, clean state of mind, the results follow us like our own shadow. The shadow doesn't wait even one fraction when we move. When we move, the shadow moves with us, it doesn't wait for us to move.

Similarly, when we are doing wholesome things we experience the benefits right away. When we do not practice metta, we cannot imagine metta. We've got to practice.

ARISING OUT OF MEDITATION

How do we activate karuna, dana, letting go, during meditation?

Letting go is a mental state you can do in meditation very easily. Karuna, or compassion, you can develop even in meditation, knowing that there are suffering living beings. It is very easy once you practice metta for you to practice karuna, or compassion, because compassion comes out of metta.

On the one hand, you wish everybody to be peaceful and happy. And on the other hand, you wish to be helpful to as many suffering beings as possible. You can cultivate that thought. And even make it active when you are out of meditation and become involved in activities out of compassion.

ILL WILL AND METTA

How does one practice metta for someone who has ill wishes toward you?

If somebody has ill wishes toward you, they may be sick, because there's no reason for someone to have ill wishes toward you. Then you have good reason to practice metta—loving-friendliness—toward that person. We wish that such a person may be well, happy, and peaceful, so that they will not have such wishes toward you.

You have to create in your own mind very wholesome, friendly thoughts toward him or her. That's all you can do. You cannot eliminate that person's ill will—that person has to work on it himself or herself. You keep practicing metta toward that person with sincerity.

METTA FOR ONESELF

I experience a lot of self-criticism. I try to practice compassion for myself—karuna—but it isn't easy. How can I practice metta for myself?

What is the opposite of metta? Anger. When anger arises, if you nourish it, are you unkind to yourself? When anger arises, it bites you. It hurts you. You don't do anything that hurts you if you love yourself. Therefore, you have to relax and let go of anger in order to love yourself.

Practice metta or loving-friendliness toward yourself. Any negative thing you do, anything that hurts you, if you let it happen, if you nourish it, you don't love yourself. It's very simple!

Look inside and see how anger hurts you, how jealousy hurts you, how tension hurts you. If you love yourself, you let go of all of this. You relax and metta arises.

METTA AND CONCENTRATION

These past few days I have meditated a lot on this retreat, much more than at home. Some sittings have gone well, others not so well. I realize I need to cultivate metta meditation in order for it to go well. Can you talk a little bit about the benefits of metta meditation?

Metta means wishing well to all living beings. That definitely relaxes our mind. And the mind becomes very pliable and workable. Because of that attainment, we gain concentration. So metta practice helps us gain concentration very quickly.

A WORLD OF HATRED

How do you practice metta in a world full of hatred, where people try to harm you?

You certainly cannot wipe out the world's hatred. Nobody has done so in the past. Nobody will be able to do it anytime in the future. We always must remember we are not trying to make the world free from hatred. It is impossible.

What we are trying to do is to liberate our minds from hatred. We make ourselves like a huge tree in the forest. Such a tree gives shade to many living beings. The tree bears flowers for insects to feed upon. It bears fruits for birds, animals, and humans to eat. It gives protection to many living beings. It is very generous and very friendly with all living beings. It does not expect anything in return.

Similarly, we aim to be full of metta. We fill our minds with metta and live with metta. We talk with metta, work with metta, think with metta. We do everything with metta.

People around us see how friendly we are. How relaxed we are. So we become an example for others to follow. We do not try to follow the example of hatred exhibited by others.

Hateful people may eventually learn to emulate us because they see us being peaceful and happy. Everybody wants to be happy. Everybody wants to be peaceful. That is everybody's aim in life. When they see somebody who is peaceful and happy, then they think, "Ah! This is the life I'd like to live, not one filled with hate."

DEALING WITH ANGER

Should we make attempts to extend metta to a specific person when our heart is not ready to do so?

If your heart is not ready, make it ready! If your heart is full of anger or resentment, deal with that particular difficulty first. When that difficulty has faded away, then you can practice metta.

When anger in the mind is strongly active, you definitely cannot practice metta. Therefore, deal with anger first. When it subsides, you can practice metta. Or wait for another time to practice metta.

SELF-FORGIVENESS AND METTA

How can we forgive ourselves through the practice of metta?

When we have done something ethically wrong and we feel guilty, at that time forgiving ourselves is difficult. And yet we have to understand that we as human beings are fallible. We make mistakes. And making a mistake is very natural for human beings.

Therefore, we tell ourselves, "When I was unmindful, I did something wrong. I don't want to repeat that action." You make a commitment not to repeat it again. You have to make this commitment sincerely. Then you are in a very good position to forgive yourself. You must think, "Every time I repeat this same unmindful action, I hurt myself and others and create suffering. Since I love myself, I don't want to say or do anything that would cause myself and others harm."

We must look at our minds honestly and sincerely and see how the situation happened that led to these actions. Then you determine that from now on you will be more patient, more tactful, more mindful, so as not to commit such actions again. That is the way you forgive yourself.

When you've forgiven yourself, it will be very easy for you to practice metta. But so long as you remain rigid and uptight about whatever happened in the past, practicing metta will be difficult.

EQUAL IN THE FACE OF METTA

Do some people not deserve our respect or not deserve our metta?

For metta practice there is no such thing as not deserving metta. There can be many people we *think* don't deserve our respect. It doesn't matter. This is not the place where we judge anybody. In metta practice there is no judgment, no criticism. We don't think about somebody's ethics and morals and all these sorts of things. These are not necessary at all. Completely ignore them.

We just know there are beings who wish to be happy and do not like pain. The worst person, the meanest person, also deserves our metta. A criminal deserves our metta. In the Metta Sutta you can see this. I advise you to read it again and again. All are equal in the face of metta.

Tonglen and Metta

In the Tibetan tradition there is a practice called *tonglen* where they teach you to visualize breathing in the suffering of others and breathing out metta to them. Is there anything in the Pali canon or commentaries about tonglen?

There is no particular mention in the Theravada canon to breathe in somebody's suffering and breathe out metta to that person suffering. But while breathing in and out we can practice metta or loving-friendliness. So while breathing in and out, we can practice metta for others.

Avoid Being Abused

How do I forgive someone who has taken advantage of me? If I don't shut him out he will continue to take advantage of me. How do I practice metta for him?

Metta practitioners cannot be simple and naive. They also must use patient, tactful, and mindful ways to deal with difficult situations. Simply surrendering to abuse is not metta practice. Practitioners also must be tough at times to avoid being abused.

Resistance to Metta

I find it very hard to practice metta. I think about the people I hate. I say the words, but they are not sincere. Do you have any suggestions?

This is a very important point. We have to make ourselves very sincere to practice metta. Once I was invited to lead a retreat in Poland. The person who telephoned me asked about what I taught.

She finally asked, "Do you teach metta meditation?" I said yes. Then she said, "I hate metta!" So, what was I supposed to do? I went there and led a ten-day metta retreat. At the end, she thanked me for taking the time to teach metta.

We keep repeating the metta phrases even if we don't feel like doing it. If you keep repeating thoughts of loving-friendliness again and again, these words will settle into your mind. And perhaps one day you may feel how wonderful it is.

Metta is a very natural state of mind that all of us have. But because of our conditioning, it is deeply suppressed. We sometimes don't even know that the possibility is within us. So we have to dig it out with some difficulty.

Until we feel it, we need patience, maturity, mindfulness, determination, commitment—all of these. Above all, we need courage to dig into our own mental states. Then it will not be that difficult. Anything at the beginning is difficult. Think about these words, and even if you have difficulty, don't give up. First, overcome that barrier. If you have anger in you, deal with that. And then practicing metta becomes very easy.

That way, we begin to feel for ourselves how wonderful our life would be if we were free from affliction, if we were happy. Also, when we recite these words our brain generates hormones that make us very calm, relaxed, and peaceful. We feel calmness, we feel relaxation, we feel peace within ourselves.

We can consider how wonderful it would be if everyone was peaceful and happy. So, first we recite metta phrases with sincerity and honesty and we think how wonderful the world would be. We must try to find some good in the person toward whom we feel hatred or dislike. Nobody is totally bad. Nobody is totally good. Once we find some good quality in the person, we should focus on it, and that will help us to practice metta toward that person.

There are many benefits to metta!

FEELING LOVING-FRIENDLINESS

Does practicing loving-friendliness help the meditator cultivate fearlessness?

Definitely. When we regularly practice metta or loving-friendliness, fear does not arise in us. And we make others free from fear. When you practice metta sitting in this meditation hall with other people, you feel everybody is on your side. Everybody behind you, everybody in front of you—all of them are your friends.

When you sit amid your friends, you feel secure. You are protected. So in your mind you feel free from fear, and everybody else around you feels free from fear. The vibration you send out from your mind and body is a very friendly, cordial vibration. It is just like when you are very angry—if a person sits next to you, that person will feel your anger because you are emitting a negative, hostile vibration.

So those surrounding you will feel your metta, human or animal. That is why one of the benefits of metta is you will be loved by human beings and you will be pleasant to nonhuman beings, like animals and other spirits. When Angulimala was coming to kill the Buddha with a drawn sword, the Buddha sent metta. When a drunken elephant was sent by Devadata to kill the Buddha, the Buddha sent metta to subdue this elephant.

Once it is very well developed and cultivated, metta can emanate from our body.

THE POLITICS OF METTA

American culture values human rights, patient rights, animal rights, and so on. Are these concepts similar to metta, or are they simply incompatible with metta?

I think these are similar to metta and compatible with metta. Because everybody deserves metta.

The problem is that when we think of "rights," people fight for such rights. That is not metta practice. We cannot fight for metta: "I will kill you if you don't practice metta!" You cannot say that. Or, "I won't talk to you if you don't practice metta!"

But I can take you to court for violating my rights. These are all political. Metta practice is not a political practice.

FROM MINDFULNESS TO METTA

When practicing metta or samatha, I try to do vipassana at the same time. It feels forced and takes me out of the meditation. Does vipassana happen naturally or do we have to cultivate vipassana intentionally? What is the clearest and simplest way to develop vipassana, or insight meditation?

The clearest and simplest way to practice vipassana is to practice vipassana. When you practice vipassana, metta evolves from that by seeing the truth. In vipassana practice, as I've mentioned many, many times, we see impermanence. When we practice metta, we understand that even metta is impermanent. So metta comes under mindfulness or vipassana practice.

Because of our mindfulness of suffering we practice metta. We have to see impermanence and suffering in order to practice metta. Not the other way around. So we practice mindfulness.

As we practice mindfulness, we become mindful of the suffering going on all over the world. To remedy and to help with that, we practice metta. When you practice metta, suddenly you realize you are practicing mindfulness. Don't worry about it. Practice mindfulness. Then you will see your metta practice naturally glides into mindfulness practice. Because you see suffering.

11

Concentration and the Jhanas

TEACHING JHANA

You were among the first high-profile Buddhist teachers of note to teach jhana practice in-depth in the West. Can you talk about that and the idea of dry insight meditation, a path that does not include jhanas?

The phrase "dry insight meditation" is sometimes used to describe those who advance on the path pursuing insight meditation without obtaining jhanas, or states of absorption. Actually, the phrase "dry insight meditation" was coined by Venerable Buddhaghosa. Buddha never used "dry insight." The Buddha simply talked about samatha vipassana, meaning tranquility and insight.

Why did commentators coin the phrase "dry insight"? They thought one can gain insight without concentration. Samatha is a concentration technique. Vipassana means insight.

Now, Buddha taught both of them and gave them equal weight. And these two must always go parallel to each other or hand in hand in order to reach the goal. They must go slowly and develop together and join at one point—and then one attains liberation. It is just like the Amazon River. There are two rivers that form the Amazon—the Solimões River and the Rio Negro. They run parallel to each other for several kilometers without mixing. Eventually, they merge and make the huge Amazon River.

Similarly, one can start with samatha practice, if the person is in that mood. At that time, they practice concentration. At another time, if their concentration is not that good, then they practice vipassana.

You alternate your practice. One day these two join together completely. That is the moment you attain the Sotapanna state, or the stream-entry state on the path to liberation. Because when you gain concentration, when the mind is very sharp and clean and one-pointed, you see impermanence very clearly. *Very* clearly! You can see it at a subatomic level. You feel impermanence. Everything is shut off in the mind. All your mind notices is the changing nature of everything.

So when you practice mindfulness, from the very beginning you see impermanence. You focus the mind on how everything is changing, changing, changing. And finally everything is equal. There is not one thing better than the other—this is impermanent, that is impermanent, this is impermanent.

This is what is called choiceless awareness. You are aware of one thing—that is, impermanence. No matter how many trillions of things flood your mind, all you see in all of them is impermanence.

You see impermanence when you practice mindfulness. You see impermanence when you practice concentration. Then these two join together to make you understand nonself, to get rid of your doubt and to get rid of your belief in attaining liberation by practicing rites and rituals. You attain stream entry.

In the Attaka-Nagata Sutta in the Majjhima Nikaya, a householder named Dasaka asked Venerable Ananda, "Please tell me what is the most important thing the Buddha taught?" Venerable Ananda gave eleven of them: the four material jhanas, three immaterial jhanas, metta, karuna, mudita, and upekkha.

Even when you practice metta, sending metta in all directions, the entire body and mind are charged with metta. You see even this metta is impermanent! This is because this metta is created by the mind. Whatever the mind creates is impermanent, so even after practicing metta you switch to impermanence. And thus you gain concentration by practicing metta.

You can gain jhanas by practicing metta. You use any subject to gain jhanas. Once you gain jhanas, you can go up to the Eighth Jhana. Then you might find you are losing jhanas. You cannot stay in jhanas forever—you are losing them because they are impermanent too. So no matter what you do, everything boils down to impermanence.

I remember my first retreat on the subject of the jhanas. In those days, meditation teachers only practiced vipassana—vipassana, vipassana, vipassana! And if somebody practiced concentration, they said, "Oh, no, no, no! That is taboo. You'll become like a vegetable, like a rock. You may go crazy! Practice vipassana."

But I took the challenge! I did research. I read everything I found in the Tipitaka where jhana is mentioned. And I found it is necessary in order to gain deep awareness of impermanence. My friend Bhikkhu Bodhi also helped me tremendously to develop this theme.

I wrote my PhD dissertation on jhana. From that time onward, I began to develop more ideas about jhana. Then, a few years after my dissertation was published, those who were against jhana began teaching jhana. Now many teachers and monks are teaching jhanas.

WHAT ARE JHANAS?

There are feelings and then there are thoughts. From your experience, are the jhanas more like a feeling than a thought? And if so, please explain why.

Jhanas actually are an experience, not a thought. In fact, as you attain jhanas you come to a state—the Second Jhana specifically—

where your thoughts subside. You will not have thoughts at that time, and yet you feel the jhanic attainment. You feel extraordinary peace, extraordinary joy, very powerful concentration.

If you are in Right Jhana, you also will have mindfulness with true concentration and an equanimous state of mind. The mind is in an advanced state.

JHANA PRACTICE AS A GOAL

Do you recommend jhana practice even for a beginner?

I recommend jhana and vipassana for anybody. It is good if a beginner begins meditation, hoping for and keeping the attainment of jhana as a goal. But you certainly will obtain jhanas if you follow the steps.

First, you have to understand what you are doing—how you meditate, what meditation you do to gain jhana. That is, gaining concentration. You have to do one thing: keep up with your morality. That's one requirement. If your morality is questionable—you do this little bit today and then tomorrow you do that—it is not going to work. You have to be honest with yourself.

Also, practice metta. Then, overcome the five hindrances: sleepiness, greed, hatred, restlessness, and worry or doubt. Overcome these five and the mind will be very calm and peaceful. When you have overcome these five, your mind naturally glides into concentration.

And so from the very beginning you do these things. If you don't gain concentration, jhana, at least you can obtain some degree of concentration close to jhanic quality. That is what you need.

STUDYING THE JHANAS

Since you have studied the jhanas for many decades, can you recommend other teachers of jhana who you think have an

accurate understanding and effective teaching about them for guidance when undertaking longer retreats?

In fact, I don't know all the teachers who teach jhanas. I have not had any discussions with them. There are many teachers' conferences that I don't attend; therefore, I don't know much about these teachers.

Your best bet is reading. And if anybody has written books on jhana, then read them and compare. I have written several times on the jhanas, in *The Jhanas in Theravada Buddhist Meditation, The Path of Serenity and Insight,* and *Beyond Mindfulness in Plain English.* If you find somebody has written even more clearly on jhana than in these books, you can read them and compare. Other than that, I cannot recommend any particular teacher.

STAGES OF JHANA

Can you speak in more detail about the flavor and characteristics of the stages of jhana?

From my reading and practicing meditation, I would say that the First Jhana is simply getting away from busy life and gaining a certain degree of concentration. In that state you still have thoughts, sustained thoughts, joy, happiness, and concentration. Only when you attain the Second Jhana is your thinking suspended. You still hear sounds, and yet your mind is not interested in sounds because joy and happiness based on concentration are very strong. As you proceed to the Third Jhana, even your joy is replaced by more subtle happiness, which, by the way, is not excitement. And when you go to the Fourth Jhana, even happiness is replaced by purified mindfulness and equanimity.

My understanding of initial thought and sustained thought is very much in line with the Noble Eightfold Path where vitakka—thought—is broken down into three subdivisions. These are the thought of letting go, of renunciation, or nekkhamma vitakka; the thought of nonhatred, metta, or loving-friendliness, or avyapada vitakka; and the thought of noncruelty and compassion, or avihimsa vitakka.

As you overcome the five hindrances—desire for sensual pleasure, or kamacchanda; hatred, or vyapada; sleepiness and drowsiness, or thinamiddha; restlessness and remorse, or uddhacchakukkucca; and doubt, or vicikiccha—the desire for sensual pleasure is replaced by the thought of renunciation. Hatred is replaced by metta. And the thought of cruelty is replaced by compassion.

When you attain the First Jhana, you will have thoughts of letting go, thoughts of loving-friendliness, and thoughts of compassion. Your mind doesn't attempt to cling to objects—sights, sounds, smells, tastes, and touch. It will not be interested in them. It would rather let go of them. This is the thought of renunciation. The mind is full of loving-friendliness—metta. It is full of compassion.

When your mind is fully charged with these wholesome thoughts, you lose interest in paying attention to sights, sounds, smells, tastes, and touch. This does not mean that you don't hear or smell, taste or touch. While in the First Jhana, you hear sounds, you may smell flowers around you. You may taste mucus if you swallow, and will feel the draining of mucus in your sinus area. Or you will feel your nerves vibrating or expanding and contracting in your chest and abdominal area.

Your concentration is not very deep in the First Jhana because of the presence of these thoughts and feelings. Your mind is far more interested in paying attention to these wholesome mental states.

When you go to the Second Jhana, you can see significant shifts from this state and you will not have thoughts. You are fully conscious of your peaceful mental state. In the Second Jhana you simply feel the feeling of letting go, you feel the feeling of metta, you feel the feeling of compassion. As your mind goes to the higher jhanas, the breath becomes so subtle that you may not even feel it.

You will notice the subtlest changes taking place in your body and mind. Then your mind naturally develops insight—vipassana.

Here, you started with concentration and ended up with insight. Any moment you begin to notice changes, you are practicing vipassana, or insight meditation. Becoming aware of impermanence is an absolutely necessary part of vipassana meditation. I must note that samatha and vipassana are equally important. These two aspects of meditation go hand in hand.

I have written several books on these topics. I recommend *Beyond Mindfulness in Plain English* as a starting place to explore further to have a better and clearer understanding of what happens to you when you attain jhana.

The Tool of Concentration

Is there any detailed understanding of which jhana you are in, or is it always to be used as a tool for insight to uproot defilements?

Concentration is the tool. You sharpen that tool by practicing jhana. When the tool is blunt, then you cannot gain concentration. So, in order to gain concentration, you overcome all these obstacles and then the mind becomes sharp and clean.

What do we do in insight meditation? We see anicca, dukkha, and anatta—we see impermanence, unsatisfactoriness, and selflessness in the most minute way, to get rid of greed, hatred, and delusion. For this purpose, we practice concentration and insight.

A Sign of Concentration

What does the nimita look like?

The nimita looks like a nimita. It is what is called a sign of concentration. That means, for instance, when the sun rises, you see the sign of the rising sun. Dawn. Seeing the dawn, you say, "Ah, the sun is rising." Similarly, suppose a vehicle is coming. You hear the sound. A faint sound. Then, slowly, slowly the sound increases and you see the vehicle. If it's at night, you see the light very far away—a car coming with headlights on. Seeing that light in the pitch dark, you say a car is coming. So that light is a sign of the car coming.

Similarly, when you are gaining concentration, before true concentration, you have a very tiny bright light in your mind. It keeps brightening and brightening and brightening your mind—the luminosity of the mind will arise with the jhana.

The Buddha said this in the Anguttara Nikaya: The mind is luminous, but it becomes polluted by adventitious defilements. Ordinarily, people do not notice it; therefore, they do not practice concentration meditation—*citta bhavana*. When they practice citta bhavana meditation, then they can reach that luminosity of mind. And the first sign of its appearance is the little spark of light that becomes brighter and brighter. Before you see the bright spark of light, all your hindrances are gone—the mind is very calm and peaceful and ready to gain concentration.

But sometimes people—without having any serious meditation background—experience a bright light. You've got to forget that. That is not a real sign of concentration.

THE HINDRANCES AND JHANA

If all the hindrances are dissolved in jhana but jhana is impermanent, do the hindrances return as before when the jhanic state ceases or when you stop meditating?

As jhana itself is impermanent, when you lose jhana the hindrances will come back. That is a normal thing. You've got to reattain it again and again whenever you lose it.

WALKING JHANA

Can a person attain jhana during walking meditation?

If the person can overcome hindrances in any posture, then that person can attain jhana. While walking, if you overcome any hindrances that arise, your body may be moving, but at the same time you can attain the First Jhana. In the attainment of the First Jhana, your body will not be 100 percent quiet and still. But after that, you may have to settle down by sitting to attain other jhanas.

KNOWING JHANA

How do we know when we reach the First Jhana? How does it feel?

When you reach the First Jhana, you know for sure. When you look at your mind, all the hindrances are not there. Your greed, anger, restlessness and worry, sleepiness and drowsiness, and doubt about the practice—they are not there. Your mind is very quiet.

Also, you have no inclination whatsoever to talk. Then you experience a great deal of happiness because you are secluded from various kinds of activities associated with sensual pleasures. Your mind is free from all these things.

The First Jhana is not a very deep, concentrated state of mind. There is concentration, but you can hear and feel and so forth. You are so focused on your experience of peace and happiness that you are not interested at all in talking. So verbalizing stops when you attain the First Jhana. Then you will know you are in the First Jhana.

TAKE IT EASY

What is the healthy, long-term approach to attain jhanas so they are natural results of effort over time? Sometimes it feels stressful and confusing to practice jhana and that more groundwork may be necessary to later on practice them with readiness.

It must come naturally. You know, friends, we use these technical terms—*jhana*, "hindrance," and so on. I don't keep thinking about First Jhana, Second Jhana, and so forth. Forget about all these terms. Just pay attention to your breathing. And whatever problems arise, you just let it go and you will be OK. You will be on the right path. Since this is a jhana retreat we have to talk about all these technical terms. I would not worry about it. Take it easy.

Don't Worry about Jhanas

Attaining jhana is not something I feel is a goal for me. I want to practice calming the mind and to develop equanimity. Is that OK?

I think this is a good question. Don't worry about it. All you need to gain true, deep, real insight is to overcome your hindrances. Just do that. Don't worry about jhanas or deep states of absorption. Overcome your hindrances and make the mind clear and concentrated. If jhana comes, don't throw it away. Accept it.

12

Mindfulness

New Moment, Fresh Moment

When I am mindful of the breath, what am I supposed to be doing?

When you are mindful of something, be mindful of that—what else? Either you gain concentration or you deepen your insight.

In order to deepen your insight, there are several things happening with your breath. If you are really mindful, you will not be bored. Because every new moment is a fresh moment. When you watch the breath, you can at first notice inhaling and exhaling. Then you notice long inhaling and long exhaling. Then you notice the beginning, middle, and end of inhaling and the beginning, middle, and end of exhaling. Then you notice when the lungs are full of inhaled breath.

You may also notice the degree of pressure. As you breathe out, that pressure is released. And then you experience a degree of anxiety about not having breath in your lungs. You breathe in again and that anxiety fades away. Then you notice the breath is either gross or subtle. Then you notice the deep breaths and shallow breaths.

Then you notice the softness and hardness of your breath. Then you notice the feeling of the breath—it's either pleasant, unpleasant, or neutral.

Also, when we become mindful of the beginning, middle, and end of each breath, eventually we will notice the end of inhaling joined with the beginning of exhaling. Then the breath will become one object, just like one cylindrical object.

There are so many things to notice! All these are happening while you are breathing in and out. But if you make your mind totally blank and watch the breath without noticing any of these things, it is really boring. You've got to watch the breath to understand the very nature of the breath.

We can also look at the elements reflected in the breath. The body has the earth, air, water, and fire elements. We experience the earth element when the breath touches the nostrils, whether it is soft or hard. That is because of the presence of the earth element in the breath. We experience the sensation of moisture or dryness of the breath—that is because of the water element. Sometimes we experience the heat of our breath, sometimes the coolness of our breath—that is because of the fire element. And we definitely notice the breath moving in and out. That's because of the air element. So, all the four elements are there.

There are many things to notice with our breathing. Of course, if you were to label all of these different features you'd go crazy. But if you simply pay attention to the breath while noticing all these things, the breath becomes subtler and subtler and subtler. And so you gain very good concentration.

When the breath becomes extremely subtle you may not even notice the breath. But you will remember the place where you focus the mind on—that will be the secondary object. The first is the breath. The second is the memory of the place where you watch the breath. That means either the rims of your nostrils, the tip of the nose, the upper lip, or inside the nose between the eyes. These depend on the formation of your nose.

Some people feel the breath touching the lip. Some people's noses bend down and they will notice the touch of the breath at the tip of their nose. Some people have a straight nose and will notice the breath at the rims of their nostrils.

Some may experience the breath touching right inside the nose between the eyes. Individuals have to breath several times to find out where the breath touches. And that locale will become a memory later on, and not the breath itself.

That's because the breath will become so subtle we don't notice it at all. And that is the time that the memory of the breath becomes our secondary object—that is called *patibhaga nimitta* in Pali. So we focus the mind on this memory. Then even the memory will be replaced by a very bright light. And then it will be a sharp, small spark of light that will disappear, giving rise to a bright, clear light. And at that time you attain concentration, a very deep, profound concentration with the jhanic quality.

That is how you gain concentration from focusing the mind on the breath. First, you will notice the details, then you develop your insight. The details will fade away and then you gain concentration. When you gain concentration, that is the time you will notice subtle, deep changes in your experiences.

At that time, you will develop the highest quality of insight—to see impermanence, unsatisfactoriness, and selflessness at the highest level. Your greed, hatred, and delusion will fade away.

These are the steps to gain the stages of enlightenment such as stream entry and so forth. Therefore, focusing on our breathing will never be boring!

MINDFUL REFLECTION

What is meant by mindful reflection?

When craving or greed obsesses our mind, our mind will become dull. When we are obsessed with craving, we have a one-track mind.

The same thing happens when the mind is obsessed with ignorance.

Mindful reflection is an awareness of our mental states, so that we may rise above such unskillful and unwholesome states of mind.

THE WHO OF MINDFULNESS

Who is being mindful when we engage in mindfulness?

This is a very philosophical question. The wording of the question should be corrected because the very wording is misleading. To ask who is being mindful is incorrect because we do not believe that there is a "who," since there is no being living inside us.

Therefore, the question should be "What is being mindful?" Or "What is happening in mindfulness?"—something like that.

This phenomenon called a "being" becomes mindful, and then what is the being? If we don't use the term "who," we have to use another term. What is a being?

There was a monk called Radha. He asked the Buddha one day, "Venerable Sir, what is a being?" Buddha gave a long, very philosophical answer—the entity that clings to form, feeling, perception, thought, and consciousness is a being. An entity that clings to form, holds on to form, is stuck in form—that entity is called a being. It is this entity that is mindful.

That means a phenomenon—we call it a being or a person or "I" for our own convenience. It doesn't matter. It is perfectly all right for us to say "I am mindful."

But behind this "I am" there is no "I." That is why it is difficult to understand. Only for conventional communication do we use the word "I." So, it is a phenomenon that becomes mindful itself.

THINGS AS THEY REALLY ARE

What purpose does mindfulness serve in our practice?

Mindfulness has a very specific function. Mindfulness makes the mind clean and pure. It also reveals things as they really are. Through mindfulness we understand the nature of the aggregates—these are form, feelings, perceptions, volitional formations, and consciousness.

Aggregates are a collection of things. For example, when we practice mindfulness and gain clear understanding, it becomes clear to us that form—*f-o-r-m*—is really like foam—*f-o-a-m*. Imagine a lot of water flowing and eddying in a creek. You'll see bubbles build up. They appear to us to be a huge pile. But you pop one bubble and there's nothing inside. Break another and inside there is also nothing.

When we pay mindful attention to our body, our form—and this superficially apparent body—we see there's nothing inside it.

Take a powerful microscope and look at any little part of the body and you will eventually see nothing in it. It is just sort of waves.

Buddha came to this insight long before people discovered this through microscopes and modern physics. When we look mindfully at our body we don't see anything in it.

CONCENTRATION AND MINDFULNESS

Can you talk about the relationship between concentration and mindfulness?

There are two aspects in Buddhist meditation: concentration meditation and mindfulness meditation. I think many of you are familiar with mindfulness meditation. Sometimes it is called insight meditation, sometimes vipassana meditation. And sometimes just mindfulness meditation.

All these are the same. Although they are related, there are some little differences. One is a linguistic difference—*vipassana* is a Pali word, and "mindfulness" and "insight" are English words.

Let's focus our attention on these two aspects—mindfulness

meditation and concentration meditation. Most meditators, when they come to meditation, they always complain, "I cannot gain concentration!" They are assuming that concentration is the only thing we do in meditation. That is not true. Although concentration is absolutely necessary—almost half of our meditation—we need the other half. That is mindfulness, or vipassana or insight meditation.

However, when we try to gain concentration we have problems. When we cannot gain concentration, what should we do? Primarily this is a result of what are known as the hindrances. When they arise, you cannot concentrate. You've got to overcome your hindrances.

In order to overcome hindrances, you've got to practice mindfulness. Only when you become mindful of hindrances and learn how to deal with them can you gain concentration.

Therefore, you can see how these two are integrated, interrelated, intertwined, and supporting each other. You are trying to gain concentration and you have hindrances. When you overcome your hindrances with mindfulness, then you gain concentration.

Some people are afraid of concentration. Especially in the West, the word "concentration" is like a taboo. You will become a vegetable, you will become stuck! You will become attached to it so that you don't hear anything or feel anything and you will become like a rock! Don't concentrate! They say just practice vipassana.

This is a misunderstanding of the whole meditation system.

We must honestly look at these two aspects of meditation. Concentration is the crown of meditation. That is why in the Noble Eightfold Path the last is Right Concentration. The seventh is Right Mindfulness. If you don't concentrate and just practice mindfulness and finish there, then you are not practicing the Noble Eightfold Path. You are practicing the Noble Sevenfold Path! If you want to practice the Noble Eightfold Path you must include concentration. But you cannot concentrate without mindfulness.

It is such an interesting dilemma that many people encounter without understanding the relationship between these two.

MINDFULNESS OF THE AGGREGATES

Can you please suggest how the Five Aggregates are brought into vipassana meditation?

The entire Mahasatipatthana Sutta (Digha Nikaya, 22) talks about how the Five Aggregates should be brought into meditation. Mindfulness of the body, starting with breathing, posture, clear comprehension, the thirty-two parts of the body, the Four Elements, and the nine stages of corpse contemplation—all these belong to the First Aggregate, mindfulness of the body.

Take, for instance, the breath, which is part of the body. We pay attention to mindfulness of the breath, to see the rising and falling, the beginning, middle, and end of each breath. We see the pauses between inhaling and exhaling, and then the expansion and contracting of our lungs and how you experience pressure and the relief of pressure when breathing in and out.

We see all of these as changing all the time, each and every part of the breath. We've got to watch and pay attention and see how they arise and pass away. We see the same pattern in our posture, whether walking, sitting, standing, or lying down. When we walk, we notice how the body changes, how the feeling changes, how the elements change.

We use everything as a subject of mindfulness meditation. We see they all are changing. Everything is permanently impermanent. Then, we see they all are unsatisfactory—everything in this entire body and mind is unsatisfactory, whether our hair or teeth or eyes or nose. Everything is unsatisfactory because they are all impermanent.

Buddha mentions many different things that happen to our eyes, ears, nose, tongue, body, skin, and so forth—they all are changing. All are subject to sickness and aging. All are subject to death.

We can see this process happening every moment, especially when we are healthy. This is a very good meditation to practice.

Look at our changes, our impermanence. That's why we do meditation on the Five Aggregates. Feeling is changing, perception is changing, consciousness is changing, volitional formations are changing, Dhamma, mental activities are changing.

STEP-BY-STEP MINDFULNESS

Sometimes when people teach mindfulness, all they teach is being nonjudgmental about thoughts and breathing in and out. What are your thoughts about that?

Breathing in and breathing out—that is not the entire practice. When we look at it superficially, it seems very simple. But that is just the beginning. Mindfulness of breathing is a very profound discourse given by the Buddha. Mindfulness of breathing is just the core of mindfulness practice.

One day, Venerable Ananda asked the Buddha, "Venerable Sir, are you still meditating?" The Buddha said that he was. Ananda said, "Could you tell me the subject of your meditation?" The Buddha said, "I am using the breath, mindfulness of breathing."

You see, before he attained enlightenment, when he was a little child, there was a festival and they put him under a rose apple tree and left to join the festivities. He was all alone, and at that moment he started practicing mindfulness of breathing. And when he was struggling to attain enlightenment as an adult, after leaving his teachers, when he was alone, he thought, "What subject should I use for my practice?" Then he thought of mindfulness of breathing.

Focusing the mind on the breath is a beginning as well as the end, because it has so many things in it to understand, when we practice it very diligently. So, teaching mindfulness of breathing is OK.

But we have to learn meditation step-by-step to further a full mindfulness practice. I have written a book on this, *The Four Foundations of Mindfulness*, where I have emphasized how to use the breath as a full subject of meditation. I'm not trying to promote my books! But if you are serious about the practice, this one is written particularly for people who are not familiar with meditation.

MINDFULNESS AND MORALITY

Meditation is now being taught in schools, hospitals, and many other places. Do you think practicing meditation without the support of morality, or sila, can make people become addicted to meditation without solving their problems in life? Can this practice increase the feelings of ego or self without a grounding in morality?

This is a very good question. Mindfulness has to be practiced with sila. Sila means observing moral, ethical principles.

Now, yes, it is true that there are lots of people who try to practice mindfulness and are not very successful because their foundation is not firmly established. The foundation of mindfulness is sila, or morality. However, if somebody were to wait until their morality was perfect to practice meditation, that person would never meditate! It is just like a man going to the seashore and waiting for the sea to become perfectly calm to swim. This fellow will never swim!

Similarly, even without perfect sila, you have to start right away. As you keep practicing, then you learn from your own experience when the practice is producing successful results. You also need to question why your practice is not successful. Because something is wrong. You correct it. And while correcting such matters, you keep practicing. Then both your morality and mindfulness will grow together.

You cannot wait until morality is perfect. It is very important to start the practice right away. As the practice of mindfulness develops, you become more aware and mindful of your shortcomings, and then you correct your behavior. These two go hand in hand.

"Secular" Meditation

Considering the growing popularity of "secular" meditation in the areas of education, business, and sports, could mindfulness during school, work, or sports be a natural extension of periodic or daily secular sitting meditation?

Meditation in the strictest sense is a very special way of training our mind. For that you don't need any particular posture, time, or place. At any time, any place, and in any posture, you can practice mindfulness.

Meditation and mindfulness practice in secular life, especially as it has grown so popular these days, has been sort of taken out of context. When you take something out of context you do not experience the full impact of the practice. Therefore, the phrase "secular meditation" is really general psychological training. You can use meditation and mindfulness in education, in the workplace, and elsewhere and it can yield results, provided that you do it correctly and properly.

In our case, that means according to the Buddhist teaching. Our understanding of meditation is a way of training the mind to remove our greed, hatred, and delusion. So if we train our mind in any way to get rid of our greed, hatred, and delusion, then that mental training is what we call meditation.

Whether at school or at the workplace or in any secular setting, if you do this training to remove greed, hatred, and delusion, then that is meditation in the Buddhist tradition.

In order to practice vipassana meditation particularly, you must train the mind to see impermanence, unsatisfactoriness, and selflessness—anicca, dukkha, anatta. When you train the mind to see these three things in any situation, whether it is a secular or religious setting, that is what we call mindfulness meditation.

MINDFULNESS AND MONEY

Mindfulness Based Stress Reduction has been an approachable way for many to gain exposure to meditation and mindfulness. Lay practitioners reduce their stress and can be trained in the practice. However, there is a fee structure in most places. Is it still OK to do this if there is money involved, or does it conflict with Dhamma?

Well, of course, people have to rent places. They have to pay rental and room fees and pay for heat and air conditioning and so forth. Perhaps people willing to pay for such instruction will feel they have gained something from this practice, since such instruction is not supported by donations.

We here at the monastery are supported by donations and therefore we don't charge. Laypeople don't receive donations and therefore they have to charge. I don't think it is wrong to charge.

CLINGING AND SUFFERING

When I become aware of my clinging and craving and feeling in situations, am I working toward ending my ignorance?

Yes. In fact, when we become aware of our craving and clinging, at any time, then we see how painful it is! As craving arises, pain arises along with it at that moment. We don't have to wait for a later time to feel the pain of craving. As it arises, we experience pain.

We all can experiment with that—that is the material for your experiment in your laboratory, you see? So, we use this to see how much suffering arises along with craving. And then we see the direct connection between craving and suffering.

As Buddha said, the cause of suffering is craving or desire or greed. And it is very true—we can experience it directly the moment craving arises. Then, seeing the pain caused by craving, we decide, "Well, every time I have craving, I have pain. Should I be foolish enough to nourish it? Or should I do something about it?"

That question rises in the mind. The next time when craving arises, we become more mindful so as not to nourish the root of craving.

How do we nourish the root of craving? By being unmindful. When we are mindful, we suffocate craving, we starve craving to death. So every time craving arises we become mindful and we don't give in to it.

Therefore, when craving arises, what do we do? We become mindful and reduce our ignorance to that degree because mindfulness weakens our ignorance. Mindfulness opens our mind, it brings light into the darkness of ignorance.

If you say ignorance is darkness, mindfulness is the light, to reduce the darkness. If you do that every time that craving arises, then, of course, you are working to reduce ignorance.

IN EVERY BREATH

At what point in practicing mindfulness of breathing do you look at the three characteristics of existence?

These actually are interconnected and interrelated. When you mindfully pay attention to the breath, you can see the arising phenomena, the passing-away phenomena, and what is happening in between. That means with every breath you can see impermanence, unsatisfactoriness, and selflessness. In every breath!

Inhaling, you can see these three things. And exhaling, you can see these things because the breath is always in the process of changing. The breath leaves through the lungs while also changing and transforming. And as the mind gets sharper and sharper, we begin to see the changes within the inhaling and exhaling. Therefore, we can see these three characteristics in every breath.

There is a very beautiful discourse in the Anguttara Nikaya. The

Buddha tells his monks, "This is very important to remember. Do you practice mindfulness of death?"

Now, when you hear the word "death," is that not something for everybody to pay attention to, since it will come to all of us at some point? When our understanding deepens, it is not an unpleasant, unpalatable, negative subject. Why? Because we are hurtling toward death every nanosecond. Every second, death is taking place if we understand it thoroughly.

So, when Buddha asked his bhikkhus, "Do you practice mindfulness of death?" there were six monks who responded.

One monk said, "I practice mindfulness of death once a week." Then another monk said, "Venerable Sir, every day I live is enough for me to practice mindfulness of death." A third monk said, "Venerable Sir, if I live long enough to go from my kuti to a village to collect alms food and return, it is enough for me to practice mindfulness of death." The fourth monk said, "Venerable Sir, if I have time to eat my alms food, if I live long enough, that is time enough to practice mindfulness of death." The fifth monk said, "If I have enough time to eat one morsel of food, that is time enough for me to practice mindfulness of death." The sixth monk said, "If, Venerable Sir, I live long enough to inhale and exhale, that is long enough for me to practice mindfulness of death."

The Buddha said these last two monks are diligent, mindful monks, really practicing mindfulness of death. Why is that? Because mindfulness of death can be seen in one inhaling and one exhaling.

That means that the inhaling breath is constantly changing—so, you can see the whole meaning of death in one inhaling. And the whole meaning of death can be seen in one exhaling. Therefore, in one inhaling we can see impermanence, unsatisfactoriness, and selflessness. We don't have to look somewhere else to see these things.

Marketing Buddhism

In every country and culture with which Buddhism has come into contact there have been particular ways it came to be practiced, such as in Thailand, Cambodia, and Japan. What are your thoughts on Buddhism in America? What are the skillful and the not-so-skillful ways you see Buddhism in America developing?

Well, the core of Buddhism does not change at all. It is the same wherever it goes. But it is outer practices, certain rituals and practices, and the language and the way of communication, these things naturally must be adapted according to the environment.

Buddha mentioned this in the Aranavibhanga Sutta (Mahjjima Nikaya, 139). He says wherever monks go to teach and bring the Dhamma, they must learn to blend with that area, use the common parlance, their language and customs, the way they do things. They must adapt to local conditions.

For instance, in my home country of Sri Lanka, monks leave a shoulder bared with their robes. But when we came here and established this monastery in the hills of West Virginia, we had to adapt to the colder weather! We cover both shoulders, we wear socks, hats, even thermal underwear in winter because we have to adapt to the environment.

But that is just an example having to do with clothing. In a broader sense, in the West many people seem disenchanted with their traditional religious rituals and they stop practicing such rituals or even leave the religion in which they were raised.

In Buddhist practice in various countries, they have adopted various rituals. So when they come to this country in the West, they try to minimize their rituals, although even in the West there are groups and sects that emphasize rituals. Some Buddhists do adopt those rituals. Generally, when people are more serious about deep Buddhist practice, they are not very enthusiastic about rituals.

Another thing in the West, often people come to Buddhism from an intellectual level, from a higher educational background. So, generally, Buddhism is appealing to intellectual people. In so-called Buddhist countries, however, Buddhism is just a common thing. Everybody follows the crowd. Therefore, they often don't care for deep investigation and studying and being very serious about it—they just take things for granted.

There is a negative side to what you might call "popular Buddhism." Without understanding the core teachings, they take this superficial understanding and rote practice as Buddhism. These rituals, these customs and cultural elements—that is not Buddhism.

Another thing one sees happening in the West is that people write various things in the name of Buddhism that do not accord with the Buddha's teachings. Some people go to a few retreats, meet with teachers for a short period of time, and suddenly they become meditation teachers and start meditation groups and centers. Then they use this as sort of a profit-making product. Meditation and mindfulness become like a commercial item.

That is the negative side. Because as meditation and mindfulness practice grows more and more popular, some people think this is an easy way of making money.

13

Understanding Impermanence

Under Your Nose

I have a theoretical, philosophical understanding of impermanence. But I still lack a direct seeing of what it practically means for attaining this understanding. Can you help clarify this?

The practical way is watching, watching, watching one's own experience. That is the best way to see. Just pay attention to your breath, for instance. Notice how quickly it changes. Pay attention to a feeling of anger when it overtakes the mind. It doesn't stay the same intensity all the time, does it?

Or examine your greed. Even that does not stay the same. For instance, notice while you are eating and enjoying whatever delicious foods you like, say, the lentils and rice served at lunch today. As you are eating, your stomach expands and fills up. And you cannot eat anymore and have no desire for another bite. Right there you experience the impermanence of your wish or desire for the food. Even the taste you so enjoyed at the beginning of the meal will no longer seem so attractive when your stomach is full—you don't want to eat anymore! So that too is an experience of impermanence.

Everything we experience is like this. We don't have to have some deep philosophical understanding of impermanence. The truth of it can be seen in the tiniest moments and experiences of our daily life.

That is the best way to conform to the theory and logic and phi-losophy that you talk about.

Right under your nose!

IMPERMANENCE IS NOT MYSTERIOUS

How do we come to know and see impermanence, since it is such an important focus of the Buddha's teachings?

First, we don't learn impermanence from others. We come to know and see it through our own experience. There is nothing mysterious about it. Impermanence is not a belief, it is not something to be proven or disproven.

But the evidence of impermanence can be found both internally and externally. The entire teaching of the Buddha is based on this immutable fact of impermanence. If you honestly pay attention to your own experience, you come to know it and see it in all things.

Knowing about impermanence intellectually, as a concept, is not enough. We must come to see how the entire Four Noble Truths are based on it. Suffering is based on impermanence. We know from our experience that impermanence itself is not the cause of suffering. The cause of suffering is craving. But what we crave is impermanent objects.

All those things that we crave and latch on to—possessions, relationships, youthfulness, fame, the latest phone, the shiniest ve-hicle—all of them are impermanent. Since they are impermanent and are bound to fade and pass away, they are also ultimately un-satisfactory. We are bound to be disappointed if we invest our hopes in them as a lasting source of happiness. They all have the mark of impermanence, unsatisfactoriness, and selflessness.

We look here and there for a permanent self, where we might find lasting satisfaction. No matter what you say is "self," the Buddha would say, "That it is not self." Then you might ask the Buddha, "What then is self?" Instead of answering your question, the Buddha would turn the question around and say, "What you call self, it is not my term. You are the one who used the word 'self.' So, you tell me what it is."

If you say such-and-such is self, the Buddha would say that is not self. He stands his ground that everything is impermanent, including what you describe as self.

Since you can never find anything permanent, you have to admit that this so-called self also is subject to the same established law of impermanence. And once you admit that everything is impermanent, then your so-called self also should be impermanent. Either you have to admit that things are permanently impermanent or nothing is impermanent.

The Buddha taught us selflessness based on the impermanence of the Five Aggregates. He said in Anattalakkhana Sutta (Samyutta Nikaya, 22.59), "Bhikkhus, form is not self." If form were self, then form would not be prone to affliction, and it would be possible to say, "Let my form be thus; let my form not be thus." Because form is not self, form is prone to affliction, and it is not possible to say, "Let my form be thus, let my form not be thus."

The same passage is repeated for the other four aggregates. The next step of his argument is based on impermanence. He said, "What do you think, bhikkhus? Is form permanent or impermanent?

"Impermanent, Venerable Sir."

"Is that which is impermanent unsatisfactory or satisfactory?"

"Unsatisfactory, Venerable, Sir."

"Is it correct to consider that which is impermanent, unsatisfactory, and of the nature of changing as 'This is mine,' 'This am I,' 'This is my self'?"

"No, Venerable Sir."

This is the argument the Buddha used for the remaining four aggregates to prove that the Five Aggregates are not self. They are all impermanent.

When we see the rising and falling and mutation of all conditioned things, then we will be full of joy—piti. When we are full of joy, we will be rapturous—passaddhi. When we are full of rapture, then we are happy—sukha. Through such happiness we gain concentration. And the concentrated mind can see the truth as it really is.

So, in this way impermanence is a source of happiness and not a wellspring of suffering!

FIRSTHAND KNOWLEDGE

What are we supposed to learn from focusing on the breath and the mind and body?

If we follow the Buddha's example and use the breath to examine our mind-body system, we gain insight into a number of essential Dhamma points. As the Buddha explains, "All Dhammas arise from attention." Among these, we gain firsthand knowledge of the Five Aggregates—form, feeling, perception, thought, and consciousness—the traditional constituents of the body and mind.

The breath-body and all other material objects including the physical body belong to the aggregate of form. We experience the touch of the breath at the nose, lungs, and abdomen. The air we breathe in is physical, and whatever is physical we call form.

The other four aggregates describe our mental experience. The aggregate of feeling refers to our sensations of the breath and the emotions we experience as a result. There is the anxiety we feel when our lungs are empty and the feeling of relief when we inhale.

Next is the aggregate of perception. We can use the breath as an object of meditation only because our minds perceive it. The aggregate of thought includes all other mental activities, including ideas, opinions, and decisions. The thought "this is the feeling of the breath" and the decision to pay attention to the breath belong to this aggregate.

The last aggregate is consciousness. It is the basis of all mental experience. We become aware of changes in the other four aggregates because of the aggregate of consciousness. But consciousness, too, is changing as the form of the breath and our feelings, perceptions, and thoughts change.

In the Anapanasati Sutta on the mindfulness of breathing (Majjhima Nikaya, 118), the Buddha tells us:

> Mindful of impermanence breathe in, mindful of impermanence breathe out; mindful of dispassion breathe in, mindful of dispassion breathe out; mindful of cessation breathe in, mindful of cessation breathe out; mindful of relinquishing breathe in, mindful of relinquishing breathe out.

When we apply these words to the aggregates of the breath, we notice that all five consist of three very minor moments: the rising moment, the living or enduring moment, and the passing-away moment. The same is true of all things that exist. This activity never stops. This is the nature of impermanence.

Forms, feelings, perceptions, thoughts, and even consciousness don't stick around. They cease without leaving a trace. Once they are gone, they are gone forever. New forms, feelings, perceptions, thoughts, and consciousness always appear.

Observing these changes teaches us detachment and makes it easier for us to relinquish the habit of clinging to any part of the body or mind.

SEEING IMPERMANENCE

Why is concentration stressed so much in Buddhist practice?

When you gain concentration you don't have to wish to see things exactly as they are because that is the nature of Dhamma. We don't need any agent, we don't need someone to initiate Dhamma in you because Dhamma is there. When you gain concentration, you begin to see things exactly as they are. Sometimes this is not an easy thing to see.

Suppose you look at yourself in a mirror. You cannot see yourself exactly as you are. If you write "MAY" on a piece of paper and hold it up to the mirror, the paper will say "YAM." Your features in the mirror are opposite what they are in real life. So, even a mirror cannot give you a real picture of the object.

But there is a real deep seeing you get when you have concentration. With concentration, what you see is your body, your feeling, your perceptions, your volitional formations or thought, and your consciousness. All of our problems arise from these five sources.

When you see them exactly as they are, you see them changing constantly and consistently. They change without giving you any prior notice or announcement. It happens naturally by itself. Therefore, we might say that all things are permanently impermanent.

Then what arises in the mind is viraga. What is that? That means not trying to hold on to these changing objects. Viraga means we do not attach to things. *Raga* signifies greed, sensuality, desire— *vi-raga* means the absence of raga, the absence of desire.

When you see this permanent impermanence, you let it go. There is no way to stop these changes. When you let go of that greed you are free from pain, remorse, and suffering.

This is what the Buddha meant in his teaching on the Four Noble Truths. The cause of suffering is greed. Greed for what? Greed for impermanent objects. What are the impermanent objects? Our bodies, feelings, perceptions, thoughts or volitional formations, and consciousness.

THE HABITUAL "I"

I think of myself as an "I" all the time. "I do this" and "I am that." Is there an "I" that exists, or is it just a figment or delusion?

"I" is a habitual pattern of our minds. You should be able to watch whatever you experience without thinking in terms of "I". In our daily conversation, we use the word "I" in order to make our communication easy. Even the Buddha did so.

But if you mindfully watch, all you notice is constantly changing activities in the mind and body. Nothing in the body and mind stays the same even for two consecutive moments.

When you are fully engaged in mindful awareness of this phenomenon of change, there will not be any room for the mind to think "I," "my," or "myself." All you notice is these ever-changing activities, not only during the time you are sitting on cushion but— if we are mindful—at every other moment in our daily lives.

MENTAL NOTING

Do we make a mental note—like a verbal comment in the mind—of insights we experience during meditation?

You don't have to verbalize your experience. The sentences "This is not mine," "This I am not," "This is not myself" are really an understanding. These are not to be verbalized. Verbalization slows down the awareness. We understand "This is not mine," "This I am not," "This is not myself." When you pay total attention to your experiences, you see all of them are changing. This is impermanence, which is not a word.

Your pleasant, unpleasant, or neutral feelings are not words. You perceive things. This perception is not a word. You are conscious of countless things. This consciousness is not a word. Your words get in between your awareness and experience. Awareness is much faster than verbalization. While your mind is looking for words, your awareness disappears. When you have found a word or phrase for your experience, the experience will have passed and then you would be naming what is already gone.

Try to be fully aware of what is going on in your mind and body without using words. Whether you experience an itch, pain, pleasure, sadness, joy, tranquility, fear, jealousy, anger, whatever it is, be aware of it. Let the experiences come and let them go. You simply become aware of the impermanent nature of all of them. Be aware of the impermanence, the suffering, and the selflessness in all your experiences.

Everything is permanently impermanent. Every fraction of a second, more than a 100 trillion functions or activities are going on inside of your body. Every cell in your body is changing, decaying, and passing away and new cells take their place every moment. You cannot verbalize all these changes, as they decay and pass away.

We should be able to use any experience as an object of mindfulness meditation. Pay attention to whatever you experience—negative, positive, or neutral. Stay diligent and mindful all the time.

IMPERMANENT EQUANIMITY

If something is in a state of equilibrium, that is to say, a balanced state, it appears to be in a state of permanent existence. Is this so?

It is said that when an equanimous feeling arises, a person who experiences the equanimous feeling gets confused. Why? That person does not see that even an equanimous feeling arises and fades away.

Not seeing the impermanent nature of equanimity itself is a

delusion. Therefore, to think that equanimity or a balanced state is something permanent is an illusion—it arises due to causes and conditions. Whatever arises due to causes and conditions is impermanent. So, even equanimity is impermanent.

PERMANENTLY IMPERMANENT

How do we use impermanence during meditation?

We can use everything as the subject of vipassana mindfulness meditation. All we see is that all phenomena are changing, changing, changing. Nothing is permanent. Everything is permanently impermanent. Then we see all these things are unsatisfactory.

Nothing in this entire body is satisfactory, whether our hair, our nails, our teeth, our eyes. Our eyes are so useful and so important. We see so many things through our eyes.

Unfortunately, these eyes are impermanent. They all are changing.

Everything in the body is subject to sickness, aging, and death. And we can see this process happening every moment. Especially when we are healthy, this is a very good meditation to practice. Look at impermanence.

That's how we do meditation on the Five Aggregates. Feeling is changing, perception is changing, consciousness is changing, volitional formations or Dhamma are changing, and mental activities are changing.

WHAT IS SO UNSATISFACTORY?

I have been reflecting on the Three Characteristics of Existence: impermanence, unsatisfactoriness, and nonself. But when I look at a flower or the ocean, I don't find that unsatisfactory. So I'm wondering, does the unsatisfactoriness arise from our clinging and attachment to things rather than from some unsatisfactoriness in the thing itself?

That's a very, very good question. It is not purely because things are impermanent that there is unsatisfactoriness. As you said, oceans, trees, flowers, birds, the earth, and so forth are impermanent. But they don't make us feel unsatisfactory.

But the unsatisfactoriness arises because of our becoming attached to impermanent things. If you are not attached to impermanent things, then they are not unsatisfactory. All impermanent things will not become unsatisfactory if you are not attached to them.

The impermanence the Buddha was talking about refers to our own forms, feelings, perceptions, volitional formations, and consciousness. Whatever is impermanent externally is also related to these Five Aggregates. And we are attached to these aggregates.

For example, take the body. If we are attached to the body—the way it is when it is young and healthy, the way the hair is thick and full when we are younger, for example—then when the body changes, as it must when we age, we become unhappy. You were attached to the image of your youthfulness, even though the fact is that we all must age, whether we like it or not.

So we experience unsatisfactoriness only when we are attached to impermanent things. If somebody asks you, what is permanent? The only thing that is permanent is impermanence. Even if you attain enlightenment, you cannot make the impermanent permanent. All you do when you attain enlightenment is you remove your attachment to impermanent things. Then you become enlightened, and impermanent things go on being impermanent.

You will never make an impermanent thing permanent. Buddha did not come to this world to make things permanent. As he said, this is one of the established Dhammas.

Buddha said, "Bhikkhus, whether buddhas come into existence or not, this established Dhamma, this element of Dhamma, exists."

Having understood and realized these truths, buddhas teach, explain, expound, and analyze for people to understand.

Impermanence is there always. As long as we are attached to

impermanent things, we experience suffering. The moment we stop being attached to impermanent things, our suffering stops.

For example, this walking stick is impermanent. It can break, burn, disappear. What is the big deal? We get another one. But if this was given to me by one of my dearest friends, I might have a deep, sentimental attachment to it. I may cling to it. Every time I look at it and think, "So-and-so gave it me. I love so-and-so! This reminds me of so-and-so!" I am attached to the stick. When it breaks, it breaks my heart. I feel sad.

But if I don't have any attachment to the stick, if I understand that like all things it is impermanent, then I won't be distraught whether it is burned, stolen, broken, or lost.

So, it is not the impermanence of the thing itself that is unsatisfactory but our attachment to impermanent things. When we attain enlightenment we make attachment null and void. Is there anything permanent we can attach to? No. Even if you say "I love Nibbana!" Then you are attached to Nibbana. Nagarjuna said, "Those who grasp at the notion 'I will be free from grasping and Nirvana will be mine' have a great grasp on grasping."

Our grasping to impermanent things is the biggest impediment.

I will give you a very simple simile for you to understand this beautiful, profound teaching of the Buddha. It is like climbing a ladder. When you climb a ladder, you have to stand on one rung and hold on to the other rung. If you keep standing on one rung and keep holding on to the other rung, you will never climb! You have to let go of the one rung you are standing on and let go of the one you are holding, right? Only then can you climb. Similarly, when you gain spiritual attainments, you protect it. But don't cling to it.

That is why Buddha said, "Bhikkhus, I teach the Dhamma as if it were a raft." What is the use of a raft? It is to cross a body of water. Once you use the raft and cross the body of water, in order to show your gratitude to the raft, would you carry it on your shoulder? No, you leave it behind for somebody else to use. If you hold on to it, you are very foolish. You are carrying a burden.

Use this body as your raft to cross over the body of samsara—and then you leave it. That means, use the body without attachment: the body, feelings, perceptions, volitional formations, consciousness—all are impermanent.

Seeing, understanding, knowing, realizing, penetrating this impermanence is our task. We don't become attached to it. If we become attached, we continue to suffer and never escape the repetition of birth and death.

So, friends, we have to understand the meaning of the connection between impermanence and unsatisfactoriness. I'm sorry it took so long to answer your question, but it is a very important one.

DEVELOPING INSIGHT

How might we act more skillfully with greater insight and recall?

According to Buddha's teachings, if we overcome the hindrances we will act more skillfully. The hindrances actually are blocking our vision and insight and even blocking our memory. So if we remove our hindrances through insight meditation, that would be of great benefit.

As our insight develops, we gain an understanding of impermanence. It's a direct personal experience. Developing greater insight comes about through mindful attention of our experiences, in order to see the rising and falling nature of all things. That will help us to stay in touch with reality all the time.

DAILY AWARENESS

In vipassana, we concentrate on one thing. In life, apart from meditation, many things happen at once. How can we bring more awareness to our daily life?

It is not actually correct to say in vipassana we concentrate on one thing. In vipassana anything you experience can be an object of your focus. Anything! Why is that? Anything you can experience is very clearly marked with impermanence, unsatisfactoriness, and selflessness. Therefore, whatever you experience in daily life, just focus your mind and see that the thing is impermanent.

You say many things are happening in your life at one time. Really, trillions and trillions of things are happening all over the universe at the same time. But we cannot focus our mind on all of them. We can focus our minds on things we experience moment to moment. And each thing we pay attention to is impermanent. And since it is impermanent, if we become attached to it, we will be unhappy—and it will be unsatisfactory.

Why? Attachment assumes we can glue ourselves to something. But our mind cannot glue itself to anything. It is not possible. But we try to do the impossible and end up in frustration. That's called suffering.

You ask yourself—you don't have to ask me—what are you trying to hold on to and attach to? Is that object permanent? This wish is unfulfillable. Therefore, you have unsatisfactoriness and selflessness.

So in daily life, although we experience so many things, if you pay attention to any of them they all are very clearly marked with these three characteristics of anicca, dukkha, and anatta—impermanence, unsatisfactoriness, and selflessness.

14

Considering Kamma

Understanding Kamma

As a Buddhist I have read that it is important to have faith in rebirth, with our kamma passing on to future lives, in order to make progress on the path. I do have faith that our actions certainly affect the progress of our current lives and the lives of those around us and our descendants. But I still have doubt about the existence of future lives inheriting the kamma of our actions. How should one overcome such doubts without having the knowledge of past lives, or the power of seeing the destinations of others, passing away?

We don't have to know anything about our previous lives to practice or follow the Noble Eightfold Path. In fact, none of us knows anything about our previous lives. We don't even know very much about this life, let alone previous lives!

But still we can follow the Eightfold Path. That means we have to understand the Four Noble Truths. We try to understand what suffering is. We must understand the cause of suffering. We must understand the end of suffering. We must understand the path leading to the end of suffering.

When we understand these Four Noble Truths, we follow the Noble Eightfold Path, without even thinking about the past or the future.

The Buddha himself many times advised us not to worry about the past, not to worry about the future. Be mindful of the present. Keep your mind in the present moment and see impermanence in the present moment. In this way, you can develop insight.

Once you develop insight and gain wisdom, you will understand what the past must have been—and how the future will be. Therefore, even if you don't know your past or future circumstances, you don't have to worry.

You certainly can practice the Noble Eightfold Path right here and now.

THE IMPERMANENCE OF KAMMA

If all things are impermanent, is kamma impermanent? Is enlightenment impermanent?

Yes, kamma is impermanent. That is why we can get rid of kamma—it wears out. As we practice wholesome kamma, unwholesome kamma wears out. It is through the promotion of wholesome kamma that finally we attain liberation.

Liberation or enlightenment, however, is not a thing. It is a "thing-less" state. Therefore, it will never be impermanent. Impermanence arises when there are things.

REPENTANCE AND KAMMA

In the sutta about Angulimala, the Buddha helped a mass murderer become an enlightened monk. How could Angulimala's bad kamma be overcome so he could become a monk? Can our own unwholesome kamma be diminished by repentance and spiritual striving?

By repenting, you cannot overcome your unwholesome kamma. But recall the Buddha's discourse in the Anguttara Nikaya, the Lonaphala Sutta, "The Salt Crystal." The discourse says, suppose somebody commits a very small act that generates unwholesome kamma, something not very serious. That person will be punished. Another person commits the same kamma and nobody even talks about it. Because that person has power. So everybody turns a blind eye toward that. Why is that? Is it because of his political power, his social status? Maybe.

Similarly, if you do an act of small karmic effect, something not very serious, you have a lot of bad consequences. Suppose somebody else commits the same kamma and that person does not suffer very much. Why? That person's small kamma can be easily overcome by doing an enormous amount of good kamma. He knows this is unwholesome, this is wrong. And then he's determined and thinks, "A person of my status, my honor, my dignity should have never done this." From that time onward that person practices morality, concentration, and meditation. He honestly and sincerely never wants to commit that type of action again.

So he builds up his wholesome kamma, practicing all the moral principles. He or she practices meditation honestly and sincerely, gaining concentration, developing insight and wisdom. Their unwholesome kamma will be overcome by an enormous amount of wholesome kamma.

The simile the Buddha gives is that suppose you take a teaspoonful of salt and put it into a cup of water. The cup of water becomes too salty to drink because there is only a little water in the cup. But if you take the same teaspoonful of salt and put it into the Ganges—or, in our case, the Potomac or Mississippi River—will you make it salty? No! There is so much river water and so little salt.

Similarly, if you create so much wholesome kamma and occasionally you do some small unwholesome kamma, the wholesome kamma is in such large amounts that this unwholesome kamma will be completely absorbed and you will never see it bear fruit.

Angulimala no doubt committed murder. But you must remember the background story. Angulimala was not a murderer by nature. He did not have a killing tendency in him. He was an innocent boy. His teacher forced him to kill—reluctantly. Just to please his teacher, he killed. And he himself hated it, as he never wanted to kill.

So the Buddha came to understand what this fellow had become—he was so obedient, he would do anything to please his teacher. And for the last of his victims, just to finish his bloody job, he was even thinking of killing his mother to get one last finger for his garland of fingers he had collected from his victims. The Buddha saw this and he saw that if Angulimala killed his mother, he would have committed the most serious kamma. The Buddha wanted to prevent that. He came and taught him Dhamma. And Angulimala confessed he did not want to kill anymore.

As soon as he turned to the Dhamma, he continued diligently to practice and attained enlightenment and there was no chance for all of that unwholesome kamma to bear its results.

DISEASE AND KAMMA

My mother has colon cancer. The doctor told her she has three months to live, so I came here to pray for her. I saw her in my dreams with children around her. She was in so much pain. Is this all her kamma?

Friends, we don't attribute everything to kamma. There are forty-seven diseases mentioned in the Girimananda Sutta, but only one of them is due to kamma. Today there may be something like two hundred thousand different diseases. In those days only forty-seven were listed. But yet only one was caused by kamma.

Therefore, it is not proper for us to attribute sickness or diseases to kamma, especially due to your previous life's kamma. Perhaps due to this life's kamma somebody may have certain diseases. I'm not saying your mother is a case of this. Don't take it personally. Don't tell your mother that Bhante G said, "This is your kamma."

Sometimes people unmindfully, through their ignorance, do certain unwholesome things in life. For instance, somebody drinks and becomes an alcoholic. Eventually that person may suffer cirrhosis of the liver. Or someone smokes cigarettes their entire life and suffers lung problems. Or somebody takes all kinds of illicit drugs and then messes up their mind. These are indeed their kamma and they experience the results in this life.

And there are certain diseases that can be due to a previous life's kamma. But we cannot say with any certainty your mother's cancer is caused by kamma she committed in this life or a previous life.

However, your compassion, your metta, your concern for your mother is a wonderful thing as a daughter or son. You can gain a lot of merit by helping her, by consoling her. Helping in whatever way she needs comfort—that is your own good kamma.

15

A Monk's Life

BECOMING A MONASTIC

Is there a minimum or maximum age for becoming a monastic?

The minimum age is at least seven years old, according to the Vinaya [the rules guiding the monastic life]. A child should be able to chase away a crow that comes and pecks on him, according to a traditional maxim. A seven-year-old child can do that.

There is no maximum or upper limit. However, in our case here in the United States, we don't ordain anybody less than twenty-one years old. We also don't ordain someone who is very old and sick, for instance, in hospice.

So, there is no maximum as long as the person can understand and practice Dhamma and live in accordance with the Dhamma. Another factor to take into consideration is whether the person can stand the discipline involved in the monastic life.

HAIR TODAY, GONE TOMORROW

Why do monks shave their heads?

One reason is to reduce the pride we take in our appearance and make life very simple.

When you have hair, think of how much trouble you have to maintain it! And when you take great pride in your hair, what happens when your hair falls out or becomes gray and brittle as it inevitably must? You feel very disappointed.

Monks and nuns shave their heads and keep the whole issue simple. If you have a dandruff problem, I suggest you just shave your head! Also, you won't have to worry about lice.

Our shaved heads help keep life simple and humble. When we ordain and shave our heads, we are also acknowledging our commitment to a different mode of behavior, a different mode of living. For these reasons we shave our heads.

FROM THEORY TO PRACTICE

Did you ever have a meditation teacher?

I never had a meditation teacher. My teachers were good in theory. They were scholars. They taught the theory of meditation, but they never taught us how to meditate and practice. But my last teacher, he was a great, learned person, and the last part of his life he spent in meditation.

I learned meditation through my own practice because I knew the theory. And that theory is not the commentarial theory but comes from the original Pali suttas, like the Mahasatipatthana Sutta in the Digha Nikaya; the Satipatthana Sutta, Anapanasati Sutta, and the Rahulovada Sutta in the Majjhima Nikaya; the Girimananda Sutta in the Anguttara Nikaya; and and so forth. There are many suttas where meditation is very clearly defined and described.

With this background I started practicing. I think that this approach helped me a lot because I could go directly to the suttas and see what I had been practicing. What we read in the commentaries and subcommentaries are in great detail and those things are there from the commentators' own experience. Each person comes up with his or her own experience and puts it down in writing. So, everybody else may not be able to follow those instructions.

But when we go to the suttas, the suttas are very clear. You can understand it even better from them.

A MONK'S PRACTICE

Your regular meditation practice has an unusual early history. Can you talk a little bit about it?

I became a monk when I was twelve, but I did not start practicing meditation until I was twenty. I had a photographic memory when I was young. At the age of twenty, I lost all of it because I did some chanting for seven days and nights without sleep, without eating and drinking. I exhausted myself and got dehydrated. Then, at the end I lost all my memory.

I became very sick. My parents and teachers tried all kind of treatments, but nothing worked. I had this instinct that if I meditated perhaps it might help. So I meditated, very quietly, when everybody went to sleep at night. I went on meditating for about six to seven months.

Then I began to recognize the alphabet. I had even lost the memory of the alphabet. By that age I had studied Sinhalese, Pali, Sanskrit, English, and Tamil. I could have learned many more languages if I had not lost my memory.

Anyway, I could not recognize the alphabet of any of these languages after my memory loss. Yet after meditating for six or seven months, I began to recognize the Sinhalese alphabet. The experience gave me a lot of trust in meditating.

I went on meditating regularly. Then I was able to read, understand, and comprehend what I read. So, since 1947, when I was twenty years old, I've been meditating. No matter where I am, I meditate. Even on airplanes, I sit cross-legged and meditate.

That is why all my books except my autobiography are on meditation. Because as I meditate more and more, things evolve or unfold within myself that I have not experienced before and have not even put down in writing.

That is how all these books came to be, along with the help of wonderful editors. My writing in English is not that good since English is not my first language. But many people have helped me to polish my English and to publish books.

COMING TO AMERICA

Did you have a dream of coming to the United States?

In fact, I never had any dream to come to anyplace while growing up in Sri Lanka where I was born. When I was a child I had a vision that I wanted to learn English. My brother taught me a few English words, which I repeatedly used. Then my friends and relatives began to tease me. They asked me what I was going to do with these English words. I was an eight- or nine-year-old boy. I simply said, "I'm going to be a monk, I want to learn this language."

I did not know where I would teach, where I would be a monk. But this is exactly what naturally unfolded. I learned reasonably good English, not the best. And I learned Dhamma and Pali and became a monk. And then I went to monastic training.

There was a Buddhist missionary school in Sri Lanka. Only ten monks were selected for the whole island. One of the monks was dismissed after a year and a half and there was a vacancy. The head monk did not want to advertise. If he advertised, thousands of monks would apply, and then he would have to go through the whole selection process.

So, through his friends he searched for a monk. Then he found me, and I entered and had to do the three-year course in one and a half years. At the end of the course, he gave a test. I was the only one who passed.

He sent me to India to serve the Maha Bodhi Society for five years. I worked with the Dalits, these poor Untouchable people. And I fell very, very sick. At the same time, I was invited to go to Malaysia for two years, and I went there. Instead of two years, I worked for them for ten years.

While I was there, an organization in Washington, DC, was going to start a temple. They formed a society and were looking for a monk. They came to know about me and invited me to come and help them for five years. So I helped them for twenty years instead of five years. Then I started the Bhavana Society in the hills of West Virginia.

It was not my dream. My dream was just to learn English and teach. Finally, the whole world opened up.

"Bhante G" Explained

Can you explain your nickname of "Bhante G"?

When I came to the United States people asked me, "How shall we address you?" As monks, we responded that since the word "reverend" is taken by Christians we wanted to use a different title. So, we said to call us "Venerable." Then people asked, "We should address you as 'Vulnerable?!'"

We changed it to "Bhante," which is similar to "reverend." And my last name is a real tongue twister for many: *Gun-a-RA-tana*. So we took the first letter of the last name, and now everyone calls me Bhante G.

Ordaining Women

You tried for many years after the founding of the Bhavana Society to establish it as a place where both men and women could ordain as monks and nuns. Do you ever see women being ordained again at the Bhavana Society, which you have stopped doing?

Traditionally, women monastics never lived together with men. Nuns and monks even in the time of the Buddha never lived in the same monastery. They had separate monasteries. In establishing the Bhavana Society forest monastery, I thought that this is a country where people talk about equal rights. So, why don't I try that? Why don't I ordain both men and women—bhikkhus and bhikkhunis—in the same place, at the same monastery. That is how I began ordaining women here.

I tried for twenty years, with bhikkhus and bhikkhunis living in this place. Of course, they had their separate quarters and kutis or cabins. But we had to come together for morning meditation and meals and evening meditation and so on.

However, there always was friction between bhikkhus and bhikkhunis. Often it would start in the meditation hall, and it would come all the way into the dining hall. It would sometimes go on all day, creating a very unpleasant situation.

After twenty years of experimenting, the situation got so bad, there were some days I was in tears because I could not solve the problem of bhikkhus and bhikkhunis living in close quarters at the same monastery.

You must remember that these people came from regular society. So they brought with them whatever was in the society and in their own home lives and family problems and backgrounds and so on. They brought it here. I did not make them here out of a mold and fit them perfectly together. I cannot do that. Living in this place—even a Buddhist forest monastery—would not solve their problems.

So they expressed this friction between each other. And I was caught in between. Every day in my mailbox beside my door there were notes telling me "So-and-so did such-and-such! What are you going to do about it?" Every day! You know, they are all adults, they are not little children. And I thought they would use their maturity and intelligence to solve their problems with each other. It was very difficult.

Finally, there were too many problems. I don't want to get into details. The nuns slowly left. And then I decided not to ordain both bhikkhus and bhikkhunis here any more—just bhikkhus.

But I fully support the ordination of Theravada nuns. Wherever they ordain nuns, if it's possible for me to travel, I go and give my full support for them to ordain. I've gone to California twice. We went to Germany in 2015 to participate in a bhikkhuni ordination ceremony. I give my full support for their ordinations. But making them live here with bhikkhus is not possible.

WHO WILL SUPPORT YOU?

What are some other lessons you have learned about trying to establish a forest monastery in the West?

The first issue was finding a suitable place. From 1976 until 1982, I was thinking about establishing such a place as this. In 1976, I met Matt Flickstein, and because of his support, in 1982, we founded the Bhavana Society.

Then we wanted to look for cheap land suitable for a meditation center, away from the city, but with good roads leading to it. We found this piece of land by a fluke of luck.

Some of my friends and relatives asked me, "Bhante, why did you select West Virginia out of all these places in the United States to start a meditation center? It has its own reputation. Since you must depend on donations to survive, we fear that you might not even be able to get your food." That made me very uncomfortable to hear!

We had some problems at the beginning, but slowly, slowly, slowly they faded away. Now it is very quiet and there are no problems.

ONE FINGER AND THREE CHAIRS

Can you talk about some of those initial problems in the community with locals accepting such a place in their midst?

Through the years there have been people in the area reminding us they didn't like us being here. But they didn't do anything to hurt us.

When I was still taking my daily walk on the road in front of the monastery after lunch, whenever I saw a vehicle I waved to the person to express my friendliness. Some of them at the beginning never responded. One man not only did not respond but frowned and looked away.

But I never gave up. I went on waving and waving.

Every single day I saw him driving a pickup truck. After about one year this man lifted one finger. I was so happy that this man had changed! After another year he lifted two fingers. Eventually he lifted all five fingers, and one day he stuck his hand out the window and waved to me.

I thought this was wonderful progress! One day I saw his truck parked on a side road. His driver's side door was open and he was smoking a cigarette. I thought this might be the time to go and talk to him.

I looked around and said, "It's a very wonderful day, isn't it?" He sort of grunted a reply, saying, "Yeah." I asked him, "Where do you live, by the way?" He said he lived under the powerlines in a little house. "Aren't you afraid of living under the powerline? I heard it generates radiation."

He dismissed the idea, but then he told me of the day he was driving in a heavy rain and a huge tree fell on his car. He was crushed and had to be cut out of the car by paramedics. They took him to Johns Hopkins Hospital where they said he remained unconscious for almost a year, with most of his bones broken in his body. "When I moved here, I could not lift my finger," he told me.

And that is why he did not move his finger in those first months of waving at him! I was so glad that he was not a bad man. Had I given up on him by his not greeting me at first, I would never have known his story. I never gave up.

So, he became my friend. When I was traveling so often, for months and months, when he did not see me one day he came here to the monastery. "Where is that little brown man? I love him," the man said.

After many years I didn't see him. So, I saw a woman coming from that little house. I said, "You know, there was a gentleman in that house before. I have not seen him for a long time." She said that he was her husband and he had since passed away.

Because of my waving to him, we had become friends instead of remaining strangers. I was so happy for that.

Despite troubles sometimes with neighbors, people would be so kind when they saw me walking on the road. They would wave back or stop and ask me if I needed a ride. Or sometimes they would bring me a bottle of water to drink. When it was going to rain, some drivers would bring me an umbrella.

One day, someone gave me a ride when it was raining. Another time I told one woman, thank you, but I did not need a ride and that I wanted to walk. Instead, she showed up at the monastery with a big box of bananas she had bought for us.

Then there was the time I stopped under a tree and sat on a log to drink some water. A local man named Roger saw me. I have known him since he was about twelve years old. One day when he was maybe thirty years old, he saw me sitting on that log. The next day he stopped and pointed to a tree. A lawn chair was leaned up against it. He said, "You see that chair? That is for you. You sit there and drink your water."

I was so happy at his thoughtfulness.

Another day I came on my walk with a friend. Then, a second chair appeared leaned up against the tree. Another day three of us took the same walk. Roger brought out another chair.

If you pass that tree on the way to the monastery on the road out front, you can see the three chairs. Have you seen them? They are still there. In 2016 he repaired these chairs. Wonderful things happened when I was walking that road!

I feel very good we selected this area in spite of many difficulties. You know, this is my gut feeling. Any difficulties can be overcome if you have patience and compassion. If you are mindful and friendly with people, problems can be solved.

LIFE MINUS HAIR

Why do monks and nuns shave off their eyebrows and head hair? Does it help them to let go?

Yes. Some shave their eyebrows, some don't. Some keep the eyebrows maybe to protect their eyes. I don't know of any other reason. But those who shave their eyebrows now belong to one particular sect. Those who do not belong to another sect. It also makes it easy to keep everything clean.

WEST VS. EAST

Do monks have different ways of teaching Western and Eastern audiences?

In Asian countries, even if you have a little piece of paper when you give a talk, they think you are uneducated. That you don't know your stuff. Everything must come from your mind, from your head. Nothing should come from writing. But here in the West, if you don't have your written paper, people think you are not prepared for your talk. "He does not know anything." See the contrast?

Here in America you have to prepare the talk, writing it down point by point and then reading it. People will appreciate it. "He is educated. He knows his stuff." It is just the other way around in the East. So, sometimes monks in the East, if they don't remember something, they write secret notes and they have a fan. And inside the fan they put the paper so nobody can see it. They see only the fan. They read their notes this way.

They don't like to show people that they have notes because they expect everything to be casual, and their audience expects monks to memorize suttas. When you are asked to give a Dhamma talk in the East, everything must come from your memory. If you write it down, they know you have not memorized the suttas.

COMPARING PRACTICES

What do you see as the differences between Western and Eastern people regarding practice?

I think Western people approach meditation from a very strong background, having tried many things in life, going through many religious practices. They have realized something is missing and they want to find out what it is. Therefore, their approach is very sincere. They are in search of what is missing.

In Asia they take it for granted. It comes to them very naturally. Sometimes they take it too lightly. However, Buddhism has been ingrained in their lives and therefore it comes naturally.

Westerners have to work hard to see what is missing. They also want to study everything in this new religion. This becomes an additional part of their intellectual search. For Eastern people, they don't care very much about learning this Dhamma. They are satisfied with whatever they already know.

FORGIVING EACH OTHER

Do Buddhist monks and nuns practice forgiveness?

Yes. On the day that a Buddhist layperson receives ordination, the very first thing they do is bow down to the preceptor and say, "Forgive me, Venerable Sir, for any offense I have committed. May the venerable receive my merits and please share your merits with me. Excellent! Excellent! Excellent."

On full-moon days and new-moon days monks assemble in the consecrated house called the Uposatha House. And they forgive each other if they have committed any offense against one another in thought, words, and deeds.

At the end of a three-month rainy-season observance, the monks gather again in the assembly hall and invite each other to point out very kindly any offense they have seen, heard, or suspected during the three months of the rains retreat.

A "SUCCESSFUL" BUDDHIST

How do you practice Dhamma every day? You are a most successful Buddhist monk. I want to know your practice, so I can follow in your footsteps.

I don't know whether I am anything different. I don't think I'm as successful as you might think. If you ask me how I practice so as to follow in my footsteps, it would take a very long time. But I will tell you in general what you have to do to be a successful Buddhist.

In the first place, you must accept the Buddha as your guide. Accept the Dhamma as your guide. Accept the Sangha as your guide. Take the Three Refuges very seriously and honestly into your heart and follow the principles of the Buddha, Dhamma, and Sangha. Then you will be a good Buddhist.

All one has to to do is take the Three Refuges. Taking the Five Precepts is additional training.

I myself honestly and sincerely am trying to follow the Buddha's teachings from the bottom of my heart. I try to follow the Dhamma to the best of my ability. I try to follow the noble Sangha to the best of my ability. That's all I do. Whether I am successful or not is another question. I'm trying to be successful.

And if you want to follow me, I would say, don't follow me! Follow the Buddha, the Dhamma, and the Sangha. I am nobody. I don't want anybody to follow me. I want everybody to follow the

Buddha, Dhamma, and Sangha. And to do it honestly, sincerely, and diligently, without a second thought.

MEDITATION RECITATION

Bhante, would you please repeat what you say at the end of the early morning sit, in both Pali and English?

I say first in Pali:

> Natthi jhanam apannassa,
> Panna natthi ajhayato,
> Yamhi jhanan ca pannan ca
> Sa ve nibbanasantike.

Then in English:

> There is no concentration without wisdom,
> no wisdom without concentration.
> One who has both wisdom and concentration
> is close to both peace and emancipation.

LOOKING BACK

How do you see your life's work from the vantage point of your tenth decade of life?

I will say—and this is not just boasting—I have tried to do so much for the world for more than sixty-three years. I have spent my life teaching Dhamma, writing books about the Buddha's teachings, leading retreats around the world. I have no interest in politics or economics or becoming famous. Nothing!

I never put my own picture up in this Bhavana Society library in which we are sitting. Our residents have put them up on their own. But I never wanted to be famous. I want to do something for Buddhism. And I have been completely dedicated to that with my whole heart.

I have written so many books for people to study. They are intended to encourage them to begin to meditate and to deepen their meditation practice in accordance with the Buddha's teachings as well as following the Noble Eightfold Path and exploring Dhamma practice in a deeper way.

I also developed the Vandana book we use here. It is available online as well, full of teachings and readings that people can experience here and then practice with at home—and Wisdom has published a beautiful edition of it under the title *Buddhist Suttas for Recitation*.

Creating the Bhavana Society is the climax of all that effort. I hope that people who come here are able to relax, meditate, and experience peace. And then they go back home and spread that peacefulness and mindfulness in their families and communities. We have had people from around the globe come to Bhavana and then return home to the four corners of the world after that experience.

Every time a person comes here and relaxes and meditates and goes away inspired or renewed, I feel very happy. I think I share part of their happiness, part of their joy, and part of their peace.

So, what I have done so far gives me a lot of satisfaction, and that is a reward for my work. I'm so happy that so many people have benefitted from that work and from their visits to the Bhavana Society. I get letters and emails from people constantly! If they were printed out, they would create quite a large volume.

But that is not what I expected or sought out when I first began teaching as a young monk. Those people who have taken any insights or peace away from all the books and retreats and teachings of the Buddha's Dhamma—that gives me a lot of pleasure and joy and happiness. I have not done as much as I wanted to, but it is how much I can do in my limited capacity.

On my birthday sometimes people ask, what do I wish for? I wish I were fifty years younger and able to do more work for the Dhamma. If anybody can give that, that's OK. But nobody can give that.

A SKELETAL GIFT

At the entrance to Bhavana's meditation hall, there is a full-size skeleton hanging up beside the door. Is this to remind us of impermanence?

Yes! The skeleton you see at the entrance to the meditation hall is to remind all of us that we will end up one day like that.

By the way, that skeleton was a birthday gift. A good friend of mine brought it one day. It was in his car. He asked me to sit in a chair and close my eyes. There was another chair beside me. He brought this skeleton and put it in the chair and took its arm and hand and put it around my shoulder. He asked me to open my eyes. Then, I saw the skeleton was hugging me. I like it very much.

Sometimes adults are afraid of the skeleton. But children like to go and touch it and count the bones. They are not afraid of it. See the difference between the adults' perception and that of children? Children are so open. Adults are often closed. They have all kinds of concepts and ideas that crowd their mind.

PERSONAL MEDITATION EXPERIENCE

What was your own experience, Bhante G, during your last meditation session?

My last meditation session was this morning. It was a wonderful experience. I sat like a rock. It was very peaceful, calm, relaxed. I didn't even feel like getting up. Unfortunately, I had to ring the bell. That was my experience. I wish that you might have that experience!

Monk Selfies

Is it OK to take your photograph with boundless gratitude?

At the end of the retreat we can do that, whether you have boundless or limited gratitude, it doesn't matter!

16

Difficulties and Challenges

THE DIFFICULTY OF MEDITATION

Meditation and metta practice are difficult. Laypeople have jobs, mortgages, children, traffic jams to deal with. With all these distractions and conflicts, is it even possible for a layperson to become an advanced meditator? Do they ever master the jhanas? Enlightenment seems unlikely.

Of course, in the Buddha's time there were not so many traffic jams! No computers, smartphones, and all these things. But even in his time, there were jobs, debts, and so forth. Perhaps not in as complicated a way as we experience these things today, but lay life had its issues then, too.

And yet if you read the Potaliya Sutta in the Majjhima Nikaya, you can see Buddha explain to the layman Potaliya how a person attains these stages. In the Kalama Sutta, he gave a talk to the Kalamas—they were all laypeople. He taught the Four Foundations of Mindfulness to everybody.

We cannot expect a perfect society, a perfect place, a perfect time to meditate and practice metta. With all the imperfections in the world, we can still practice metta and meditation. And imperfections can even be seen as a blessing and an encouragement for us to practice metta.

If everything were perfect, we wouldn't need metta and meditation. Since things are not perfect—there are so many problems in daily life!—we need to practice metta and meditation. Therefore, it is possible—even with traffic jams, paying a mortgage, having a spouse and children and jobs—to practice meditation, metta, and mindfulness.

If we want to find excuses, we can find thousands of excuses not to practice. I ask people, how many excuses can you come up with to avoid practicing metta and meditation? People are not used to giving an excuse *to* practice meditation. But they certainly can come up with excuses *not* to practice!

Friends, if there is a will, there is a way. I think it is not impossible, although it is difficult. But it is not impossible to practice as a layperson. And many, many laypeople have attained the jhanas and enlightenment.

Attached to Meditation

If you are too attached to meditation practice, can this lead to an egotistical attitude?

When we practice mindfulness sincerely and with understanding, then slowly and gradually we chip away at the notions and habits of the ego.

In our meditation practice, what do we normally see? We see everything is always changing. Everything is impermanent. Everything is permanently impermanent! Everything—without any exception! Everything is marked with three characteristics. You will never miss them if you really practice mindfulness. What are the three things? Everything is impermanent—anicca. Everything is unsatisfactory—dukkha. And everything has a selfless nature—anatta.

Things are always changing, changing, changing. And since everything is impermanent, nothing can be ultimately satisfactory.

The Buddha's aim was not to say things to please others. He wished to tell the truth. Truth, in the Buddha's eye, is the sweetest of all the sweets. Among all the tastes, the best taste is the truth. That is not what we normally hear, right? The truth is bitter, we say. But if our mind is pure, clean, and unbiased, we really will enjoy the truth.

The third characteristic of all things is their selfless nature. Deep down at a subconscious level there is something we want to keep permanent and immutable. But within this ever-changing entity we live in, we can never find something permanent and everlasting. Everything is continually changing.

In mindfulness practice these are the three things we invariably see. There's not one single thing in our entire personality that we find to be permanent. When we see impermanence, unsatisfactoriness, and selflessness, there is no reason for one to become proud, attached, or egotistical. Why? There is no ego. In true mindfulness training, one learns this.

So, this is a very important question. If someone honestly practices mindfulness, one develops morality and sees these three characteristics in one's self. You may not see all three at once. It is not easy, since we are trained to think there is an ego. And to let go of it, not to accept it all of a sudden—that is very difficult. In the time of the Buddha, it was just like now.

Once I wrote a paper, and I got one of my friends to edit it. He took the paper and disappeared for about six months. After six months he came back, and as soon as I saw him I remembered my paper. I said, "Let's go for a walk." Even during our walk, I did not want to bring up the paper. I thought I might hurt his feelings. But I finally raised the subject. "You must have been very busy and probably didn't have time to see my paper." He said, "Bhante, I read the paper. But when I came across one sentence that said there is no self, no ego, I got so angry, I threw away the paper!"

I never saw the paper again. This man was very angry. How can we live without self? That is the core of our experience. What are we—just a mere bottomless abyss? How can we exist? This is a very normal reaction people have when they hear this. This is the way we have been trained and conditioned.

In mindfulness meditation don't try to fool yourself and white-wash things and sweep something under the rug. Friends, in mindfulness practice you've got to accept the whole package!

So when we really, honestly practice, then there is no room for us to become egotistical or to become attached to the practice. Attachment even to the practice also will fade away if we practice honestly and sincerely.

THE WEIGHT OF ANGER

The first verses in the Dhammapada, "The Pairs," talk about how, "If with an impure mind a person speaks or acts, suffering follows him like the wheel that follows the foot of the ox." What does this verse signify?

Remember the cart that the ox pulls. The cart is not an empty cart. It is full of supplies. It is very heavy. The ox that pulls the cart is not doing it with pleasure, joy, and happiness. When he pulls the cart, he has to drag it up a very rugged, rough, winding, often uphill road. And the driver also is not a compassionate person. Given all the conditions, when the ox pulls the cart he does not enjoy it. It is very heavy on his shoulders.

Similarly, whenever you create hate or anger in the mind, you are the one who experiences its weight more than anybody else. Therefore, you've got to think before you say anything or take any action. Think about whether you are saying something with hatred, anger, or delusion to hurt somebody.

If you do so, you yourself will suffer more than the person toward whom you aimed your anger, causing pain and suffering. This is the message we have to remember from the first stanza of the Dhammapada.

JUST PRACTICE

When practicing metta for myself sometimes I feel numb, and at other times, vulnerable and wounded. I try to extend metta to those parts of myself that are calling for care and attention. Yet the teachings say there is no self. This feels confusing. How do we honor these feelings while still not clinging to self?

"Self" is a very common, conventional term. We use it all the time. In the conventional usage of "self," it is very important. In fact, without the word we cannot communicate. Therefore, it is important for that purpose. But in reality, it does not exist.

For instance, I ask you, what is today? Saturday, isn't it? Have you seen Saturday? Have you touched Saturday? Have you heard Saturday? No. But we use the term. Tomorrow is Sunday, yesterday was Friday. We use these terms very conveniently and practically. Similarly, longitude, latitude, or January and February. Have you seen January or February? We use these names, but we have never seen or touched them.

So, how can we prove they are there? There is no way. Society agrees we call this particular period of time Saturday. We all agree and we use it. But in reality, there is no Saturday, Sunday, Monday, and so on. Remember this.

Similarly, "self" is such an important term that we have to use it. But in reality, it does not exist. When we practice metta we practice metta for all beings. And for our entire being. Because suffering exists in our entire being.

Suffering is also a conventional thing because it is impermanent. This impermanent thing I use for the benefit of that impermanent thing. Just like this convention that we use for that convention. Then, there is no problem.

I would not worry about nonself, or even self. Just practice metta.

PRESENT-MOMENT AWARENESS

True or false? If I see things in the past or future while meditating, does that mean that vipassana doesn't have to be in the present moment?

It doesn't matter whether you feel it is in the past or future—it happens now, in the present moment. So vipassana really is present-moment awareness.

When experiences from our past come up, normally people don't look at them as past experiences and put them into a bundle labeled "past experiences." The problem is that people don't do that—they go into details and then they keep thinking, thinking, thinking. That is where they get into trouble.

So, I suggest you put such thoughts into one bundle, whether it is thoughts of the past or future. For, you see, both categories of thought—thoughts of the past and of the future—actually happen in the present moment.

And the present moment is very easy to deal with. Look at the mind in the present moment. Notice what happens in the present moment.

WHO SHOULD NOT MEDITATE?

Is there anyone who shouldn't meditate or for whom it will do more harm than good?

Perhaps if somebody is under the influence of alcohol or drugs or mentally not sound and stable, then that person should not meditate because they can get into all kind of mental states and meditation could be harmful.

Forgiveness and Meditation

How can we develop or cultivate forgiveness for someone who has wronged us?

Forgiveness is a part of meditation. When we meditate we definitely must learn to relax, and this is the reason we recommend metta meditation at the very beginning.

In meditation you can remember all sorts of things, especially if somebody has wronged you, which may have left a deep scar in the mind. That might become prominent in your meditation and you find you cannot meditate well. Therefore, in order to make your meditation easier, start the practice with metta.

The person who has wronged you may have done so out of their own suffering. If you think you are innocent and have not done anything to hurt the person and still the person hurts you, it means that person has some suffering. Therefore, if you practice metta it will be easier for you to forgive the person, to forgive the wrong.

Through meditation we come to understand impermanence. This is my central theme these days—and not because I am already old! Even you are impermanent! It is good for even young people to think of impermanence and that we are moving along an impermanent road.

Therefore, when you remember somebody who has wronged you or hurt you, then you think, well, this moment is impermanent, the situation is impermanent. The words and deeds of the person are impermanent. Those things are all gone—it happened in the past. That is why I say, don't get caught up in the details of the past.

See the impermanence of the situation. Also forgive this person because the person himself or herself may have problems.

One thing to consider is that if you keep nourishing the root of anger or nourishing the root of hatred toward that person, then your anger and hatred will continue to be strong.

That is why I say look at your mind. If you can forgive and let go of that hatred, then you will be very comfortable and it will be easier to forgive. Forgiveness and patience are considered to be among the highest practices in Buddha's teaching.

LEARNING FROM THE BREATH

One day while meditating, I was completely absorbed in the breathing process. I was not aware of my surroundings, and at last the man closing the door to the meditation hall asked me to leave. I came out to my car and could not drive at first as my mind was still absorbed in the breathing process. After that episode, when normalcy returned, I felt a sense of well-being in the body, which I had never felt. I regretted not being able to continue my meditation. Then, about five years later, I had an experience in which I felt I was about to die and only my breathing was there. The feeling of "me" or "I" was not there. I was so afraid that I was going to die instantly. I reasoned out that, well, I am still breathing, hence I could revert back to my usual state. A few minutes later, I regained the feeling of "I" or "me" and things seemed back to normal. My question is, what are those experiences that are beyond my control?

Both experiences you have explained are not unusual. Stay fully alert and mindful, paying total attention to your experience— breath, contact, feeling, perceptions, thoughts, and awareness. If you are not conscious of anything around you except the breath, pay attention to it and notice its rising and falling along with the feeling.

You will notice the feeling of the breath is also rising and falling.

Don't try to think or say "I am breathing" or "I am feeling." Without verbalizing or conceptualizing, simply become fully aware of the rising and falling of your breath and feeling.

If the mind is wandering, then become aware of the fact that the mind has not really gone anywhere. It simply brings up anything you have stored in your memory bank from your childhood into the current moment. Just become aware of the memories' impermanent nature.

When you gain concentration, you will notice the impermanence of anything you experience. You will notice that nothing is there for you to cling to. Everything is slipping away. Any attempt to grasp something is a futile effort, for your mind cannot grasp anything.

Just imagine that you are trying to balance a mustard seed on the tip of a moving needle. You will never be able to do it! Similarly, since everything is fading away and disappearing, your mind cannot hold on to anything. This is how you learn to let go of any experience—pleasant, unpleasant, or neutral.

If you cannot gain what you have lost, don't worry about it. What you have experienced is not permanent events. You will have similar experiences again. Simply don't force yourself to get them back.

HANDLING ANGER

Anger causes us to act in unskillful ways. How can we deal with it arising?

It doesn't matter how beautiful you are. You can become ugly very quickly when you get angry. Anytime people criticize you—even if someone makes very constructive, positive criticism—you may get upset and angry. At that moment, look at your face in the mirror. You look very ugly!

It is not only in this life. Because of these unwholesome, unskillful habits—akusala sila—you build up these habits. So even in your next life, you will look ugly and be unpleasant looking.

The remedy for this is to be very patient, relaxed, and comfortable. Try to understand if somebody criticizes you. If somebody becomes very critical about your behavior and activities, just listen very carefully, very mindfully. Then you will see yourself grow relaxed. You will not look very ugly and unpleasant in this life.

The same thing will happen after your death. In the next life you will be a very pleasant, very peaceful-looking person. It all depends on what you do at that moment when somebody criticizes you.

So, this is very beautiful and practical advice Buddha has given us: don't get too upset and angry and don't try to hate others when they criticize us.

Self-Inquiry

Does Buddhism claim that the only way to reach a state of freedom from the rebirth process is through vipassana meditation? Will self-inquiry not get you to that state?

When you do "self-inquiry" you are practicing vipassana meditation. That is exactly what we do in vipassana meditation. We honestly look at ourselves. With no biases, no pretense, we look at our own body, feelings, perception, volitional formations, and consciousness—the Five Aggregates.

In this way, we come to understand impermanence, suffering, and nonself—anicca, dukkha, anatta, respectively. This is vipassana meditation. Nobody can be free from suffering without a perfect realization of anicca, dukkha, and anatta.

Measuring Improvement

How does one measure improvement in the practice? Sometimes it is easy to be satisfied with the mere act of meditation.

How does one push personal practice to keep it engaging and challenging and evolving?

You can measure the improvement by looking at your own state of mind. Friends, sitting on a cushion and just focusing the mind only on the breath and falling asleep and getting up after one hour is not meditation at all! Ask yourself, "Have I been meditating honestly and sincerely or have I been sleeping on the cushion? And how often do I meditate?"

If you meditate only once in a blue moon—which happens only once every three years, by the way—and expect to attain enlightenment, it will never happen. If you meditate every day, more than once—at least twice day—only then can you assess your attainment and improvement. Then you can see.

If you started five years ago, recall how you felt back then. How emotional you were, how angry you were, how impatient you were, how unhealthy you were, and so forth. Compare it to today. See how you are now. Are you still impatient? Are you still angry? Are you still greedy? Are you still restless?

Compare. There is no machine to precisely measure your improvement as a result of meditation. Perhaps a biofeedback system could give some external measurements. But that is only external. You have to measure yourself, assessing your own practice.

Ask yourself, "How often do I meditate? For how long?" If you keep a record of it very clearly you can see how regular your practice is. Encourage yourself!

Friends, every moment we meditate—every moment we meditate!—a certain amount of difficulties and defilements fade away.

HANDLING HATRED

Sometimes I feel very strong feelings of anger about some individuals, even to the point of hatred. How do we deal with such strong feelings?

When hatred arises within yourself, you recognize its existence. Then you deal with it. You need to do something about it. You try to get rid of this hatred.

We can feel the impact of hatred within ourselves. When you feel the impact of hatred you really feel it in the body. You feel the palpitation in your chest, it increases your blood pressure. You feel how hatred creates a very unpleasant and painful experience. You feel how it destroys your peace. It makes you very uncomfortable.

Hatred affects the body in so many ways. This is how to think about the disadvantages of feeling such a strong emotion as hatred.

Then you have to analyze the aggregates. Ask yourself, "Which of the aggregates of that person do I hate?" The form of that person? Or the feeling of the person? Or the perceptions of that person? Or the thought of that person, or the state of mind of the consciousness of that person? Is that what you hate?

Or do you hate the situation that precipitated hatred in you?

Then you will see, when you look analytically at the situation, you will really see you don't hate any one of those single things. You may hate the situation. But after some time you will see that the situation that precipitated the hatred is gone. It is not permanent. Then you know that you had hatred at that time, but now the situation is gone. You don't have any reason to sustain that hatred within yourself. That is one way of dealing with hatred.

Another way to get rid of feelings of hatred is to think of someone who is greater than yourself. In our case, we always think of the Buddha as our model, as he is one who managed to get rid of his hatred totally, never to return again.

There is a very humorous incident in the Buddha's life. This incident is important to remember when we are dealing with hatred. There was a man whose name was Akkosaka, which simply means "one who doesn't get angry." But this man was the embodiment of anger. This man got angry at every tiny little thing. He got angry with people for not getting angry.

That is why he was angry with the Buddha, as recounted in the Akkosaka Sutta (Samyutta Nikaya, 7.2). He was angry with the Buddha for never seeming to get angry.

One day he thought of provoking the Buddha to see what he looked like when he got angry. He went and scolded him, using all sorts of abusive words, calling him names. He scolded him until his vocabulary was exhausted. The Buddha listened to him very mindfully and quietly.

At the end, he asked this man, "Sir, do you have friends and relatives?"

He said, "Yes, of course, I have many friends and relatives."

"Do you visit them?" the Buddha asked.

"Yes, I visit them very often," said Akkosaka.

"Do you carry any gifts to give them?" the Buddha went on.

"Surely," the man replied. "I never go empty-handed when I visit them."

The Buddha then said, "Suppose when you give a gift to a friend, they don't accept it. What would you do?"

Akkosaka said, "I'd take it home and enjoy it myself."

Then, the Buddha said, "Similarly, you gave me a gift. I don't accept it, it is all yours. You take it home and enjoy it yourself."

You see? He turned everything back to Akkosaka in such a humorous way. And he was able to do that because he did not get angry.

We have to remember that when we try to deal with our own anger. This is a beautiful story to remember.

HANDLING HATRED, PART 2

But anger and hatred can be such strong emotions. How do we let such emotions dissipate?

When we tell stories to children, we tell very simple, beautiful tales. This story is very simple and good not only for children, but I'd like to tell it now for you also. It is a story of a quarrelsome fox.

This fox always wanted to quarrel. One day he found a peaceful fox. This quarrelsome fox told the peaceful fox, "What are you doing sitting there doing nothing? Come, let's fight!"

The peaceful fox said, "There's no reason to fight."

The quarrelsome fox said, "I'll give you a reason! Let me go and bring a rock and put it in front of us. And I will tell you this rock is mine and you say it is yours. Then I will get angry because I brought the rock and said it was mine. Then we can fight."

So the quarrelsome fox got the rock and put it in front of the peaceful fox. "This rock is mine!" he cried. Then the peaceful fox responded, "If it is yours, you take it!" So, the quarreling was over before it began!

If your motive is to be peaceful, you can always find a motive to be peaceful. If you always think of not getting angry, you will always find a way *not* to get angry.

Therefore, when we have anger, we have to think of a way of getting rid of it. Or we have to think of a way not to get angry in the future. Always keep this thought active in your mind. When a situation arises that might lead to anger, we latch on to that thought of peacefulness and bring it to our mind and stay calm.

By cultivating loving-friendliness you are able to get rid of your anger or defuse it. But as soon as you get angry, don't try to cultivate loving-friendliness. Your mind is not yet ready. You are furious, burning with the flame of anger.

As you calm down, as you become aware of your mental state, then, when you cultivate loving-friendliness, your hatred will disappear.

When hatred arises you deal with it like this and let it go. After some time, if it arises in the mind again, be mindful of it. When it disappears, you realize, "Hey, my hatred is gone, it is no longer there! I can proceed with the practice of dana, or generosity."

THE SUPREME BLESSING

How do we avoid people who act in unwholesome and foolish ways?

Sometimes people ask, how can we disassociate from such people? You will have the tendency to pick up their behavior. Trying to help these foolish people is not going to help. You will be dragged into the same pit. Therefore, the Buddha said, until you attain enlightenment, don't associate with them. Or if you have good willpower and have trained yourself for a long time in practicing Dhamma, then you will be strong enough to teach them.

In the Mangala Sutta the Buddha was asked to describe the supreme blessing. He said don't associate with fools—leave them alone. That is very good advice. There is no end of correcting them. They will do the same foolish thing over and over again. If you want to clear your mind, don't associate with them.

The Buddha was asked how to recognize a fool. Buddha said the fool speaks untruths, tells lies, and always steals. A fool is one who is very arrogant and very angry. A fool thinks that everyone else in the world is just like dirt. They have no respect for anybody.

And a fool is one who gets angry all the time. A fool is one who does not care for oneself, does not care for this life, does not care for the next life. When we associate with the fool, that is another condition for cultivating the three unwholesome characteristics of word, thought, and deed.

The Buddha said, try to find a good friend, a spiritual friend, a kalyana mitta. When you mindfully reflect on what is happening to you in your own life, you see you are going upstream or downstream—and by downstream the meaning is you are going down the drain in your spiritual practice.

But when you are making progress, that is because you are associating with good friends.

UNSKILLFUL MEANS

Is it ever OK to use unskillful means to achieve wholesome results?

No. We are not supposed to use any unwholesome means to achieve wholesome results. Unwholesome means that it leads to unwholesome results. Say, for instance, you plan to support your parents through stealing or robbing someone. You support them but you create a lot of unwholesome kamma. By supporting your parents you will have some good kamma. But the way you do that is very, very unwholesome. So you acquire two types of kamma.

Supporting your parents is a good thing. But the merits will not be as great if you support them in an unskillful way, using illegally acquired things. You have weakened your efforts to support your parents by gaining things unlawfully.

The Buddha never advised anybody to acquire anything by wrong means to achieve wholesome ends. This means the mind should be very clean and pure when giving. What you acquire should be acquired with right means, otherwise the result of your dana, of your giving, will not be strong.

A THIEF'S DONATION

Suppose a criminal offers dana to the Sangha. Should we accept it even though the person giving is a criminal and might have gotten the dana by bad means?

If we know that he's a criminal and has stolen something from somebody and wants to give it to us—if we know this—then we should not accept it. If a criminal stole food from a store and someone told us that, and the next day we are presented the food as dana, we will tell him we cannot accept it because we had heard that he got the food by illegal means. If you accept it you will encourage him to do the same thing.

LAZINESS AND MEDITATION

What are the teachings on discipline? Is it ever acceptable to stray from daily practice because of laziness?

No excuses! No way. I would never recommend this. Always try to find excuses *to* meditate. Don't try to find excuses *not* to meditate. That means it is so important that it is sort of a mandatory requirement. I would not advise anyone to stray from the practice of daily meditation because of laziness. Laziness, sleepiness, and drowsiness are something you have to overcome.

17

Benefits of Practice

CLEANSING THE MIND

I do chanting every day in Pali—the Metta Sutta for my mother and father, animals and spirits. Do you think they all receive merit for this?

Honestly, we practice metta, we chant suttas, we practice meditation to cleanse our minds, to get rid of the defilements from our minds. We do these things to make us calm, relaxed, and peaceful and to develop our insight and understanding and liberate ourselves from suffering. We do this for ourselves.

With that state of mind, you can wish that all other living beings may also experience peace, happiness, and liberation. Whether they receive these merits or not is not your concern. It is not possible, after all, for you to sit in one place and cause another person in another place to attain liberation. But you can wish them peace, happiness, and so forth. And that would increase your merit.

The way to share merit with a living person is to go to the person in person. Or these days you can use the Internet to share your practice. You may say, "Mom, I meditated today for one hour. It was so peaceful. I practiced metta for all living beings. You should also consider meditating."

Your mother will be happy to hear that you are meditating. That is the way she shares your merit—you create an opportunity for her to be happy. Write a letter. Email. Telephone. Text. Whatever!

The Four Unlimitables

How do we focus on loving-friendliness, compassion, appreciative joy, and equanimity—the Four Unlimitables?

In order to obtain the First Jhana, you have to overcome hindrances. One is anger, which is just the opposite of metta, or loving-friendliness. When we overcome resentment and anger our mind becomes very relaxed, calm, and peaceful. Then metta arises in your mind naturally.

The thought of nonhatred triggers metta—that means it comes to us naturally. When metta arises, noncruelty arises. When metta and karuna or compassion arise, then whatever success anyone else gains, the thought of appreciation arises in our mind, not jealousy.

It begins even from the First Jhana. It arises naturally as the hindrances fade away. Because as we naturally let go of our resentment and anger, then we feel that the whole world is one breathing, feeling unit. That is how it happens. No negative thought can arise at that stage because the hindrances have totally subsided.

The Power of Thought

How can we generate happiness for ourselves?

You don't have to look for somebody outside to make you happy. You can make yourself happy. All you have to do is look in your mind. There are so many beautiful things you can think and beautiful words you can utter if you think with compassion, loving-friendliness, joy, peace, and happiness.

When you see somebody in the morning, with a very pure, clean, compassionate heart, you say, "Good morning! How are you?" And in the evening when you see somebody going home, you simply say, "Have a nice evening! Have a good rest." If you say this with a sincere, honest heart, see how much happier you will be. You can think of your words later on and you will be very happy you made somebody happy for a short period of time.

This happiness did not come from the person you spoke to. It comes from your own mind. Because you have a very clear, pure state of mind. Whenever you do something with a clear, pure state of mind, the Buddha said to repeat it again and again and again.

Don't think your thoughts don't have a powerful effect. Whenever you cultivate a thought again and again, that becomes a habit. That is called *kusala sila* in Pali. When you cultivate this wholesome habit, you will do it almost automatically.

Where did that happiness come from? It does not come from outside. You create it in your own mind. And then you express it through your thoughts, words, and deeds. And that's what we have to do. Then we will always be happy.

It is just like your own shadow that follows you all the time, very faithfully, without departing even for a second. Wherever you go, you have your shadow. Do you feel any weight from your shadow? No!

I think this message is a very important one for you to remember.

No Greed, No Need

Western consumer society is all about achieving happiness by acquiring things and seeking out new sensations and experiences. In the Buddha's teaching we are told to let go of so many things. Can you talk about this difference?

What do we look for and search for? We search to satisfy our greed. We research the Internet to satisfy our needs and desires. But when there is no greed and no need, what is the use of searching for such things?

When we come to that kind of understanding and wisdom, then we become disenchanted with this constant urge for pleasure and the gratification of our incessant desires. Because by letting go, you get everything. It is sort of paradoxical. By collecting, by accumulating, you lose everything because you experience the inevitable disappointment of the loss of your possessions as they age and break down, as they must.

But notice the effect when we practice seeing the impermanence at the heart of all things. When we develop mindfulness of impermanence, we reach permanence. That is Nibbana.

By seeing unsatisfactoriness and suffering, we come to a painless state that is minus suffering. By practicing meditation on death, we come to a deathless state.

All of these are very meaningful paradoxes. When we practice mindfulness, we look at our own mental states. By letting go, we can attain peace and happiness.

So, friends, mindfulness meditation, insight meditation, Buddhist meditation—whatever you call it—through such a practice we peel off, we remove layers and layers and layers of mental impurities until we reach the purity of peace and harmony.

By analyzing things, by thinking about them alone, it will not happen. So I encourage you to meditate. This is a subject that will never go out of date! It is always current and fresh.

I hope you will enjoy your practice. I don't mean enjoy it as if you are going to a party. That is a different type of enjoyment. That kind of enjoyment just makes you excited, agitated, and ultimately tired. The enjoyment of meditative practice makes you refreshed and calm, peaceful and happy.

Therefore, seek out this sort of enjoyment—the enjoyment of peace, the enjoyment of lasting happiness.

TAKING REFUGE

It feels unfair that I can come to a place like this and take refuge in the Buddha, the Dhamma, and the Sangha when others cannot.

It is good that you can go and take refuge and practice in a most sincere way. Then, through your behavior, someone who follows you or observes you will think you have been doing something different, something wholesome and beneficial. That person observing you may be inspired by your behavior. In that way, we can help others to take refuge.

But deliberately, on our own, we cannot force others to go for refuge. That is not our way of practicing Dhamma. So we let others follow our example. But if somebody asks you questions about taking refuge in the Buddha, the Dhamma, and the Sangha, then you can explain it in the way you understand it.

18

Generosity and Dana

GENEROSITY

What are the benefits of generosity?

When you share things with other people, you may think you are losing what you have given away. In fact, you are enriching yourself. You become rich in your heart. If you don't share, you become stingy. It is a samsaric habit.

I remember when I was in Sri Lanka as a boy, I used to travel on the bus. A beggar came onto the bus from one end and went down the aisle, stretching his hand to both sides, begging for one penny. Those days, one penny was very big money!

He stretched his hand to this side, and nobody gave him any money. He stretched his hand to the other side, no one gave him any money. So finally he walked out the back door of the bus, saying, "I have the habit of asking. You people do not have any habit of giving. So I'm leaving."

This is a samsaric habit. Once we learn to give, it is almost irresistible that we want to give. The giver becomes rich in heart, rich in wealth in this life. And he or she becomes rich in the next life, in heart as well as in material wealth. That is wonderful, practical advice that Buddha gave to all of us.

SIGNIFICANCE OF DANA

What is the significance of dana, or generosity, in Buddhist practice?

In Buddhism there are either ten perfections or six perfections. In the Mahayana tradition there are six perfections while in the Theravada tradition there are ten perfections. The number one of them is dana, or generosity. And there are three pillars of Buddhism. These are the three cornerstones, sort of like a tripod. One of them is dana. So dana is a very important thing.

Why is it so emphasized? What is the significance of it?

In the Buddhist tradition dana, or generosity, is a fundamental principle of our liberation from saṁsara, the endless round of rebirth. What is the opposite of dana? Greed or stinginess. Stinginess is an unwillingness to share what one has. When we are stingy, we build a fence around what we have. We want to protect it. The more we try to protect what we have, the more insecure we feel and the more nervous we feel. We don't want to share our wealth.

Stinginess comes from the greed to possess, to hold on to things. In vipassana meditation we always mention that holding on to things is inevitably going to be very painful. And letting go of things is very relieving, relaxing, and comfortable.

So, fundamentally, for this reason, for our own piece of mind, generosity is emphasized in Buddhism. You know the word *Nibbana*—the *ni* means absence and *vana* means craving. You could say the absence of craving is called Nibbana.

Sometimes people wonder why, if dana is so important, is it not mentioned in the Noble Eightfold Path? I even have read a great scholar who has written an article on dana and he mentioned that dana is not listed as one of the thirty-seven Factors of Enlightenment. There are thirty-seven factors to attain enlightenment, and dana is not mentioned! The writer asked why.

In fact, if we mindfully and carefully investigate the Noble Eightfold Path, we can see dana very clearly mentioned in different words. For example, the phrase used in the Noble Eightfold Path is *samma sankapa*, or Right Intention. What is Right Intention? It is the thought of letting go of things, of renunciation. *Avyapadda sankhapa* is freedom of hatred. The third is *avihimsa sankapa*, the thought of nonharming. So, the thought of generosity, of loving-friendliness and compassion make up Right Intention. This is a very important factor.

The first step on the Noble Eightfold Path is Right View and the second step is Right Intention. The thought of letting go of things does not really mean letting go only of material things. That is, of course, an expression of generosity. But in a real deep and fundamental sense, generosity is the thought. Therefore, when we practice generosity there are certain conditions to make generosity real, actual generosity.

We have to have a very clear state of mind before we give something away, both while we give something away and after we have given it. Why do I want to give? To have my name listed on a wall? Or to become famous? Or to win friends? Or to receive some favor? Or just because everybody gives so I also want to give something?

No, we have to keep in our mind when we give something that we are cleansing our mind of attachment, clinging, craving, and holding on to our things. We are minimizing and reducing our greed.

You know, if you clench your fist very hard, you feel pain. If you have long fingernails you may even hurt your palm if you press too hard. But if you open your hand and let go of this tightness, then you feel comfortable.

Similarly, the harder we hold on to things, the more painful it is. As we let go of that grip, we experience relief of tension. And that is exactly what happens when one attains enlightenment.

Another word for the attainment of enlightenment means to lay down the weight, the heavy burden that we carry in our hearts and minds. That burden keeps us down, it keeps us weighted to the ground. We cannot move easily because the weight is so heavy. When we let go of this weight, we feel very light.

So, enlightenment means lightening your heart and mind. Not only lightening it but brightening it. That is what we want to achieve.

Therefore, keeping that goal in mind, we practice generosity. Just to relieve our own mind. Before we give away something, we have to keep this in mind—I give something to reduce this greed in my mind.

When we give something away with reluctance, we may gain some merit. But it is not as great as having pure thoughts while giving. After giving, we should not have regret, "Ah, I should have thrown a party with that donation and could have celebrated with my friends!"

This is another reason many people find not to give. Maybe I give a couple of dollars to somebody. The next moment you see the person walk into a liquor store or that person may take my money to go gamble. You will be utterly disappointed that this man or woman is using your money for wrong things.

You should never be disappointed! Because of your disappointment, after giving you will not be able to enjoy the results of giving.

When you try to share your things with somebody, don't think of the quality and attributes of the recipient.

Before the Buddha attained enlightenment, he was called Bodhisatta. He practiced dana. He achieved the perfection of dana. Nobody else was as pure and compassionate as he was. He was so full of loving-friendliness. Whenever he gave his gifts, everyone else was inferior to him. If he had been generous with his time and with his gifts only to a perfect person, he would never have found that person.

Therefore, when you give away things, don't look for perfect recipients.

KINDS OF DANA

Are there different kinds or levels of dana?

There is individual dana and communal dana. *Puggala dana* means giving to individuals. *Sangha dana* means giving to the whole community. When you give something to an individual—no matter how great the individual is—that is still an individual. And the merits you gain could be conditional merits by giving to an individual.

Why? When you give to an individual, automatically you may think, "To whom am I giving this? Is it a friend or relative? What do I get in return? If I don't gain anything in return, why should I give?"

But if you give to the whole community, you don't know who receives it. Not knowing who receives your gift is more meritorious for you than knowing who receives it. So giving things to a community is more meritorious than giving to an individual.

Dana can be practiced at many different levels. There is the level of perfection (*parami*), higher perfection (*upaparami*), and highest perfection (*paramatthaparami*).

One time, in one of the many stories about the Buddha's past lives as a Bodhisatta, he was practicing the perfection of dana. He saw a tigress who was very hungry. For several days she could not find food and she had several cubs. Finally, she was going to eat her own cubs, and the Bodhisatta saw that. He saw the tigress with the cubs in a cave and thought, "This is the best time for me to sacrifice my own life to save these little cubs." So he immediately jumped into the cave.

You know what happened? This was just an illusion. This was a creation of the king of deities to test the perfection of generosity of the Bodhisaṭṭa. As soon as he jumped into the cave, the tigress disappeared and the Bodhisatta found himself quite alive. But the thought that occurred in his mind at that moment was a wonderful thought.

I will tell you another story that occurred in Washington, DC, in 1982. On Friday, January 13—a very auspicious date—an Air Florida jet crashed into the Potomac River. It was an icy winter day. Helicopters came and TV crews were right there. They began to telecast the rescue.

We watched on television as a helicopter came and brought a rope to rescue people. The first time they dropped the rope, a man in the water directed it to another person. And the second time, when the rope came he gave it to a woman and the helicopter rescued her. The third time the helicopter dropped the rope, this man was gone and he was drowned. He saved two lives.

I think he was a bodhisatta born in America, practicing *dana parami*—the perfection of giving. That story struck me very powerfully. I will always remember this man's generosity. When we see a situation in which we can sacrifice our life without any ulterior motive—that's the highest perfection of dana.

And there have been many such people who stood for noble principles. During World War II, when many millions of Jews were massacred or tortured, there also were many wonderful Germans who rescued and saved some Jews.

These are people who under very dire circumstances and difficult situations stood up for their principles. They risked their lives, but they never gave up their principles. They loved human life and were ready to sacrifice even their own lives.

THE BENEFITS OF DANA

The Buddha spoke highly of the benefits of giving, or dana. Can you talk about why he stressed this?

The Buddha said, "If you know as much as I know about the benefits of giving, you would not eat even the last morsel of food without sharing it with somebody else." This is a wonderful statement. It is actually the giver who enjoys the gift and becomes happier than the one who receives it.

I like to tell the story of a man who lived in Sri Lanka in 1944 during World War II. That was a time when food was rationed. Every person got a small quantity of food, just enough for one person. This man thought of giving dana to ten monks. The quantity he received was hardly enough for himself. Yet his intention of giving was so great.

He collected maybe one teaspoonful of rice every day, one half teaspoon of dal every day, a little pinch of salt and chili, one small dry fish, and so forth. He collected this food for the entire year. Then he had enough to give dana to ten monks.

The problem was in finding the recipients because that was when the Japanese had dropped a bomb in Colombo, so all the monks had left the area.

This man was so intent on finding monks that he went to a bus stop and he saw a monk coming to catch the bus. From a distance, he said, "Venerable Sir! Please help me." The monk said, "I have nothing to give you!" The man ran after the monk, and the monk ran away from him.

Finally, this man said, "Venerable Sir, I want to give you something. I want to give dana to ten monks." The monk said, "You are really crazy. How can we find ten monks in the city right now?"

The man said he had a car. So, they went to many temples and finally found ten monks. This man gave this dana, the food he had had so much difficulty in collecting through the year. He was not a rich man and it was not an easy time to give dana. He was so happy.

One day, I went to Houston to participate in the opening ceremony of a new temple. This new temple was donated by a couple who came to this country as students. They did not have much

money. They had a baby and could not even afford to get a babysit-
ter. So they brought the baby to the temple with a little milk. The
monks in the temple took care of the baby. In the evening the couple came to temple and picked up the baby.

After several years this man became a doctor. Then he invented a
catheter to use for heart bypass operations. A company bought the
patent and gave him 10 million dollars. The couple bought a piece of
land for the temple and donated it to the monks who had cared for
their baby. I was invited to the opening ceremony of the temple in
1991. The man who had given dana to ten monks in Sri Lanka also
was there, as he was the father of this young woman who married
the man who became a doctor. The man told me the story of how he
gave dana at that most difficult time in 1944 in Sri Lanka. Even at
that time, in 1991, tears of joy were rolling from his eyes.

See? It was forty-seven years later, and he was telling me the
story—still he enjoys the giving. This is why the Buddha said if you
know the benefit of giving, you will not eat even the last morsel of
food without sharing it with somebody else. And this man is a very
good example of how beneficial giving is.

Dhamma Dana

What does *Dhamma dana* signify?

There is a saying in the Dhammapada: "The gift of Dhamma excels
all other gifts."

A religious place, a temple or shrine, a monastery or meditation
center, stands for peace. It is a place for people to assemble, to learn
Dhamma, to meditate. It is a place to relieve tension and to experience some joy and happiness.

Therefore, when somebody builds a temple, that person gives
everything. Sharing Dhamma—the Buddha's teachings—and
teaching Dhamma is like sharing immortality. Why? Because it is
the Dhamma that puts our life on the right path, relieves us from

suffering, liberates us from pain, and brings us to the attainment of enlightenment.

Somebody may say, "Well, I don't know Dhamma well enough to teach." But you don't have to stand in a pulpit to share the Dhamma. You can discuss whatever you know about it, without any ulterior motive.

And there are many ways of sharing Dhamma, too. One can print Dhamma books or contribute financially to their printing and distribution. One can discuss and explain various points of Dhamma to anyone they come across.

I have seen the benefits of sharing Dhamma. Above all other gifts, the gift of Dhamma is considered to be the highest dana.

Now, I know I said when you give away something don't expect anything in return. But there are certain things we can expect. And those things we should expect are wonderful, noble things.

When you give away something, for instance, to a religious group or sangha, you expect the sangha to live a moral, decent life. That is for the benefit of the sangha. Your expectation that the monks, the nuns, the community of the sangha lead a pure, decent, and moral life—that is a wonderful expectation.

We hope that our gift will help those who receive it to attain enlightenment. We may wish, "May this gift help this person relieve their pain and suffering. May this person be happy, joyful, and peaceful because of these gifts I give."

19

On Death and Loss

CONFRONTING DEATH

How can we meet death skillfully? When we know it is imminent, how can we best invest our remaining moments?

I think you cannot all of sudden get into a very calm, peaceful state of mind without preparing in advance. If somebody dies very slowly over a long period of time, because of certain illnesses, then that person has time to think and to practice meditation on death.

I just attended a funeral. That person lived for about eighteen years with several massive heart attacks, pacemakers, and all that. She learned meditation. Then they signed her up for hospice, but she lived for another five months.

During that time, she knew she was going to die and she had plenty of time to meditate. And I heard she talked to her husband and consoled him. One morning she passed away. I think she had time to prepare. Not everybody is so lucky. But if we keep meditating, meditating, meditating, then the mind is prepared to face death at any moment. So, I encourage you to meditate.

LIFE AFTER LIFE

What is meant by "relinking consciousness"?

This is the consciousness that links this life with the next life. And this life will connect to the future life because of relinking consciousness.

You cannot explain Dependent Origination without explaining how consciousness arises dependent on volitional formations. Through volitional formations we form thoughts, words, and deeds—willing them intentionally. As consciousness arises, thought arises. But Dependent Origination explains how consciousness arises dependent on volitional formations and links this life to the next life and to the previous life.

This is difficult because we cannot perceive it, we cannot confirm it through any scientific experiments. Of course, we have to accept this with a certain degree of faith. Faith in the Buddha. We have faith in someone who has seen this and experienced this. "Volitional formations" simply means kamma. Dependent on our kamma, consciousness arises in a suitable place for beings to take birth.

LOSING LOVED ONES

How do we let go of those whom we love?

Suppose we love someone dearly. And that person dies. Of course, we feel sad. That is very natural. We acknowledge the sadness. At the same time, we should not lose sight of the truth of impermanence. We acknowledge the sadness and understand, "I'm sad because I have attachment to this loved one. I must understand that even loved ones are impermanent. I have not understood this. I simply have clung to my loved one and, therefore, I have this suffering."

We mindfully look at the whole situation as we experience pain, sorrow, and sadness, and we come to understand at the same time it is because of our attachment to the loved one.

So, what to do? Even loved ones pass away. We understand it, console ourselves, and always look to the Dhamma, the truth. Then, gradually, we increase our insight into this reality and decrease our sadness toward losing our loved ones.

IMPERMANENCE AND MOURNING

The Buddha often spoke of how impermanent all life is. Yet how do I stop myself mourning the loss of loved ones? I know it is the natural end to things. But I still miss them—they are gone, not to return. Is this selfish?

Honestly speaking, yes. We may not like to admit that. We are so attached to our loved ones! I say it is selfish because, what is it that you are missing? You miss the person's touch and appearance. You miss their voice. You miss the things you've done together or that they did for you. All the support you got from that person is gone. All the benefits you got from that person—emotional and material, those feelings of security and companionship—we miss all these things when someone passes away. And these are the things we're attached to.

That is why we mourn so deeply when we lose somebody—a mother, father, brother, spouse, sister, or children. And this is the very truth that Buddha spoke about—he said it thousands of times. The more we are attached, then the more suffering, pain, and mourning we will experience.

Alleviating such mourning will not be easy without examining the sources of these feelings. I warn you, you may not like to hear this, but the Buddha said don't cling to loved ones. From attachment and clinging arise pain, sorrow, grief, lamentation, and despair.

So, what is the wisest approach toward our loved ones? We should, of course, have healthy, loving relationships with everyone, our relatives in particular. At the same time, we should keep in our minds: "This person will pass away."

All unions end in separation. This is one of the things we must reflect upon often. One day we will separate from our loved ones. That is the truth! We must always remind ourselves of this truth. When we keep repeating this kind of thought, we condition ourselves to accept this reality when somebody passes away.

When it happens, we are able to see, this is what we've known all along. It has finally happened. Nothing has changed, this is nothing unusual. We feel pain for a while, but it slowly goes away. The tears will dry, the pain will not linger in our mind forever.

When we train our mind in this way, when we rid ourselves of our clinging and attachment, we will not experience the kind of grief you describe.

It's a matter of mindfully training ourselves.

DEALING WITH DEATH

I have had friends die recently and unexpectedly, including one who died of a heroin overdose. I have survivor's guilt in that he considered me a spiritual friend. Sometimes I was not able to help him. How have you been able to cope with deaths in your life, and what are your own feelings about death at age ninety?

I myself have been thinking about, talking about, and advising people on how to deal with death for a long time. When my mother died in 1976, until the funeral was over I was holding it together. As soon as the funeral was over, I broke down.

A few years later we had a conference in Dallas, and President Ford was also there. It was a big ceremony. We all were supposed to give a talk on gratitude, and I wanted to speak about my mother. I stood at the podium—and I could not utter a word! I just cried. On the one hand, it was very embarrassing. On the other hand, it was a great relief. That was my honest response to the emotion.

Now, when my sister died at age 104, I had better prepared myself. She was exactly like a mother to me. She was married before I was born. Then, she had a baby five months older than me. She would come to our house, and my mother and father would go out to a little paddy field to work. My sister took me to her lap—she put me on one side, her daughter on the other side, and breastfed us both!

She treated me like a son until she died. I had so much attachment to her just like my mother. When she died I stayed calm because over the period of the many years since my last cry for my mother's death, I began to think about it and prepared myself for another death in the family—because surely we must expect these things to happen.

A friend who was exactly like a family member to me, a wonderful man, some years ago had a liver transplant. This month his wife telephoned me and said, "Bhante, my husband is in hospice." I said, "What? Can I talk to him?" She put the phone up to his ear. He had been a robust man. That day, he was whispering and said, "I cannot talk. I am supposed to die today." But he didn't. So, every day I talked to him.

The day came when he could no longer talk. But his wife put the phone on his ear, and I kept on talking and talking and talking— and two hours later he died. It was a very sad situation. He was Jewish by birth, but because of our association he became a Buddhist. A temple in Tucson gave him a Buddhist funeral.

By that time I had contemplated death even more seriously, so I did not have any sadness. Of course I miss him, but I was not emotionally upset.

My turn also is coming. I don't know how soon. I've been preparing for my own death a long time. Every night I go to bed thinking that I may not wake up in the morning. When I wake up, I continue my work.

You may recall the story I tell in my autobiography of the time I was flying in an airplane from Hawaii and through the window I saw one of the engines burst into flames. In that moment I thought, "Well, I must die one day, so why not now?"

But I wanted to spend this time in meditation, so I kept on meditating on mindfulness of breathing while enjoying the fireworks spewing from the engine—sometimes they were blue flames, sometimes yellow, sometimes they moved in a spiral. The other passengers all seemed half dead already out of fear, making the sign of the cross, crying and hugging while little children kept playing.

But the plane did succeed in returning to Hawaii. And then the emergency doors opened and an inflatable chute came down. They told us to jump out the exit door and slide down the chute. When my turn came I just jumped. I was forty-nine and that was the first time in my life I had ever jumped down a chute—I even enjoyed it!

So, the entire time it was just like a movie for me. On this side were fireworks, on that side were half-dead people with little kids playing nearby. That was my attitude to my own death—I don't know how it will happen and what I will do. But I am thinking even at the moment of death—if I am conscious, if my mind is not completely confused—I want to know how it happens.

Not too many people have that kind of curiosity, since they are so afraid of death and are afraid of the manner in which they will die—whether they have to be bedridden and somebody has to clean and change them. I have seen some old friends die in such a fashion.

There was a monk friend of mine in Sri Lanka who was close to ninety when he passed away. For about ten years he was bedridden. He had diabetes and was reduced to almost a skeleton. He could not move his hands or legs, so somebody had to feed him. When I visited him, first he would cry and cry and then he would laugh and then he would cry.

I was also there when another friend in Malaysia died. The first five days he talked to me. The sixth day he put his arm on my chest and looked at me. He was crying because he could not talk, but he was fully conscious. I had lived with him for ten years before that time.

So, I have seen many of my relatives and friends dying. And for some of them, in the last few years or months, they suffer. That's the kind of thing that causes us fear. In my case, that is what I have in mind and work on—not to be afraid of death itself.

After all, no matter how afraid of death we are, we cannot stop it—it comes. But we can try to remain awake, mindful, alert, to know how it happens. We must prepare well in advance, by practicing mindfulness, by working with our emotional states, by being alert to everything that arises, moment to moment.

Of course, we all hope we die peacefully and without pain and discomfort. I want to die like a friend of mine in Atlanta died. He and his wife were watching TV. He had his legs up on a reclining chair. They were watching a movie. After watching the first part they were talking and joking. His wife went to make tea and asked him from the kitchen whether he wanted a cup. He didn't respond. "What's the matter with you? Are you angry with me?" She came back into the living room and found him dead, just like that!

That is the kind of death I'd like, a very desirable death.

20

The Buddha as the Teacher

A TREATMENT FOR SUFFERING

Long ago I read somewhere that upon enlightenment the Buddha became free from all suffering, but that he chose to participate in the sorrows of the world. Can you elaborate?

It is not true, therefore, I'm not going to elaborate! But I will say something about it. Why do I say it is not true? Even learned people believe this. There is a statue in Sri Lanka of the Buddha. One of our very learned archaeologists interpreted the meaning of that statue to say that it represented Buddha suffering for all the suffering beings in the world. And he even coined a term: *para dukkha dhukikkita mudra*. That means that he suffers for the suffering of others.

Friends, if Buddha were to suffer for the suffering of others, he would never have had one single moment of peace. Because the world is full of suffering! There are millions of beings, trillions of beings, suffering! If this were true, he would have simply become an embodiment of suffering.

So, that is not true.

The first part of the question is correct—Buddha overcame suffering, he got free from suffering, and he never suffered after that. He may have had aches and pains here and there from growing old, but he never had any suffering. He had compassion for suffering beings and he tried to help those beings without himself suffering.

It is an ordinary person who suffers from the suffering of others. That is, in fact, unhealthy. Suppose you are a doctor or nurse. A doctor sees so many patients crying in pain. If the doctor suffered from all the suffering experienced by his patients, he would cry with his patients just as they cry or experience suffering. But they don't do that. Just like nurses, they are steady emotionally in order to treat patients. If they want to cry with the patients, they cannot do their jobs. They must remain steady, alert, and mindful to help their patients.

And that was the position of the Buddha. He knew the suffering of others and was so mindful of it that he offered a full course of treatment for that suffering.

"RIGHT" AND "WRONG"

What is meant by "Right" Concentration? Does this mean there is "Wrong" Concentration?

In the Noble Eightfold Path you see there are Right View, Right Intention, Right Speech, Right Action, Right Livelihood, Right Effort, Right Mindfulness, and Right Concentration. All are qualified with right, right, right, and so on. That implies that there must then also be wrong, wrong, wrong, and so on, doesn't it? If there is Right Mindfulness, there must be Wrong Mindfulness.

In fact, some people say there cannot be wrong mindfulness. If there cannot be wrong mindfulness, why did the Buddha qualify it as Right Mindfulness? This was for good reason, because even mindfulness can be wrong mindfulness. And concentration can be wrong concentration.

So, wrong concentration is concentration without Right Mindfulness. And mindfulness can be wrong mindfulness without Right Concentration. We have to understand what Right Mindfulness and Right Concentration are.

When Siddhartha Gautama Bodhisatta attained concentration, suddenly he thought, "Ah, this is so blissful, so pleasant! How can I proceed?" He realized, "No, I don't have to worry about it, I don't have to fear this concentration."

Why? Because this concentration had nothing to do with carnal pleasure. It had nothing to do with sensual pleasure. This was concentration that did not make one attached to this blissful, peaceful state. And it was free from the hindrance of greed. After all, you can have concentration with greed. You may focus your concentration intently on the slice of double chocolate cake you see in the bakery!

But Right Concentration does not have greed in it. Instead, with the attainment of Right Concentration you gain the tremendous freedom of letting go. You don't attach to anything. The mind becomes clear and pure because of the presence of equanimity.

When the mind is balanced like this, it doesn't go to one side or the other, to greed or to hatred. It remains equanimous. Why? Because it has overcome greed and hatred as a hindrance. Restlessness, worry, and doubt are also overcome because the mind is clear.

Finding a Teacher

If a meditator doesn't seek proper guidance from a qualified teacher, is there a danger of practicing in a way that is detrimental? I mean to say, perhaps dismantling the ego in such a way that it may become difficult to relate to or function in daily life?

If you want to meditate, I would suggest that you seek out a teacher who knows meditation and does not have any ulterior motives. That would be someone who can honestly and sincerely guide you from the teacher's own meditation experience.

If the person has not meditated and does not know anything about meditation and simply claims to be a meditation teacher, then definitely that person could mislead and misguide you.

Therefore, practicing meditation can sometimes be very dangerous without a teacher. You need some guidance, some guidelines to start your meditation practice. It is better to do dana and practice generosity, to undertake sila or moral discipline, until you find a good meditation teacher.

The other thing is to read good books. Read the Mahasatipatthana Sutta. Read the Digha Nikaya, the Majjhima Nikaya. Read the Anguttara Nikaya. There are so many beautiful discourses Buddha has given, laying out all the necessary and sufficient information for somebody to practice meditation.

If you don't find the person in the flesh and blood to call your teacher, then go and read these teachings and you can get a good knowledge of meditation. Otherwise, just don't follow somebody who claims to be a teacher.

SEEING THE DHAMMA

When I read the Maha Jayamangala Gatha (Great Verses of Joyous Victory), I see the phrase "By the power of the Buddha, may all misfortune be destroyed, may all suffering cease for me." My question is about the power of the Buddha. If the Buddha died and achieved paranibbana, what power is this? Does the Buddha still have power to dispel misfortune?

Yes, even though the Buddha has passed away, we still can receive the blessings of the Buddha and Dhamma. Whether the Buddha exists or not, if we establish our mind in the qualities of the Buddha, the Dhamma, and the Sangha, we receive blessings.

There was a monk called Vakkali. He was a very devout monk, with a lot of saddha, or faith. He became a monk because of his faith. He wanted to see the Buddha all the time. One day he fell seriously sick. Buddha visited him and asked him how he was doing. He said, "Venerable Sir, I'm suffering enormously and the pain is excruciating."

Then the Buddha asked him, "Vakkali, do you have any remorse? Have you done anything serious that you are now regretting?" He said, "No, Venerable Sir. I have not committed anything that makes me remorseful. But Venerable Sir, I am very sorry that I will not be able to see you as often as I used to."

This monk was so sick that he could not go and visit the Buddha, and that made him very unhappy. Then Buddha said, "What is the use of seeing this body? It is subject to change and is impermanent. But he who sees Dhamma, Vakkali, sees me."

This is an important point. When can we not see the Dhamma? We can see the Dhamma right now, anytime, anywhere. So long as we have these Five Aggregates, we can see the Dhamma. And if somebody sees the Dhamma, they see the Buddha and definitely receive blessings.

Seeing the Dhamma, we see the Buddha. Therefore, right in front of us, anytime, we can see the Buddha. And how shall we pay respect to the Buddha? We follow the Dhamma. When we follow the Dhamma, we receive blessings.

So, when we recite the Jayamangala Gatha, we receive blessings because we try to emulate and follow the noble principles taught by the Buddha.

Of course, people recite words like parrots sometimes, without thinking about their meaning and significance. But if we know the meaning of each word of the Jayamangala Gatha and recite them, we will receive the blessings of the Dhamma.

Friends, anytime we honestly follow the noble principles, we receive blessings. Whether Buddhas are alive or have passed away, we receive blessings. So long as the Dhamma exists and we see the depth of the Dhamma, we see the Buddha and receive his blessing.

The Focus of the Teachings

At age ninety have you adapted your views and understanding of the Buddha's teachings over your life, or have they changed in any way over the course of your teaching career?

At the beginning I just had faith and I obeyed my teachers. I played it sort of by ear, so to speak, according to the situation. When I first gave Dhamma talks, I told a lot of stories. My understanding of Dhamma was not very deep. When I became a novice monk, I was only twelve years old. At that time I did not understand anything. As I grew up, slowly and gradually I began to understand some basic principles, but not very deeply.

Only after my thirties did I begin to understand the teachings more deeply. Initially I had sort of a shallow understanding of certain Buddhist concepts.

As for things that I teach differently, I would say metta practice is a good example. I started practicing the same way everybody else did, as described in the commentaries and subcommentaries to the Buddhist suttas. These recommended that meditators start metta or loving-friendliness practice with oneself. I described such a practice myself in many of my books, even until recently.

Then I began to see the shortcomings of such an approach. I went back to the Buddha's own discourses. There are many other interpolations by other people in discussing metta practice. But when I went to the Buddha's own teachings, the basic principles, I saw that metta practice should be boundless. So in the practice we must begin with this idea in mind. That is, it is boundless.

For instance, you practice metta toward one direction—the east. When you focus your mind on the east, that direction has no end. It can go to infinity. Similarly, living beings in that direction will be infinite. In a similar way, you direct metta in all the ten directions—south, southwest, west, northwest, up, down, and so forth. This is called boundless practice.

When we do that practice, we forget ourselves. We don't think of ourselves at all because we also merge with all other beings. And afterward, when we have practiced metta in that way for maybe ten to fifteen minutes or a half-hour, then the mind gets tired. When the mind returns to ourselves, we feel very relaxed because when we practice sending metta toward others, we eventually feel how wonderful this practice is. Our own mental state becomes very lucid, relaxed, and peaceful.

And so I decided in recent years to teach metta in that way— directional metta. Forgetting myself.

Also, these days I talk more about impermanence. Some people, as soon as I talk about impermanence, they start laughing, "Oh, there he goes again!" But that is what the Buddha called the root of Dhamma, established Dhamma, the law of Dhamma. These three terms the Buddha used: *Dhamma-dhatu,* the root of Dhamma; *Dhammatthita,* or established Dhamma; and *Dhamma-niyama,* the law of Dhamma. Here *Dhamma* means the nature of everything in the entire universe.

Because things are impermanent, we suffer. And also because things are impermanent, we don't have anything in us that is autonomous. Our body, feelings, thoughts, perceptions, consciousness, and so forth—there's no way to control them.

If there really were anything called "soul" or "self," then that would have autonomous powers to control all the aggregates and everything that happens to us. But nothing is there to control us because things are changing all the time!

This can be found to be 100 percent true in science. Quantum physics, chemistry, biology, wherever you look, all will prove that nothing—nothing!—remains the same for two consecutive moments. Yet not understanding this principle, people wish to grab on to something, to cling to something. But you cannot cling to anything. It is just a thought and that thought arises from ignorance and desire.

These two work together to make us deluded. Ignorance deludes us. Greed deludes us. Everything boils down to greed, craving, and ignorance. When the mind is obsessed, a person will be completely confused. They won't know what to do, and cannot make a decision between right or wrong. It is just like an arrow that goes in one direction, the mind becomes so narrow!

Similarly, ignorance leads to the same result. Just imagine when these two combine together. So much confusion results. Yet if one understands impermanence, that person will not be so deluded.

That is why the Buddha said, "*Ponobhavika nandiragasahagata tatra tatrabhinandini, seyyathidam kama tanha, bhavatanha vibhavatanha.*" It is a beautiful definition. He says, "This craving is re-becoming." It repeats itself again and again and again. Because of our attachment to a momentary feeling of desire, we experience a moment of pleasure. The mind goes to this and enjoys it for a while. And the feeling fades and then goes to the next pleasure and enjoys that for a while. And then the next and the next and the next. It keeps repeating all the time.

Each time, the mind gets some pleasure and then wears it out and yet seeks more and wears it out and the process repeats. The grass is always greener elsewhere! That kind of delusion is created by desire.

When I think of this process, it becomes clearer and clearer in my mind. And therefore, I talk a lot about impermanence these days!

SMILING BUDDHA

What is the role of laughter in spiritual life? Did the Buddha ever teach or speak about laughter?

The Buddha did not say much about it. But in the commentaries to the Pali canon there are various degrees of laughter mentioned—they actually list five of them. These start with the very mildest smile to very loud giggling. Buddha did not say anything about laugher specifically, but the suttas do record him smiling on several occasions. These occasions are recorded because these smiles have a very deep meaning.

One day, for instance, he saw a beggar. Seeing him, he smiled. But that is not something funny at all, to see somebody begging. You might wonder if the Buddha was being sarcastic or insulting. His attendant, the Venerable Ananda, asked him, "Sir, why did you smile at seeing that beggar?"

Buddha said, "You know, this beggar was a millionaire. Now, see what he is doing now?" Buddha said if he had better spent his money and energy when young, he could have become the richest person in this country. But he wasted that opportunity. And if he had practiced Dhamma, he would have attained full enlightenment. He passed up that opportunity. If in his middle age, he had used his money diligently, mindfully, he could have become the second richest person in the country. And if he had followed the Dhamma with determination, he could have attained the third level of enlightenment, the Anagami stage. And if he had used his wealth in the latter part of his life, he could have become the third richest person in the country. And if he meditated, he could have attained the second level of enlightenment. Instead, he wasted his time and energy, his money and opportunities, by abusing his money, becoming involved in gambling and drinking. He wasted everything and now he is a beggar. That is why he smiled at how foolish this person had been.

So, in his smiles there was always a very deep meaning, something for us to learn. We laugh and smile when we hear a joke that doesn't make any sense; it simply makes us giggle. A meaningful smile can be very spiritual.

RITUALS AND ENLIGHTENMENT

The Buddha says rituals are empty and enlightenment is not found in rituals. How does one separate seemingly wholesome customs from rituals?

A certain practice becomes a ritual if one believes that it brings enlightenment. If somebody practices certain behaviors—say, for instance, even lighting this candle behind me in front of the Buddha statue. We may do it almost as a ritual or as a custom. But while lighting this candle, if you think you can obtain enlightenment from the observance of lighting a candle or burning incense and bowing to the Buddha, then that becomes a ritual.

Instead, we can light the candle with the understanding that its illumination dispels darkness. In the same way, we may wish that our practice of meditation may illuminate the truth and dispel the darkness of ignorance. With this intention, if you light the candle with this mindset, this gives you the right understanding.

We offer the Buddha puja at lunchtime as a custom and sometimes place small containers of food before the Buddha. We all know the statue doesn't eat anything. But as a custom we put the food there.

While putting the food there we think, "I make this offering to the Buddha as I feel the Buddha has done so much for me and the world. Out of gratitude, I put this food out as a symbolic gesture of respect and honor."

In so doing, that makes our hearts fill with joy and happiness through the act of respecting the one who helped the world and who has helped us. But if we think that the food we offer the Buddha will result in some kind of magic result, then that's a ritual.

No Other Refuge

I facilitate two meditation groups. One person said, "Oh, you're a very good teacher." I responded, "I can't accept that term." I say that I facilitate. I can sit in the chair. I have the gong and a watch. I can tell you which Nikaya and which sutta, but then you go and find it. But please don't call me teacher. There are so many people now who say they are teachers of Buddhist meditation, but they are teaching something so watered down, so diffuse—stress reduction in the office through mindfulness, for instance.

I think that's a very good approach that you describe: providing the sources for them to do research. I think if we can quote the Nikayas and a particular discourse or at least the essential gist of that discourse, that is even better. And then encourage them to read on for more detail.

So, they know at least this isn't your own invention, your own creation. You learn something.

It is very good for all Buddhists to say, "I have no other refuge, the Buddha is my refuge. I have no other refuge, Dhamma is my refuge. I have no other refuge, the Sangha is my refuge." It's easy to remember—these are the Three Refuges of the true practitioner. Then expand on that. What is Buddha? What is Dhamma? What is Sangha?

So, one who grows in the teaching will grow with this understanding of Buddha, Dhamma, and Sangha.

Love, Oneself, and the Universe

What was the Buddha referring to when he spoke about looking out across the universe and finding no one we loved more than ourselves?

You find it in the Samyutta Nikaya, in the Mallikaa Sutta, 3.8. The story is of King Pasenadi of Kosala, who had a very beautiful and intelligent wife called Mallikaa. One time they were together, and in a romantic moment the king asked his queen, "Tell me honestly, whom do you love the best?" She said, "Your Majesty, the one I love the most is myself." The king went to the Buddha and told him about her answer.

The Buddha responded, "With my mind, I surveyed the whole world in all directions to see whether there is anybody who loves someone more than oneself—and I found none. Nobody loves any-body better than oneself. Therefore, since you love yourself more than anybody else, don't hurt others, recalling that if you hurt them, they also love themselves and therefore you just compare yourself to them."

The implication is that you ask yourself, "Do I like it if somebody hurts me?" Therefore, in order to avoid hurting others, we practice nonviolence, not killing or harming any living beings. The Buddha said this is what one must think and keep in mind all the time—that just like me, everybody else loves oneself.

MASCULINE AND FEMININE

Did the Buddha teach anything about the balance of masculine and feminine energy within us, like the yin and yang in Taoism? One reason that I wonder this is because many statues present a more masculine image of the Buddha, and some a more feminine aspect.

Actually, the Buddha did not talk about masculine and feminine energy. The yin and yang is a familiar concept, but you cannot find any reference to it in the Buddha's teachings.

The Buddha spoke of energy—especially spiritual energy—to arouse our spiritual urgency. He spoke of beginning effort, or *arambhadhatu*. And continuous effort, or *nikkamadhatu*. And the effort to accomplish your practice, or *parakkamadhatu*. These sorts of energy the Buddha talked about. But he did not distinguish energy between the feminine and the masculine.

THE TWO DARTS

As I grow older, one of the teachings that really leaps out at me is the Buddha's teaching on the two darts, that with birth comes inevitable physical or emotional pain and discomfort.

But it is the second dart—how we react—that causes so much suffering. Can you talk about that?

Actually, with birth comes the birth of suffering. One of the aggregates is *dukkha khanda*—the aggregate of suffering. In his teaching on Dependent Origination, Buddha concludes, "Thus is the arising of this mass of suffering."

Being a being of any sort—human, animal, divine, and so forth—equals suffering. Being equals suffering. Because a being—in this case, a human being—has to at least, if nothing else, maintain oneself. How many things one has to do to maintain one's existence!

We try to stay healthy. But often we fall sick and we have to do something about it. We experience hunger and have to eat time and time again. Hunger is always there, so we have to eat. And we don't want to be thirsty, but we get thirsty and we have to drink. Defecating, urinating, all of it.

At the very least, we are experiencing these six things all the time: cold, heat, hunger, thirst, defecation, urination. We must address these six again and again and again and again. Even if everything seems 100 percent satisfactory in our lives, at any one moment these six things will constantly claim our attention.

Of course, it becomes clear that no life is satisfactory all the time, as we have to do so many things just to maintain our existence. When you want to eat, food doesn't fall into our laps from the sky—we have to get the food. And in order to get the food, how many things do we have to do? Get up in the morning, go to work, come home—the same treadmill every day. Why? To eat? To feed and clothe ourselves, to pay our bills. To pay for medicine and housing.

We have so many things we need to do just to survive. And none of them comes easy! Suppose you own a little plot of land and you are not working for anybody. You have your own house inherited from your parents. But you have to maintain that house and that land. And that is not easy.

So, that is the suffering we are born with and the situation we face just in order to maintain ourselves and our lives and families.

But in addition to that there is the second dart of desire. We want something, some pleasure. If we don't get it, we suffer. We want something and we get it—are we happy? Maybe for a short while. But then we have to maintain it, whatever it is—a beautiful new car, a new house, a brand-new phone. Why? Because it is impermanent. So there is no win-win situation. There is something always arrayed against us.

However, if we learn to be content, understanding that this is life—this body has to be maintained, these are the basic things necessary for survival—then we will not experience that second dart of suffering.

At the same time, we realize we don't wish to be on this treadmill. We think, "I don't want to repeat this again in the next life and the next life after that." Therefore, the person must learn to minimize greed. And understand the Dhamma, the truth of Dhamma—which leads us to liberation.

SPIRITUAL FRIENDS

You have often described yourself as a kalyana mitta, or spiritual friend, to your students. What do you mean by *kalyana mitta*, and what does the definition of "teacher" mean to you?

Of course, even a kalyana mitta can be a teacher. A teacher is one who shares his or her knowledge with others. An ideal teacher is one who shares knowledge without expecting anything in return. They are not interested in any reward, they have no aim to increase their number of students or to become famous but just wish to impart knowledge. That is the kind of teacher I like to be myself.

And a kalyana mitta has even more noble qualities. A kalyana mitta is always very compassionate. He or she speaks and listens well because their intention is to help others. There is no way they would mislead anybody. A kalyana mitta is mindful to give right instruction and right advice to people out of compassion.

So, he or she is always there and available to help people. A kalyana mitta is a selfless person who serves others without expecting anything in return.

BEING A BUDDHIST

Does one need to be a Buddhist to gain benefits from Buddhist meditation?

Up to a certain point, no. "Up to a certain point" means until you gain concentration and even attain jhanas. One doesn't have to be a Buddhist to attain the jhanas.

Even before Buddha came on the scene there was meditation and there were meditating rishis and mendicants in India. And some of Siddhartha Gautama's teachers before he obtained buddhahood, such as Alara Kalama, were meditators and they had attained these stages. He learned their system and learned all the eight stages of jhanas.

But then he found their system was not complete. Those systems bring you to a certain level and beyond that they cannot go. He thought there must be something more to this because this repetition of birth and death continues even after obtaining these states.

He wanted to stop the seemingly endless repetition of birth and death. Therefore, he broke away from all of them. He explored his own vipassana meditation. He introduced this mindfulness system, to see impermanence, unsatisfactoriness, and selflessness.

He came to realize that until you get rid of your greed, hatred, and delusion by understanding these three marks of existence, you will continue to be bound to the cycle of rebirths. So he introduced this and practiced, and he attained enlightenment.

Therefore, anybody can practice meditation up to that point—up to the point of the Eight Jhanas, the eight stages of attainment. But they cannot go beyond that without the Buddha's teachings.

They will exist in samsara for a long period, even in many pleasant places. But wherever you are born, no matter how blissful the place, suffering is there. So long as existence is there, then impermanence is there. So long as impermanence is there, suffering is there. So long as impermanence and suffering are there, there is no autonomous power to control these states of being.

As I've often said, we refer to the self, but it has no autonomous existence. It is just like today is Friday—but does Friday exist? Have you seen Friday? Have you seen Monday? Tuesday? January? March? December? Longitude? Latitude? Nobody has seen them, but we use them for practical purposes, just to communicate place and time.

The notion of self is absolutely necessary for communication purposes. For instance, "I," "you," "she"—we use these terms with this provisional understanding.

But, in reality, there is nothing permanent there that these terms signify. If there were something that should be autonomous with all powers to control, to manipulate, then we would have control over our condition.

Instead, we fall sick, which we don't like. There are six "sicknesses" for which there is no permanent cure, although there may be temporary cures. What are these sicknesses? Cold, heat, hunger, thirst, defecation, and urination.

When it is cold you can put on warm clothes and heat the room, but cold still does what it does. As for heat, you may turn on an air conditioner and become cooler, but it is a temporary measure. Heat continues to do what it does. And hunger? You may fast one or two days, but you cannot fast forever. And you may quench your thirst temporarily, but then you become thirsty again.

So, we experience these six sicknesses as long as one exists. Therefore, even if, like so-called divine beings, one doesn't eat anything, still their bodies change and eventually they pass away.

When they are going to pass away, they are going to have the same anxiety, worry, and fear as we have.

As long as anxiety and fear exist, suffering exists. Therefore, no matter how long a person exists in samsara with all kinds of luxuries—with all your beautiful cameras and cellphones and Internet connections, your big TVs and expensive cars—no matter how many of these things they possess, the inner suffering remains.

Buddha wanted to find a way to escape from this cycle. So he introduced vipassana meditation.

To answer your question, you can meditate without being a Buddhist up to a certain point.

We say Buddhists have the complete system of meditation that can lead us to enlightenment—that is called samatha-vipassana.

STICKING WITH THE PATH

Buddhist cosmology can seem overwhelming with mention of innumerable eons we have wandered through the cycles of rebirth. What do you say about sticking with it when we wonder if we will ever have what it takes to achieve enlightenment or when it seems like such a distant goal?

Actually, if somebody does not start to practice, it can seem so scary. Then the goal seems not within any imaginable distance. It is too far. But if one starts and practices with understanding, with diligence, and makes it a regular, consistent practice, then as your inner ability and your skill slowly unfold, you see the distant goal coming closer to you.

I say very often there are four types of people when it comes to practice. One is a quick-witted person (*ugghatitannu*). The second is a little slower (*vipancitannu*). The third (*neyya*) is slower still but can still attain the stages of enlightenment because he or she knows the importance of associating with kalyana mittas—spiritual friends—and of discussing Dhamma. They realize the importance of practicing consistently, following instructions, listening to seasoned teachers, and so on.

But the fourth category of person will feel like the goal is beyond the horizon. They cannot even see it. Why? His interest is in reading, pada parama. *Pada* means word, *parama* means paramount. Such an individual will talk, talk, talk. Endlessly, he will talk. And he will seek out many lectures by many teachers. And read, read, read. He will count the number of words in the Tipitaka, the Buddhist scriptures. He will spend his entire life seeing, hearing, and discussing the Dhamma—and never put the Dhamma into practice!

But the goal of enlightenment will only come into view if we practice.

All difficult things become easier only if we take up the challenge and start doing them. Many a time people ask when we explain things, "Bhante, it is easier said than done." I say, "It is easier done than said!"

The problem is, people don't like to undertake the challenge. They are sort of cowardly: "This is so intimidating! How can I do it with all my other commitments, activities, and obligations?"

I say it often: people are very smart in giving excuses for not doing wholesome things. But have you seen anybody who gives an excuse to do something good? They must learn to give an excuse to do something good and beneficial to oneself.

I think of the moment that Buddha attained enlightenment. Every time I think of the Buddha and that moment, I have no way to express my gratitude, my amazement, my thankfulness that he decided to teach.

You know, soon after his attainment of enlightenment, he was reluctant to teach. He thought, "My goodness, how can I teach people who are so engrossed, so deeply sunk in the quagmire of greed, hatred, and delusion?"

The story in the scriptures tells how he was convinced to teach at the urging of Brahma Sahampati, the highest god of the highest god realm. He said that there would be some people who would understand the profound realizations the Buddha had come to know about suffering. The Buddha realized there would be some people in the world "with little dust in their eyes." And so he began to teach, and his followers began to attain liberation.

That is true for this century as well as into the future. There are a few who wake up to the challenge, face it, and achieve it.

So, it is certainly possible. But only if we begin to practice.

THE CONCEPT OF SIMPLICITY

You have talked about the Buddha's teachings getting lost amid the pomp and circumstance of ceremonies and festivals. Can you elaborate?

That is what happens even in some expressions of Theravada Buddhism, the oldest tradition of Buddhism, where popular Buddhism has led to all kinds of elaborate Buddhist rituals and ceremonies.

People find it extremely difficult, even in a Buddhist country like Sri Lanka where I come from, to engage in the simple, traditional offering of a Kathina robe, the robe given monks at the end of the three-month Vassa period. They do several things to make money out of the robe—they send the robe to one family and they collect the money. And they send that money to the temple. And they send the robes to the next family and the next one. They collect a lot of money and send the money to the temple. If there are one hundred houses, each has to collect money.

There are also these big, big celebrations. They feature elephants, drum beaters, dancers, singers. There is a big procession a mile long. In all of this, where is the concept of simplicity? The concept of just donating a simple robe? The Kathina robe is given to a monk as if it came from heaven.

It used to be only the person who gives the robe knows that they give the robe. Now it is surrounded with all kinds of embellishments, ceremonies, rituals, commercials, money, and so forth. If you attend one of these ceremonies, you wonder, what is happening? Why are there elephants? So many drum beaters! So many dancers!

Even giving dana in Sri Lanka—now there is catering for dana. In the past, offering dana meant you prepared food yourself and you offered it by yourself as families still do here at the Bhavana Society.

The Buddha's instruction was for the monks to take their alms bowl and go from house to house and collect only what the monk can eat. He can eat only this much. If he goes to two houses, he will get enough food. He doesn't have to go to too many houses. Somebody might be overburdened by giving food. That was the original Buddhist monastic practice. Now people bring food to the temple. I don't know how many monks you see going on pindapata or alms round in Sri Lanka. Some of them don't like that. They think that is demeaning and degrading. And why is that?

Some temples became very rich because kings in the Sri Lankan tradition offered them buildings, paddy fields, coconut estates, forest lands. They gave thousands of acres to the temples, and so temples became very wealthy. They became landlords. Now you see these large celebrations, pageants, and carnivals. You see stilt walkers and all sorts of things. When someone goes to one of these big events, they will think, "Oh, this is what Buddhism is about."

But these people will not get a clear image of the Buddha's original teachings because everything will be all mixed up with so many things.

After saying all this, I cannot go to Sri Lanka! Since I am out of Sri Lanka, I can say this.

But some Western monks have gone to Sri Lanka and they engaged in regular meditation practice. Then, some Sri Lankans became interested in meditation. Now meditation is sort of a fashion in Sri Lanka. "Where are you going?" "I'm going to meditate." But the real meditators are very, very few.

That will happen with Buddhist practice here in America, bringing all kinds of things into it. And the risk is losing the essence of the Buddha's teaching.

AMERICAN BUDDHISM

Can you talk more about what you see as American Buddhism?

With the American version of Buddhism, in many cases it is very difficult to point out whether they are offering Theravada or Mahayana or Zen or Tibetan teachings, as there is sort of a mixture. I've even encountered some teachers who I thought were teaching only Theravada vipassana meditation, but I found they don't have any particular branch of Buddhism in their mind. They just blend all the branches of Buddhism.

I think one day soon—in my lifetime it may not happen—there may be a new form with a new name. Like you say "Chinese Buddhism" and "Tibetan Buddhism," there will be "American Buddhism." But will it retain the Buddha's actual teachings over time?

There is a short sutta in the Samyutta Nikaya called the Ani Sutta, or "The Peg." In those days, when kings wanted to summon people, they set out a big drum and a drummer would beat it. Hearing the sound of the summoning drum, the people would come. Whenever the drum would split, they would put a peg in it to hold the drum together. They would keep doing this over time. Eventually, you don't find a drum, you find a bunch of pegs! And the drum will no longer be able to be heard. That will happen to the Buddha's teaching, when there won't be a particular group or individual who still puts their finger on what the Buddha originally taught.

You also find in the Samyutta Nikaya the Saddhammapatirupaka Sutta. The message of the sutta is that as long as artificial gold does not appear in the market, real gold will have real value. But as soon as artificial gold appears, it blends with the real gold and eventually you cannot recognize which is artificial and which is real. This applies to the Buddha's teaching.

Now we have a sort of watered-down Buddhism. People want to make a very shiny, attractive Buddhism. But it is shiny and attractive only for the intellectuals or people who are just skimming the surface of Buddhist teaching. They want an easy and popular Buddhism.

THE BUDDHA'S GUARANTEE

You said that in one of the Buddha's teachings he issued what amounts to a "seven-year money-back guarantee." That if we practice diligently we can obtain enlightenment in seven years, or seven weeks or even seven days. Does this require we heed the Five Precepts or the Eight Precepts?

Observing the Five Precepts is enough to have this money-back guarantee. Buddha talked about this in a discourse he delivered to people in Kuru in a market town called Kammassadhamma in the Satipatthana Sutta (Mahjjima Nikaya, 10). The Buddha gave several beautiful, very profound discourses in that particular place.

When he gave this discourse, his listeners were not bhikkhus or even meditators. We don't know how many bhikkhus were there, but he addressed everyone as bhikkhus: "Bhikkhus, there is one direct way of attaining enlightenment . . ."

Many of his listeners he met there were not bhikkhus; they were laypeople. So, it is to these laypeople too that he gave this guarantee. Observing the Five Precepts is absolutely necessary— and observing the Eight Precepts is an additional qualification to make progress on the path even quicker for whoever practices seriously.

CORE INSIGHTS

How would you say your own understanding of your experience of the Buddha's teachings have changed?

My own understanding has changed in several ways. Even in the teaching of metta meditation, as I have mentioned, I no longer teach the same way. I first began teaching metta in what you might call the "individualizing" method, focusing on oneself, then on one's parents, family, friends, and so on. You will see this in some of my books.

But these days I have been emphasizing the directional method of metta, as I felt the other method was too narrowly focused. The Buddha taught metta as just a directional practice, directing metta to all beings in the north, south, east, west, and above us and below us.

Also, I talk more about the core insights gained from vipassana—anicca, dukkha, anatta—or impermanence, unsatisfactoriness, and selflessness. I particularly stress and emphasize impermanence these days. Because I have seen through all these years so many things happen. They rise, they pass away, and are gone. Now, when I think and think about it, all these things are just like dreams, with no substance. They appear and disappear.

So many of my friends with whom I closely associated are no longer here. All that remains is fading memories. My relatives, my brothers and sisters, everybody in my village in Sri Lanka where I grew up—they are gone. Everybody who was there when I was born, everyone who was there when I was five or ten years old, everyone is gone! In the village where I received ordination, all of them are gone. Thousands and thousands of people that I knew are already gone. All I have is a memory of a few here and there—others are not even in my memory.

Therefore, all these turn out to be just concepts. Mother concepts, father concepts, brother concepts. Just concepts. Maybe if you have a photo, occasionally you can see the picture and look it it. But it's just a picture, not a person. It cannot talk and move.

And I feel very deeply sometimes that it is all just a dream. The meals I have eaten, the things I have seen traveling the globe, the sounds I have heard, the places, the situations, the experiences, even the talks I have given—so many trillions of experiences through my senses are mere concepts now with no substance.

Even now when I meditate, very seldom do individuals appear in my thoughts. Only concepts appear. And when I very closely get into that concept, it is just sensation. That kind of understanding, I get now. Therefore, it is very easy for me to let go. To let go of anything that happened in the past. To let go of anything that is happening now—because in them there is not any substance.

That is how my understanding changed.

So, I deeply appreciate the Buddha's teaching of established Dhamma, the root of Dhamma and the law of Dhamma. That is all that exists. There is the Dhamma-niyama Sutta, in which the Buddha says, whether or not Buddhas come into existence, all conditioned things are impermanent, all conditioned things are suffering, all phenomena are without self. There is this established condition of Dhamma, this fixed law of Dhamma.

These things are very, very clear in my mind now. I mean to say, more than in the past. Therefore, especially when I meditate, I see the instructions the Buddha gave to Bahiya. It's very clear to me now. You remember what instructions the Buddha gave to Bahiya who was so hungry to learn the Dhamma?

> Then, Bahiya, you should train yourself thus: In refer-
> ence to the seen, there will be only the seen. In reference
> to the heard, only the heard. In reference to the sensed,
> only the sensed. In reference to the cognized, only the
> cognized. That is how you should train yourself. When
> for you there will be only the seen in reference to the
> seen, only the heard in reference to the heard, only the

sensed in reference to the sensed, only the cognized in reference to the cognized, then, Bahiya, there is no you in connection with that. When there is no you in connection with that, there is no you there. When there is no you there, you are neither here nor yonder nor between the two. This, just this, is the end of stress.

And, as the sutta recounts, Bahiya was instantly enlightened and died soon after when he was attacked and killed by a cow with a young calf. So, he died as an arahant after that quick and succinct teaching went right into his heart and immediately opened his wisdom eye.

That teaching to Bahiya strikes me very deeply when I meditate. I can see the truth of that. There are many short but very profound suttas like that in the Pali canon. Those are the things I enjoy now.

QUOTE THE BUDDHA

You encourage your students not to quote you but to quote the Buddha. Why do you make this particular emphasis, given how people like to refer to the sayings and teachings of their own Buddhist teachers?

That is what I tell all our people here at the Bhavana Society, "When you teach Dhamma, don't quote Bhante G! Don't say 'Bhante G says such and such . . .' Quote the Buddha! Buddha said such and such. You give the source and cite the Nikaya and give the name of the specific sutta."

Why?

When you quote a Buddhist teacher, it is like copying. And then from that copy you make another copy. From the second copy you make another copy and so forth and so on. When it comes to the hundredth copy, it will be just blank paper. You will not be able to even see any letters!

That is why I don't like to quote Buddhist teachers. Instead, quote the original teachings. The Buddha's teaching remains the same. Find a good translation from the Pali. So whether you quote a teaching or your own student quotes a teaching, it goes to the same root.

But the other way around—quoting a teacher's teacher's teacher's teacher—finally you don't see its meaning. It is like trying to find a needle in a haystack. You cannot find Buddhism!

This is a trend in Western society. They always like to quote "my so-and-so says such-and-such." Some people write books only on their teachers. We have many such books in our library. They prefer not to quote the Buddha's teachings because perhaps they feel it is archaic, old-fashioned.

Sometimes, when I go somewhere to give a talk, if I mention the Four Noble Truths, people respond by saying, "Bhante, that is child's stuff. Let us talk about something deep!"

You can see the mentality—the core teaching is "child's stuff." I ask them, "Well, what is the real stuff?"

We must remember that after forty-five years of teaching, Buddha said, "Bhikkhus, I teach only suffering and the end of suffering." That is all he taught.

Everything else is peripheral.

I have seen this happening when it comes to Buddhism over the course of my life. Therefore, we will see what happens in the future.

Index

About the Author

 VENERABLE HENEPOLA GUNARATANA
was ordained as a Buddhist monk at the
age of twelve in Malandeniya, Sri Lanka.
He is the bestselling author of *Mindfulness in Plain English* and several other
books—including his autobiography, *Journey to Mindfulness*. He travels and teaches
throughout the world, and currently lives at
Bhavana Society Forest Monastery in West
Virginia.

More Books by Bhante Gunaratana from Wisdom Publications

Mindfulness in Plain English

Eight Mindful Steps to Happiness
Walking the Buddha's Path

Beyond Mindfulness in Plain English
An Introductory Guide to Deeper States of Meditation

Meditation on Perception
Ten Healing Practices to Cultivate Mindfulness

The Four Foundations of Mindfulness in Plain English

Journey to Mindfulness

The Mindfulness in Plain English Journal

Loving-Kindness in Plain English
The Practice of Metta

The Mindfulness in Plain English Collection

Start Here, Start Now
A Short Guide to Mindfulness Meditation

About Wisdom Publications

Wisdom Publications is the leading publisher of classic and contemporary Buddhist books and practical works on mindfulness. To learn more about us or to explore our other books, please visit our website at wisdomexperience.org or contact us at the address below.

Wisdom Publications
199 Elm Street
Somerville, MA 02144 USA

We are a 501(c)(3) organization, and donations in support of our mission are tax deductible.

Wisdom Publications is affiliated with the Foundation for the Preservation of the Mahayana Tradition (FPMT).